JAMIE**DOBB**

A SEASON IN THE LIFE OF A
MOTOCROSS WORLD CHAMPION

JAMIE**DOBB**

A SEASON IN THE LIFE OF A
MOTOCROSS WORLD CHAMPION

JAMIE DOBB
with Adam Wheeler

TEMPUS

All photographs by Ray Archer

First published 2003, Reprinted 2003

Tempus Publishing Limited
The Mill, Brimscombe Port,
Stroud, Gloucestershire, GL5 2QG
www.tempus-publishing.com

© Jamie Dobb and Adam Wheeler, 2002

The right of Jamie Dobb and Adam Wheeler to be identified
as the Authors of this work has been asserted in accordance with
the Copyrights, Designs and Patents Act 1988.

British Library Cataloguing in Publication Data.
A catalogue record for this book is available from the British Library.

ISBN 0 7524 2880 2

Typesetting and origination by Tempus Publishing Limited
Printed in Great Britain by Midway Colour Print, Wiltshire

CONTENTS

ACKNOWLEDGEMENTS

IN THE past two years, my life has been one hell of a rollercoaster ride – one that has had its fair share of ups and downs. After all is said and done, I would not change a single thing, but the journey has meant a great deal of hard work and sacrifice from a lot of people whom I would like to thank because it would not have been possible without them.

Naomi, my best friend, my soul mate, my wife – from the first moment I saw her, I knew she was the one for me. Since then we have become an awesome team, and for all her support, love and understanding, thank you.

And Gracie, my angel, you have helped me more than you will ever know.

Mum and Dad, what can I say, twenty-nine years but we got there! Richard, Sarah, Julian – I appreciate so much all the sacrifices you have made and the support you have given me. Thank you for never giving up on me. Kurt – thanks for believing in me and giving me the chance when many others wouldn't.

Fred and Kirk – I couldn't have done it without you both. Craig – cheers for all the long hours and late nights, at least it was worth it. Thanks also to Toby, Leighton, Kev, Wilfred, Andrea, Vincent, Morgan, Gunter, Hans, all at KTM, Steve H, Matt 8, Eddy, Shirty, Spanner, Matt G, Gino, Sandra, Mark, Jordan, Abigayle, Olivia, Elliot, Christian, Annette, Alex, Des, Dan and Andy F.

Adam, patience is a virtue, good job you've got it – thanks for telling my story.

ABOUT THE AUTHORS

JAMIE DOBB was born and raised in the Midlands and has emerged as the most successful and widely known Motocross racer this country has produced in the last ten years. After winning all over Europe as a junior, he started his GP career at the tender age of sixteen, riding for the Cagiva factory in 1988. Dobb is one of the most experienced riders in the paddock and few can claim a longer career at the top level. In the last four years, he has finished in the top five of the World Championships, including winning the 125cc number two plate in 2000 and then the title in 2001. He has won 11 Grand Prix and ridden for five manufacturers. Jamie is married to Naomi with a baby daughter, Gracie Dalas Mae, and lives close to Donington Park.

ADAM WHEELER worked for three years in television before moving to Barcelona, Spain, to fulfil a role as TV journalist for the company that held the commercial rights to the Motocross World Championships. His first season in the off-road world coincided with Jamie Dobb's world title-winning campaign, and the writer has been a friend and colleague of the rider ever since. He has just completed his third full season in the sport and now writes for various publications and teams in the paddock.

PROLOGUE

I DIDN'T feel the collarbone snap until I hit a braking bump around the far side of the Swedish circuit. The sensation of pain came before the realisation of what had happened, but only just. It was as if someone had stuck a knife in the back of my shoulder and, instead of standing back and admiring his handiwork, was giving it a twist for good measure.

The qualifying race was over for me and I managed to guide my bike around the jumps and narrow track to the pit lane. Taking the slow route back and watching the others vanishing into the distance, the adrenaline started to wear off and the pain increased. Only ten minutes before, I had been super-confident and pumped for the first qualifying heat race in the 125cc Motocross Grand Prix of Sweden, round seven of fourteen events in the World Championship. I was halfway through the season and had already won five trophies. To say I had felt primed and on top of the world with my riding was an obvious understatement.

As I examined the start gate five minutes prior to the off, along with most of my racing peers, I could not help but think that I would sink on the bike, rather than leap forwards off the line and plough headlong to the first corner of the track a mere 100 yards away. Strangely, the organisers at the Uddevalla circuit felt that they needed to cover the firm mud on the short start straight with broken seashells to absorb any moisture the clouds overhead threatened to deliver.

The two 125cc qualification heats held on Saturday to whittle the sixty or so entrants down to the thirty fastest riders – who will line-up behind the drop-down metal barrier that kicks off a Motocross Grand Prix – are usually pretty hectic affairs. The aim is to finish in the top twelve and secure a starting position for the main event on

Sunday. With many young faces and unknown talent keen to make their mark in front of the factory teams, the heats can be a test of preservation; it's a matter of getting a result that provides a decent pick of positions in the gate, but also staying free of trouble and qualifying unscathed for the Grand Prix race. This was exactly my thought and objective as we filtered through onto the line Saturday morning.

I had been telling people two days before the GP got underway that the first corners in Uddevalla, a long S-shaped chicane that swung either side of a gully, were too tight and there was bound to be an accident when thirty crazed motocross riders bombed towards the curves with scant regard for personal safety. I certainly didn't expect to get into trouble, firstly because my factory KTM machine was one of the best on the grid and I knew I'd get out of the gate quickly ahead of many others, and secondly because this was only a qualifying heat: taking the 'hole-shot' - when you enter the turn first - was hardly a priority. Slithering across the broken shells as we dipped to the right on the first bend, my start wasn't amazing and I think I was fifth. I felt a nudge from behind and moved slightly wide as we made our way uphill.

What happened next took place so fast that it wasn't until much later and with the help of several television replays that I managed to piece together the sequence of events that led to the accident. An Italian rider called Alex Belometti gunned his bike off the banked wall of mud on the outside of the circuit — an addition to the track placed by the Swedish motorcycle club to make sure we didn't just drift off the course as we tried to squeeze through the section. At this speed many riders who were pushed, or had chosen the outside line, were using the wall to keep up their pace — he clashed with Erik Eggens, my nearest rival for the Championship, and sent him onto the floor. Eggens was also riding for KTM and I barely got to notice the differences on his paintwork before his bike skidded across the track under mine and launched me over the handlebars.

The ground rushed up pretty fast and my left shoulder and neck took the full weight of the impact. The bike was looping away somewhere, and while my position wide on the outside of the circuit meant that I was perfectly positioned for Eggens' careering KTM, it also, quite fortunately, meant there were not many people following me. Aside from the obvious disadvantage of falling on the first corner of a race, which, believe me, I have done many times before, the biggest fear is a swarming pack of motorcycles bearing down on you and being unable to escape. Luckily, this time being trampled or hit by someone else was unlikely as I was lying on the top of the uphill left turn while everybody was heading down and into the last part of the S-curve.

Crashing in a race – especially in motocross where the speeds aren't always as high as other motorsports but the distance to fall is greater and more 'final' – there is always a rush of panic, frustration and desperation just afterwards, followed by a sense of urgency in getting back to the bike, getting it kick-started and trying to catch up. The technical demands of the sport mean that skill, ability, timing and judgement count for so much and, unlike many other motorsports, decent equipment is not always necessary. If you are in good physical condition, have no shortage of talent and a real fire in your belly, then it's surprising what you can achieve. Motocross is so much about the individual – your style, your approach, your professionalism – a factory bike is more or less essential to win a World Championship and compete at the highest level, but a motorcycle bought over the counter can also bring success at your local track if you have the ability and dedication. Motocross has always been called a 'poor man's motorsport', but when I look around I'm not sure if there is any other discipline that allows so much richness of individual expression. Our sport probably relies less on the standard of your machinery than any other in the world.

So when I found the bike stationary, oddly, my first thought was one of a challenge. Although the slightly bewildering shock of travelling at speed one minute and then being motionless on the floor the next was still there, I was almost bubbling. All season I had been winning my qualifying races and now I had to work my way through the disappearing pack; if I was not hurrying to retrieve the bike so much, I might have even rubbed my hands at the prospect. There was no problem heaving the KTM upright and I glanced across at Eggens who was also trying to recover his race bike. Mine fired first time and I sped off to keep my meeting with the braking bump.

★ ★ ★

I thought the physiotherapist was going to run out of tape. He was certainly patching up my shoulder very tightly just prior to the Grand Prix of Namur in Belgium, only four weeks after the drama of Uddevalla where I was an unwilling spectator for the first time in the 2001 season. Since then I had returned and gained a respectable second position at the intermittent GP in France, but only one race after the qualifying heat prang, I had a new problem. I looked at the scar on my collarbone, my 'gift' from Sweden and the subsequent operation, and then glanced across to the other shoulder that was currently being strapped. Now I had a matching pair.

The after-effects of the break from several weeks ago were, surprisingly, not bad and I could easily put pressure on my left arm. Once the X-ray had confirmed the fracture in Sweden, I was naturally concerned, but I had a good lead in the points standings and knew that missing one GP would not be a disaster. As it turned out, I was able to race two weeks later in France and everything seemed to be okay, even if I wasn't functioning anywhere near 100 per cent. This latest development was troubling my confidence twice as much. Sitting in the team awning, convincing myself I could get a result on the tough and most physically challenging circuit on the calendar, I was honestly starting to believe that perhaps I was not destined to win a World Championship.

A British rider had never won the 125cc crown and I was definitely not going about it the easy way. My wife, Naomi, was also in Belgium because she had driven over with my family from home in Derby. She was heavily pregnant with our first child and joined a posse of people making the trip to watch me race. Scandalously, there was no event in Britain on the 2001 calendar, despite our excellent tradition and history in the sport; I won the GP there at Foxhill in 2000, and I can honestly say it was one of the finest moments of my life – Namur represented perhaps the geographically closest Grand Prix. The baby had already changed my life and adjusted my focus, and I can't express how much its imminent arrival meant to me, but now I just felt more pressure and knew that this race would be vital if I was to go on and make a little piece of history.

My second broken collarbone, completing the set, hurt a lot more than my rendezvous with the Swedish mud. A crash while training only a few days before I was due to travel out to Belgium had separated the shoulder, and now my upper body was crying out for a rest. I had thrown the bike into a berm – a groove of mud formed by bikes ploughing through the soil – and the thing just disintegrated as soon as I hit it with the weight of the bike. The KTM got out of shape, threw me off at speed and I smacked the shoulder on the ramp of a jump. A tiny piece of me was glad it wasn't the freshly-repaired limb, but it hurt like hell. It was simply a case of bad luck, there was no over-exuberance on my part and sometimes these things just happen.

Crashing is a big part of motocross, not least because of the whole unpredictable nature of the terrain and weather conditions. The sheer number of crashes means a high injury toll; if you were to go into a GP paddock now and interview every rider and ask if they had any small injury problems, then I'd be surprised if fewer than eighty per cent said 'yes'. Sadly, a collection of operating scars or a permanent hobble or limp is almost a trademark sign of a retired MX pro.

The shoulder was a mess and because of Uddevalla, I had spent hardly any time in the gym, so I felt like I was losing my edge – my physical strength and advantage over the other riders that had already let me dominate the first half of the season. My rivals for the title were not so far away, and to miss another race would give the momentum to a nineteen-year-old Belgian called Steve Ramon, who was riding for the Kawasaki factory. His consistency now made him the guy most likely to ensure that I didn't walk off with the main prize so easily. Ramon was gearing up for his home GP and as I took a pain-killing injection prior to the thirty-five-minute and two-lap race, I sensed even more that this was the moment to prove myself, stake my claim and make everybody see that the elusive title, which I came so close to grabbing in 2000, was not going to be denied me in 2001.

Namur was round nine. I had a 64-point lead (each victory earning 25 points) with six races to go. It had rained the night before and lightly through the morning prior to the start of the 125cc, 250cc and 500cc race programme. The steep inclines of the Belgian hillside track cut through a woodland that was narrow and dark in places, and which also had heavy, wet and clumpy mud that seemed to make my bike and riding gear weigh twice as much. I got an average start and managed to slip and slide my way to second place inside several laps.

I cannot describe quite what propelled me that day. Determination was the over-riding emotion in a race that seemed so important for me and my career at the time. I was thinking of my shoulder, I was thinking of my baby, I was thinking of my family and our fourteen-year struggle to get to a position like I was in right now. I rode quite beyond myself and have rarely experienced a more spiritually enriching moment on the racetrack. I passed a Dutch rider called Marc De Reuver and went on to win by seven seconds.

When I crossed the finish line, I felt a sense of immense and supreme satisfaction. Ramon completed the race in second but I didn't care much; the psychological damage was done, in my opinion. I was beaming all the way to the podium. If I could win in this state then I knew there was no stopping me. In my mind I earned the Championship in Namur. Now the gathering of points seemed to be a formality.

★ ★ ★

I could see the finish and it drew closer and closer. The bike practically rode itself over the final small jump. I saw this scrum of photographers and people charging from the pit boxes, up the hill to where I was slowing down and cruising.

In round eleven of the 2001 World Championship, at Gaildorf in Germany, I had finished fourth, and sealed my (and Britain's) first-ever title in the 125cc class with three races remaining. At the age of twenty-nine, I had also just achieved my dream after twenty-four years of messing around on motocross bikes and devoting the majority of my time on this earth as a professional. I was emotionally, physically and mentally exhausted and felt like the 2001 season had been going on for fourteen years. To be honest there was no explosion of emotion or happiness, no delirious air punching, no tears; it was over and when I breathed, I let out all the frustration, pain, rejection and tension that I had been carrying around with me for God knows how long.

The sense of relief was the first thing that hit me. Then I felt almost embarrassed by the wave of attention that followed. I am actually quite a shy person in a motorsport world where supposedly ego and confidence are vital ingredients for any success. Naomi, my parents, my brothers and sister, my friends and my trainer, Kirk, who had worked so hard with me, had travelled out in anticipation that Gaildorf would be the day. There are several touching photographs I have from the post-race blur where I am kissing Naomi's bump, but I don't remember a great deal apart from the fact that I was truly knackered and felt slightly bad for the three riders who had just finished on the rostrum in the race and were being virtually forgotten in the bevy of media.

Also, my result gnawed at me. From ten GPs I had only one DNF in Sweden and hadn't finished off the podium all year, so to win the Championship was awesome but to accomplish it with fourth place took a coat of polish off the day. I went on the podium after the top three riders had sprayed their Champagne and stood there looking at the bouncing group of people all decked out in bright orange t-shirts, the colour of KTM, displaying the words 'Jamie Dobb: Two broken collarbones, one World Championship, now the opposition hurts'. I held the number one plate and couldn't take my eyes off my family.

Only two weeks before Gaildorf, my team boss, Kurt Nicoll, had approached me about riding KTM's new factory bikes for the 250cc class for next season. After spending the last five years in the 125s, I had decided before 2001 got underway that it was time for a change. With the powerful Austrian manufacturer, perhaps the biggest set-up in the paddock to have won honours in the 125s and 500s, deciding to build and race a two-stroke 250, I was in the right place, felt more confident than ever and snatched the opportunity to show my Championship mettle in the most competitive motocross category in the world.

24 March 2002: Round One
Dutch Grand Prix, Valkenswaard

AS I watched out of the window, I couldn't help but think how my mood matched the Dutch grey skies unloading their heavy complement of water onto the top of the motorhome. Thursday afternoon at the first Grand Prix of 2002 in the paddock of the Valkenswaard circuit in Holland, barely twenty minutes' drive from the city of Eindhoven, was a wet one. A typical March day in Northern Europe, the weather was grim and at this moment in time I wasn't looking for sunshine on just one horizon. I was facing my first-ever GP year as a World Champion.

The draining events of Gaildorf 2001 felt quite far away and now my mind was pre-occupied, almost too much, with the problems I faced with only two days until the opening 250cc race of the season. In short, I was shitting myself. I knew I wasn't prepared. Personally I had done everything possible to make sure I was set for the first round of twelve races in the series, but numerous incidents out of my hands now meant that my chances of success looked as bleak as the clouds rolling overhead. I felt an all-too-familiar sense of nerves; the start of another motocross racing calendar and a way of life that I have lived for at least fifteen of my thirty years on this planet. Now that I had realised my ambition and entered the small elite club of world title winners I was determined that I would not fall into the comfort zone and this new 250cc challenge, in the sport's premier class, was proving to be a tough assignment.

Gracie Dalas Mae, my lovely little six-month-old daughter, was trying to push herself around the floor of my new, shiny and somewhat opulent motorhome, and as I contemplated beginning my sixteenth season competing at the highest level of motocross it was almost uncanny to think that I had been hearing the blast of dirt bikes at more or less the same age as her.

★ ★ ★

My dad, John, was a local man from Sutton-in-Ashfield, Nottinghamshire, and he worked his socks off doing numerous jobs starting with going down the coal mine in the mornings, followed by running a mini-bus service and then being off to feed the pigs he was breeding. He even had a paper-round going at one point, on top of indulging in some occasional boxing! He started working on a farm before he left school and bought his first farmhouse when he was twenty, after he and my mum had earned and saved. They would have a fish and chip supper once a week and also go to the cinema and that would be it. He worked damn hard to get where he is now and he made sure a good ethic was present around his children.

My mother, Cynthia, was a dental assistant and my nana used to go to the surgery where she worked. My dad was a bit of a Jack the Lad around town at this stage, and when my nana said that she had met a lovely person at the dentist and he had to stay away from her, he ended up booking an appointment and worming his way in from there.

When dad was away working or selling, my mum would be out feeding the pigs. Occasionally he brought one home to cut up and I used to be there, merrily chopping away on pieces of pig with my dad. I was born on a farm on the second day of 1972 and moved around three other farmhouse properties while I was growing up in the Derby area in England's midlands.

The place where I entered the world was a big and very old house with nearly fifty acres of land surrounding it. I was the baby of the family. I had two brothers – Richard, who was ten years older than me, Julian, who was six years older, and also a sister, Sarah, who was eight years my senior. Living on a farm was fortunate in many ways. It was a fantastic time and great environment in which to grow up, one I would love to give my kids. There was so much we could do and I felt so free, my parents didn't have to have any worries about where we were. When you woke up every morning, you did not know what was going to happen that day.

There was a stream running through the centre of the land and we used to jump in it and mess around, trying to catch the small fish and lifting up big rocks looking for bullfrogs. I'd be gone all day just wandering around this huge adventure playground. In the summer, we would sit and watch the machines cutting up the hay.

My dad's brother, uncle Robert, was big into bikes and his enthusiasm proved to be infectious with our side of the family and that's where it all started. In the area where I lived, having a dirt bike was a popular and almost essential toy. I got my first bike for Christmas, a week before my third birthday. It was a yellow Italjet and I learnt to ride around the front garden. I would also ride my brother's bigger bikes. They would push me off and I would have to jump to one side and run with the bike if I wanted to stop because I was too small. I had a good and competitive relationship with my brothers and, being the youngest, I always wanted to try to beat them or out-do them to gain some sort of status. I guess that's why I wanted to ride fast and the little rivalries started me into a routine that constantly involved two wheels.

We left the first house when I was almost ten and I preferred the second place. It had a small sand quarry and we marked out two tracks inside. Another lucky advantage to a farm upbringing was all the equipment around that made building a track or some jumps a simple process, and my brothers were just as much into it as me. We had a SX track with some jumps and obstacles; more than enough to occupy a young kid on his bike. When I wasn't on a motorcycle I liked football a lot and was quite good at it. I played for the county and also for Notts County junior team (I had a choice between them or Forest). Centre midfield was my position. On the farm I also used to run around doing the usual boy things like building camps, shooting guns and revelling in the space and environment, finding and discovering things to do.

The Italjet eventually gave way to a Suzuki 50 and I had my first race on that bike at a track in Chesterfield. I remember it being quite an exciting time, but at the age of six I can't say that it was a pivotal moment in my life because all I was doing was an activity that I more or less took part in every day. There were a few more other kids around which made it different and for sure I had the butterflies but it felt so ... easy.

My dad patted me on this old yellow-and-black helmet with a big facemask and said, 'Off you go, son' and that was it. I was nervous in a relaxed way. It was more of a stage fright. I still have a picture of the day somewhere; I think I finished third or fourth. As a kid, I would always have these grubby little yellow overalls on and would be running around making motorbike noises. I watched my brothers race from a pram and it seemed impossible that I would head in any other direction. Anyone who has grown up in a family that has any kind of special interest or passion, whether it be a football team or a particular sport, will say how easily it becomes a way of life. Motocross bikes, mud and the excitement of going fast just seemed a natural existence.

The British GP was always a regular fixture that our dad took us to and so was an event held on Good Friday, I believe, at Matchams, Ringwood. They used to have some big names turning out in the old days: riders like Brad Lackey, Gerrard Rond, Hakan Carlqvist. The top guys from the 125s, 250s and 500s all used to ride on 500s against each other. I have good memories of travelling down there. Riders in those days seemed like gladiators to me, a mysterious pack of guys thundering past. I was fixated, inspired and afraid. Motocross racers to me then seemed like a herd of untouchable heroes and I dreamed of being a part of the group.

Other kids may have had ideas of climbing mountains or playing professional football but for me, from riding a bike almost every day of my childhood to being hypnotised by the professionals, racing and going fast was all I ever wanted to do.

My steady progression in the racing world began. It was a matter of competing when my dad could take me until I reached the point whereby I was appearing at the same little meetings as my brothers and we would all pile in the van.

I started to become successful all over the UK in junior events and had to look further afield for challenges. I was winning everywhere we could afford to race: Holland, Belgium, France, even some supercross stuff. 1983 was the year things started to go into overdrive – I won my first Schoolboy National Championship and something like sixty-three out of seventy-five races. I started to travel out to America from 1980 at the age of eight and had a few little races over there as part of a three-week stay at a small training-ranch course that provided the bikes and gear.

It became a yearly treat and I would do well stateside as well, beating guys like Jeff Emig and Mike LaRocco. I missed a bit of time from school because of my riding in my early teens, but I was a good kid at school and even found it enjoyable. I never got into trouble and I never started a fight because I always wanted to get out as fast as I could and get back home to ride my bike. Mum would quickly make me sandwiches while I was getting my gear on and then I'd be gone until it was dark. Home again for tea and then I would have to do my schoolwork until 11 or 11.30 every night. Homework was the worst part of school and maths was my favourite subject, but studying numbers did not stop me leaving when I was fifteen without touching one exam paper. I took all the mock tests and passed with As and Bs but never made it to the real ones because I had to go testing with Cagiva in January (in comparison, there was no clash of priorities). I knew what I would be doing with my life from when I was eight years old, so a relatively incomplete education was not a worry. I didn't have any negative thoughts about a career as a motocross racer and never doubted the fact that I would not have to work after I had retired!

In the early years of schoolboy motocross, my racing became a ritual and competing became second nature. We'd pack the van and travel to the meeting; I'd win or come in second, return home and stick the trophy on the mantlepiece. It used to be horrible to hear the music from *Tales of the Unexpected* on television after having a bath on Sundays because I knew school was the next morning and I'd have to wait another five days.

I was British Schoolboy Champion in 1983, 1984, 1986 and 1987. In '87 I also held a dual licence and took third in the proper British Championship at the age of fifteen. Before 1987 I was wanted by several teams and was ready to turn professional. I decided to mark my first year as a MX pro with the Cagiva factory. The deal was confirmed in '87 and I had to wait until the beginning of 1988 before I was the right age to start a career, sign the paper and pick up my first pay cheque, which was a princely £12,000. The only problem was that you had to be eighteen to legally complete this document and I was only sixteen. My brother was twenty-one so we went to the offices in Italy to get our first payment, collect the bikes and begin testing.

I was told that I couldn't sign without my dad. The old man was really busy on the farm and unable to travel over for a week or so, which meant that we had to survive by nipping into the Cagiva canteen for lunch and then eat bread and water the rest of the time. We used to fill our plates up as much as possible in the afternoon. Living that way for a week or two was certainly sobering and character-building. I recommend the experience to anyone, and it wasn't the last time that I was living on the threads in my pockets.

My first-ever GP was with Cagiva at the opening round of the 1988 World Championships at Castiglione Del Lago, Italy. I had never seen mud like it. It took two people to lift my bike onto the stand after the race. I made thirteenth in qualifying which meant I had the thirteenth pick of positions in the starting gate. Former double World Champion Georges Jobe was riding in the 125s that year to see if he could complete the title treble. His team-mate Alain Lejeune was in twelfth and was saving a space for Jobe, and when I entered the gate and tried to take the spot next to him he told me to 'piss off' and find another slot. I said, 'Too late, I'm coming in' and lined up.

In those days for a muddy race they didn't wear face guards and Lejeune was there in his goggles, occasionally turning his head and spitting on me. I was extremely nervous, just this little sixteen-year-old kid in his first GP! I thought, 'Screw this, I'm outta here'. I'll never forget the scene going into the first corner. Alex Puzar was first, Jean Michel Bayle was second and I was up there in third! Then the incident that would come to be the story of my season occurred. After the second jump, the bike started to cough and splutter and I went from third to last in two corners. In both motos I was in the points until the final laps, and it was the first step of a disappointing year.

It became difficult when I turned pro because it took a long time for me to switch onto the fact that being a professional motocross racer who gets paid to compete is a full-time committed job. That's where I messed up and probably lacked guidance because I didn't see that I had to change: why should I? I had been successful the way I was and couldn't recognise the need to vastly raise my level of professionalism and even mental approach. My brother Julian really helped me out, more than I can express. He stopped riding in 1985 and decided to put all his efforts into me, perhaps realising that he didn't have what it took to go all the way. He used to do everything for me: organise the race entries, prepare the bikes and negotiate the deals. He was my mechanic, agent, manager and secretary on top of being my brother. There were many, many good days spent racing with him.

We went our separate ways in 1992. He had met and fallen in love with Annette, whom he went on to marry, and she had ideas about life which were different from those of the family. It was a change of life and direction for him and it differed from what I wanted and needed.

Motocross took up a lot of my days as a child and teenager, but I never felt like I was missing out on other stuff. I had my friends at school but then I also had this other life at the races where we used to park up the family caravan next to the same people wherever we went, like a little community, and even now that camaraderie and travelling troupe is a major part of the lifestyle.

★ ★ ★

2001 had ended amazingly in my personal life but on a disappointing note professionally. After taking the Championship in Gaildorf, it had been some time since I had been able to train, thanks to the collarbones, and because the quest had been completed with only a fourth-place finish in Germany, I really wanted to win the three remaining rounds. So we headed out to Holland to get some testing in before the GP of Dutch Brabant at Lierop.

A few days before the race, I pushed myself hard – training for the first time in many weeks – and it took its toll on the upper half of my body, which had been battered enough as it was. I went into the local clinic for a massage and told the specialist that I'd had some problems with my collarbones and was feeling tense around my upper back. He checked me out and I was trying to relax when suddenly CRACK, CRACK! He yanked my neck two or three times before I could stop him. Somewhat alarmed, I left the building and felt uncomfortable trying to sleep that night. At about 4 a.m., I woke up because it felt like my neck was ready to explode. Of all my broken bones and injuries, I have never had pain like it.

Early in the morning I was referred to a local doctor, who managed to do a few things to make me more comfortable. It was the first day of the GP by now, and I attempted the initial free practice session. I got halfway around the track before I came off a big jump that takes the circuit into a lengthy forest section and the neck cracked again. I had the stinging pain sensation and had to endure a long ride back to the pit, where every bump in the sand sent a shockwave down my back. I was as white as a pot of Dulux and I went to the physio once more for some relief but I could not even lie down; the pain was unbearable.

With all the recent bad luck concerning my collarbones, I don't think the team could quite believe it when I told them there was no way I could ride, and for the first GP as world number one, I was forced behind the fence with a neck brace. The final prognosis was a prolapsed disc and they gave me a recovery period of six to eight weeks, ending my season of glory with a resounding thud. I didn't even travel to the final two races, and while Naomi's expanding tummy meant I was drawing close to an awesome life experience, professionally I was more down than I had ever been. One moment I was soaked in champagne, the next wrapped in bandages and tape. Luckily, Naomi and our soon-to-arrive little person provided a welcome distraction. Having a baby is quite exciting and in true 'tell your grandchildren' style I had to make the affair a dramatic one.

About a week before Naomi was due to deliver (a total of five weeks after Lierop), the doctor finally cleared me to start doing some light exercise because my neck had improved. I asked him if I could play football and he remarked that running around was okay, but he advised against lacing up my boots because heading the ball or straining my neck would not aid my recovery. In typical stupid style, I left the surgery at 5.30 p.m. and by 7 p.m. I was in the middle of a match. By 7.15 p.m. I was off the field having broken two metatarsal bones in my foot. I couldn't believe it. I thought 'What are you doing, man?'

It was quite comical arriving home to my heavily pregnant wife hobbling on one foot; she thought I was winding her up, but by the next morning she looked at it (being a trained sports therapist) and said I should get down to the hospital again. Another cast. I called my friend Russ, who is the physiotherapist at Wolverhampton Wanderers Football Club, and asked if he could get me one of the 'blow-up' boots (the sort that David Beckham wore when he broke his foot just before the World Cup). So he sorted me out and actually brought it to the hospital as Naomi was going into labour.

I was finding it hard to walk because the foot hurt so much and I had to use crutches as my wife was in the next room huffing and puffing. The comedy started again when they didn't have any scissors in the delivery suite, so there's Naomi with her mum going through her breathing exercises while I'm at the other end of the room, frantically trying to rip off this cast so I could move around. Finally I got the boot on, pumped it up and made it to her bedside without managing to crash into everyone and fall over all the equipment. It was a hectic time. Naomi was in quite a lot of pain by this stage so, feeling a bit useless, I thought I'd try to crack some jokes; asking if she wanted a cheeseburger didn't go down too well actually.

I find that whole 'moment of life' a really exciting and special thing. I had wanted it to happen to me for a long time. Naomi actually had to have an emergency Caesarean because the little sucker was stuck in there – 'star-gazing' they call it. She had twisted around the wrong way. You think these babies are delicate little things, but when you see the doctor tugging away you have to think, 'Wow, tough little so-and-so'. It took about two minutes for the baby to make any noise and when she gurgled for the first time it did bring a tear to my eye. They laid her wrapped up on Naomi's stomach and it was such a strange feeling to see the 'bump' now a little person in front of me. Her nose and mouth were identical to mine when she was first born and it was a truly heart-melting moment to know that we had made this little miracle.

Gracie Dalas Mae arrived on 2 October, right on time. She was conceived on 2 January and finally popped out of her mother's tummy a full forty weeks later. She was a lovely little thing and I felt like I could look at her for hours in the hospital. She had been the inspiration for my success on the track that year. Since the first day we found out we were expecting a family, she was the last thing I would think about every time before heading out onto that start line. In Teutschenthal for the GP of Mitteldeutschland, the fifth round of the series in April, I was listening to my music as usual before the race and I had just seen the first ultrasound of Gracie. The track 'Silence' by Delirium then became my anthem of victory. I won in Germany that day and I still do not know how I managed to obtain a Championship in a season when I broke both collarbones. I had an operation on one, but I could do nothing about the snapped ligament and cracked bone in the other shoulder. Perhaps it's a good example of mind over matter; proof of how strong and potent sky-high confidence can be. I won that title for Gracie and she won it for me.

The mental strength I had that season was such that I believed absolutely nobody could beat me, especially with the package I had and the team that was wrapped around me. Grand Prix motocross is a 'head game' and you need more than the bike, skill and physical condition; the backing of your team is a vital ingredient to that 100 per cent mix if the Championship pot is going to be sitting on your shelf at the end of the year.

What a lot of people still don't comprehend (and never really see) is the level of commitment that goes into being a professional sportsman. It's difficult because on the face of it I have a dream life, especially to all those people who love motocross or motorcycle racing, but in reality I'm working just as hard, maybe even harder, than the guy next door.

It's a full-time, day-to-day existence that I've had for more or less twenty years. Sure there have been dips. There have been numerous times when my friends have been out and I've joined them because I've wanted to go mad and have a laugh, but then I end up riding to thirty-fifth position in the world. With motocross, there is no middle ground, you either make the sacrifice or you don't and have to settle with being lapped every race. The work isn't only about forty-five minutes on a Sunday afternoon. The intensity at which I train, ride, and race every single day is on another level.

The mental side is just as demanding as the physical element and is something even the people very close to me do not understand.

Thinking about your racing and psyching yourself up, for want of a more technical phrase, is a twenty-four hours a day, 365 days a year load on your mind. In fact, when you do get a break, it can be difficult to switch off.

I think it's human nature to tire of a single thing after constant repetition, and while I live and breathe motocross to such a high extent, I am so glad for my family, sports agency business and other aspects of my life that I have to help myself take a step back.

★ ★ ★

The 250s for 2002 is where I wanted to go. For the majority of my career I have been racing in the 125s, and after finally realising a dream I was ready to move on and try new challenges. After GPs in the 125s, with Cagiva in 1988 and then Honda Britain in 1989 (where I finished thirty-fifth and twelfth), I moved up to the 250s in 1990, still with Honda, and ended up ninth.

The following torrid season with Yamaha was wiped out through injury and gave me a twenty-third while, in 1992, in alliance with a skint Kawasaki effort, I claimed tenth. From three years in the 250s, I won two motos, one in 1990 and another in 1992, before the prospect of moving to America full-time was too tempting to resist. In the States, I became the first non-American ever to win a National US 125cc race.

After supercross and several decent results in the 125s, I returned to Europe in 1997 with Suzuki, joining Honda again in 1998 before riding for Rob Hooper's Suzuki team once more in 1999. KTM boss Kurt Nicoll gambled on a wavering British talent for the 2000 season and the rest is 125cc GP history.

For 2002, I believed that I could win and would make a sizeable impression with a view to heading to the 500cc class the year after, that's how confident I felt after 2001. 'Bring it on', I thought. Riding the way I was that season, I had the belief in my ability to beat anyone in the world.

I don't think people look down on the 125cc class because it's the newest (the first World Championship was run in 1975) or because of the smaller engine size. The 250cc has always been the traditional premier category, while the 500cc has a history all on its own. The gap in engine sizes is quite great in road racing, where the speed differential is vast. In motocross, particularly national series, it's not uncommon to have all three sizes of bikes racing against each other, and the 125 riders more than hold their own in the company of 500s and 250s because a rider's technical ability can count for just as much as extra horsepower, depending on the terrain and the twisty nature of a circuit. The skills necessary to climb aboard a larger machine and go quickly are not a world away from what we already have. Sure, you have more power to play with, but it's not a whole different ball game.

With KTM at the start of the 2000 season, I identified a team with which I thought my Championship dream could be made a reality; a good supporting unit of people is nigh-on essential to earn that number one plate. That team happened to be in the 125cc class, and it was also the category where the Austrian manufacturer had a very strong motorcycle. I always enjoyed the 125. It is a proper race bike and you have to go like the clappers on it – go like hell. With a 250 you have to be more patient, with about fifteen more bhp, and adapt your style to be a bit smoother.

People have asked me if I ever wanted to move classes before 2001 and, in truth, I suppose the answer is yes. I've made mistakes in my career. I haven't worked hard or had the lucky breaks and I'm pissed off with myself for not waking or wising up earlier in life. Maybe I could have won a Championship and moved on and accomplished more things; as it is I'm now thirty and the clock is ticking in a sport that demands so much of your energy, time and dedication. I raced my first factory bike when I was twenty-eight years old. Until then, I was thrashing production motorcycles with special bits trying to get somewhere; sometimes with a lot of effort and little help.

★ ★ ★

November is where a GP season starts for me. I usually have October free just to unwind and take a holiday and then begin the fitness programme and riding all over again. In 2001, I was taking a forced October break because it simply wasn't possible to start working out and Gracie had just arrived. Around the end of November, the foot was fine and the neck was good, so I was able to get the training into full swing, which normally means six days a week in the gym with Saturdays free. I still couldn't ride so it was a perfect time to rebuild my condition, which had been slack for some time.

I get my base training out of the way by hitting two sessions a day and it can be a miserable slog. It's usually cold and wet outside and you are getting out of bed at six in the morning to drive to the gym, but it's those factors and sacrifices that make the success and the fun all the more sweet.

Everything had been fine until flying back from America after my usual end-of-year month-long visit in 2001. Travelling to California is vital for winter riding, mainly because of the weather. In England the conditions are usually pretty grim which means riding every day can often be a wash-out or the ground is frozen solid. In the sun-oven of western USA, this is not a problem. We left just after Christmas – I always enjoy going to the States, especially since I already know many people out there from my four years competing in the mega-bucks show that is USA motocross and supercross.

My body was back to normal and my fitness was virtually in race-condition; I had put a lot of work in with my trainer Kirk Gibbons, who had flown out there with me for four weeks. I had never taken a trainer stateside before, and I really put a lot of effort into that period. I was very optimistic.

On the bike I practised two thirty-minute motos with a twenty-minute break in between and was getting faster and faster lap-times, trying to break my record right until the end of the 'moto'. The 250 was working well, and any little niggles the bike had at that stage I just ignored, because I knew there were bound to be some teething problems and we would get everything fixed.

We had rented an apartment in Corona, where there is a big community of motocross riders and plenty of tracks. I always stay there and it was the location where I actually lived for several years. I felt awesome and so fit coming back from the States, I had good vibes and was ready to get underway with testing work.

As soon as I arrived back in Europe, the shit started to hit the fan. We went to Italy to test in the hope of finding some decent weather, but we had no luck with the circuits. It had rained a lot the week before we arrived, and the conditions were not good for trying to get the best out of a brand new motorcycle. To be honest, I'm not the most patient of test riders. I can get bored quite easily on a motorcycle if I'm not pushed to go wide open, hang the bike out and be shoved into a competitive environment. After a couple of days' riding, I had already had a couple of near misses with crashes and misjudging the track surface, which was changing quite a bit throughout our endeavours. On the last scheduled day of testing, I slipped off in a big way.

The Castiglione Del Lago track was poor. There was a strip, or a racing line, of about eighteen inches that you could bomb along; veer off that course, and the stony ground either side would be like riding on ice. I entered a turn a bit too quickly and ran wide off the line. The front wheel slipped away and I went straight down on my shoulder and also gave the mud a whack with my head. I felt quite groggy for a while and then found out a bit later that I had ripped the deltoid muscle in my upper left arm. This muscle basically controls the wide range of movement in the shoulder. The incident naturally put a downer on things.

My progress was not quite halted, but it slowed down dramatically. I could still ride but was in some discomfort and certainly could not ride at the speed that I wanted. Later, as it turned out, the worst thing was not being able to train in the gym. Fitness work is vital for me, just as much for the mental side as it is for maintaining my strength. The top motocross riders in the world have to work in the gym, there is simply no other way of getting your condition up to a competitive level. We are athletes and as such need a complicated training and diet programme to make sure we hit our physical peak when the first big race comes around.

Getting hurt in pre-season is every rider's nightmare. When the GP racing calendar eventually begins (depending on the severity of the injury you've had and what you have been able to do), you might be unfit, unfamiliar with your race bike (in my case, the machine was brand new and needed as many miles as possible) and inwardly afraid, because mentally you know that you cannot cast any influence on a race.

At the top, you are competing against the best in the world. You can bet the other guys have been working just as much, and possibly even more, than you have. To carry a physical disadvantage, with your bike, or a mental one to the start line is like already conceding the champagne to another rider.

One of the main reasons for finally taking the world title was my strength on the bike in 2001. Nobody could match my power or will in that season. Now I was facing my first-ever year as a World Champion (in the toughest class with a bike that had been only a schematic several months previously) and I was losing precious time.

Like track and field athletes getting ready for the Olympics, we also race in several meetings to make sure our speed is starting to click before the first GP. At Hawkstone Park, the venue for one of the traditional big pre-season meetings where all the GP guys get together with all of their new teams and machines for the upcoming World Championships, I managed to get away with it. The race was in mid-February and only a couple of weeks after the Italian 'job'. My shoulder felt better, but not great. It's always a reassuring feeling to be riding in front of your fans and, being the only 125cc World Champion Britain has ever had, my profile had risen to an all-time high – I will admit that I enjoyed the attention.

I won the meeting overall by coming first in all three motos. I quite surprised myself by beating current number one Mickael Pichon and some other future opponents. Just after the Hawkstone success, as I suspected, the win served only to cloud the problems that were affecting our preparations and create a false sense of illusion that would work against us in the coming weeks. I said to Naomi when we arrived home, 'That was possibly the slowest I have ever ridden in my life to win a race.'

The bike was coming along slowly, but I was still a little surprised about how far away we were from a really strong machine. In America, the tracks were quite choppy, but nowhere as rough as they get in the GPs, and some more faults with the bike were emerging that I hadn't originally noticed. I could circulate quite happily, but when I tried or needed to go fast, the thing was hopping about and throwing itself everywhere. The rate of development on the KTM to turn it into a motorcycle that had to beat the factory Suzuki of 250cc World Champion Pichon, who had won ten out of fourteen races in 2001, needed to be accelerated, and fast.

Looking back, I was a tad naïve. I was in the hands of the team regarding the bike. Why would I doubt them? In 2001, my 125 was faultless and near perfect. KTM's pedigree in the 125s and 500s is well known. Most of the leading guys in the 125s were on orange bikes, and the 500cc four-stroke had already won two titles in four years, thanks to Belgian Joel Smets. My new team-mate Gordon Crockard, twice a British Open Champion and winner of two 250 GPs in 2001 riding a semi-factory Honda, was also hypnotised by KTM's commitment to winning Championships in all classes, and rejected offers from numerous other teams to ride alongside me.

Crockard, at twenty-three years of age, was younger than me but we got along okay. I was a World Champion but Gordon was the 250cc expert, so a lot of development work centred on him, especially while I was unable to clock up hundreds of practice and testing laps. Despite being mature beyond his years, he was no better at setting up a bike than I was, and maybe his inexperience in life and racing did not exactly help. Bouncing around on the 250 for the first time in a few years, I did not have much of an idea if the bike was really good or really bad in the current climes. It felt like it had potential and I felt quite fast; something that my Hawkstone victory helped re-iterate. The next major pre-season meeting was the following week at Beaucaire in the south of France, near Nîmes, and here I was to find the depth of my self-deception concerning the new 250.

I had bought the motorhome by this stage. My status in the sport was as high as it's ever been and the financial rewards had reflected that over the last couple of years. I've always been one to re-invest in my racing, whether in image, which I believe is very important and ignored by a lot of other professionals, or in terms of equipment or little bits and pieces. My view was that if I was happy in the paddock and feeling more at home, then that would have a positive effect on my racing, rather than being holed up in some grimy hotel, which was the situation a couple of times in 2001. I had a family now and I wanted them with me. The motorhome may have looked like an extravagant purchase, but to me it was ideal.

Following the four weeks in which I had returned from America, started testing, injured my shoulder and won in Britain, I now sat in a windy paddock in France, ruing the fact that I had not completed a single full day of training since the fall in Italy. The GP season was three weeks away.

Beaucaire was a miserable time; I did not have the right attitude and maybe should not have been there. Aside from the strong wind, it was sunny and the track was very hard. It was the first time that we had really pushed the bike on a surface like this over three motos, and some more problems with the 250 came to light. In the first race, I took fourth from being back in something like fifteenth.

In the second, I had to pass a lot more traffic again, and just ended up riding round the last few laps for a fifteenth as the bike was becoming unpredictable in its handling. I virtually gave up in the final moto when I almost had three or four huge crashes and backed right off. Only a few weeks before the season, it was stupid to take risks, and the state of the machine under dry and hard racing conditions gave serious food for thought.

The main problem was the suspension. It was difficult finding a set-up and handling that I liked. The team was also confused because we won in the slime of Hawkstone the week before and now suddenly the bike wasn't working. Inevitably, they were looking at me, when the reality was that we were firmly at the beginning of the road of development. I expected it to be a short one. I was doing a pretty good job of hiding a weak shoulder and was just hoping it would soon go away. 2001 was certainly going to be a hard one to beat. Within one year I had got married, won a Championship and had a baby; it had been a mind-boggling time, and certainly not easy to forget.

The 2002 250cc World Championship was twelve races long and visited, in order, Holland, Spain, Germany, France, Italy, Austria, Bulgaria, Sweden, Belgium, Germany, the Czech Republic and Russia. There were two fewer rounds than the previous year, and Australia had been scrubbed from the calendar, which was a shame. It's always important for sponsors and the sport to have global credibility and not to remain so focused on Europe. We were visiting eight circuits that had held a race in 2001; of that total, I took victories at three. Bulgaria and Russia were completely new venues and were built especially for the World Championships, so they would be neutral ground for everybody. Interestingly, the time programme had been switched for television reasons, meaning the 250 race would be the first moto of the day, with the 500s second and the 125s last. In 2001, the 125s were the first to the gate, so there was no major change for me.

For 2002, I placed my affairs in the hands off Neil Calvesbert. Neil had sorted me out with a good deal when he worked at Fox

Clothing and was now part of a new brand called Alloy. I had no problem being the only rider to wear his prototype gear throughout the season, and sold 'myself' as a package, with regards to helmet, boots and everything, through Alloy. I had already confirmed my goggle contract with Smith, and I've had an association with DC Shoes for years.

Approaching the first race of 2002, niggly little things were really holding me back from being ready. I went riding to try and do training 'motos' (a practice period where you simulate a race distance and speed) on almost thirty separate occasions and could not finish one. The bike was a brand-new model, and this meant that the factory did not yet have enough spare parts for certain things such as the mounts for the cylinder head. It was vibrating a lot and every time I thrashed it, the spark plugs would fail; after twenty-five minutes it was never running that well, and we could not last a GP race distance of thirty-five minutes and two laps; more or less just under three-quarters of an hour.

Naomi, Gracie and I would pack the van, drive an hour to my practice track near Mansfield and would not be able to complete a session. Being a factory team, the trouble should have been more or less fixed straightaway, but there seemed to be a problem with communication. The KTM racing set-up has become extremely big now. People who had worked with me in the past had moved around into different departments, stepped up the ladder and new guys were learning from more new guys. I let the communication hiccups get to me and, with the benefit of hindsight, the unsettling influence did not help in the build-up to the first race. I had had a terrific unit around me from KTM for the last two years and I expected it to be the same, but I wasn't happy with the re-structuring – I felt some details were missed and I didn't feel enveloped in terms of support and attention (however much of a prima donna sentiment that appears to be) by the team, due to its size and re-organisation and the fact that we were trying to work with a prototype.

In 2000, the 125 Championship was its own entity and had its own calendar, and in 2001, when the triple-header GP format was introduced (bringing all three series into one weekend), the small factory 125 squad was still separate from the 500 guys. For 2002, Gordon and I were sharing the large working area with 500cc riders Joel Smets and Yves Demaria and their respective personnel. The whole crew had expanded and fragmented. Smets didn't care about anybody else and went off to do his own thing and Gordon adopted that kind of attitude a little bit as well. I found on several occasions that I would want to test or work on the bike, and the trucks or technicians would be away with Gordon. Then I would end up in the predicament of having to ride only weeks before a GP out the back of a small van like some privateer. We were not functioning as a team and that made life difficult.

Gordon was rapidly becoming a competitor more than a team-mate, and we were working apart – and even against each other – rather than together. Again this was a contrast to 2001, when my Italian team-mate on the 125, Thomas Traversini, did a hell of a lot of riding and we'd always share notes and make suggestions. Gordon was like a closed book on occasion, and not quite as passionate about the whole racing scene as me. I can accept that we are all trying to win our own personal World Championship, but we are also representing KTM and have that development angle to wade through; if we had worked together more, then maybe the technical difficulties would have vanished quicker.

We had varying views on the team. I'm very much a team player and like to work and interact with those around me, presenting the KTM race squad in the best light that I can, but Gordon came in with a very set and determined view of winning the Championship and not really giving a shit about anything else. I think he found it hard to blend into the surroundings, coming from a relatively small team with whom he had spent most of his career. Gordon and I both had very different tastes and wishes as to how we wanted the bike to work, but two heads are better than one when tackling the bigger picture and general trouble-shooting. I accept some of the blame for the fraction and Gordon isn't a bad guy. I sensed that he wasn't going to share or help me out, so I also threw up my defences and was equally as childish. It's like were we both peeking over the top of our own little walls within six feet of the KTM awning.

Essentially, a GP racing team is a development and testing project in a competitive environment. We promote and market a new bike by doing our best to try to win, thereby selling motorcycles. KTM have a new 250 and the problems I had pre-season and throughout the year were merely part of an ironing-out process so the consumer would have a better quality end product. On one hand, this is what I am employed for and I can accept the hassle, but it's also frustrating to endure that side of the business when you are a competitive sportsman.

As the start of the season drew near, I rode every day and things were beginning to pick up as we made some progress in different areas on the bike, although it was hardly turning into a bed of roses; I was still facing obstacles. One day I was nearing thirty minutes into a moto, when the thing suddenly threw me over the front end, and I thought, 'What the hell was that?' I got back on the bike, started it up and tried again. Going into the next corner, I grabbed the front brake and the bike just crunched. The carbon-fibre front disc had crumbled. The dead leg lasted a week. Valkenswaard was almost upon us, and Naomi could see that I was upset. I know what it takes to become a World Champion and, in my opinion, I was nowhere near that state of readiness.

I was nervous sitting in the motorhome in the paddock, but not because it was the first GP. After twenty-odd years, the butterflies still get you from time to time, but here I was taking a step into the unknown with an unpredictable bike on the biggest motocross stage in the world. Through a combination of factors, I had not done my homework.

I think of myself as an honest person, and I was the first to put my hand up and express my doubts going into the race. I told the

KTM bosses I was not fit, but this was not through a lack of effort. I was determined not to whinge about my injury problems, but I wasn't keeping quiet inside the team about the bike's ailments. Mechanically, it was sound but not yet a winning package, and the pre-production problems of small things breaking and there being a lack of spares delayed any progression.

The Valkenswaard circuit had changed a little bit in terms of its layout. Located in Holland, it used to have a very flat orientation with some big jumps and a nice rhythm section of triples and doubles around the back. This year, they had taken out a few of the twisty turns, which made the wide sandy circuit a pretty fast place. We were hitting times of one minute fifty, which was quick for a 1,750m track.

Come the start of the weekend and there were quite a few people around, including a lot of press, and the riders were trying their best not to show their nerves when talking amongst themselves in the paddock. I was doing the rounds with Gracie, who was in her element with all the attention she was getting. It was great to see some old faces again, and during the brief moments when the race isn't at the forefront of my mind, I savour the time and conversations I have with people I see only for seven months of the year. The gathering of bright colours, revving bikes, expectant fans, young kids running about fetching autographs and the best riders in the world in one place creates an amazing atmosphere that is really special. No other race is the same as the opening GP of the year. Everyone is placed at square one, we all have zero points and nobody knows what will happen in the next two days. The only pressure you have is that which you exert on yourself. As the season goes on, people embark on their own individual Championship campaigns, be they successful, political, disastrous or injury-prone, and the mood never quite reaches the same fever pitch as the first race when we are all equal in the eyes of the grand prize.

As a World Champion from the previous year and one of the senior riders, I was now one of the leading figures in the paddock and was delighted to see a large British crowd had travelled over the channel to cheer on myself, Gordon, Carl Nunn, Paul Cooper, Stephen Sword and Billy Mackenzie. Despite the underlying excited tension mixed with the behind-scenes nervousness, there were also some ugly feelings and political wranglings occurring due to Dorna's new pass system, which was another change from 2001. The riders now did not have a permanent pass for the season, and were made to buy extra paddock tickets if they had any family or friends attending. As you can imagine, this went down like a lead balloon with Pichon and the other guys. I wasn't particularly impressed either, and had already had a problem getting clearance for the motorhome.

Qualifying largely went off without a hitch as I posted a couple of quick laps and hovered around fourth or fifth, which was good enough for a decent pick on the gate; I finally ended up in fifth.

Trying to eat breakfast on Sunday morning can sometimes be difficult. Your mind is not with you and it's like being a little drunk because you can miss what people say and you are not completely tuned into what is going on, thinking instead of what will happen later, your start and how the race will map out.

There is usually some time to kill after the warm-up (an opportunity to look at the track and see if any rain in the night or work after Saturday's practice has changed the terrain on the circuit at all), and this is when I can feel the butterflies going, especially if I am racing in front of a lot of my fans. About an hour before the off, I start to listen to music. There have been a lot of pictures and television shots of me wandering around with a set of earphones, and everybody always asks me what I am listening to and why. It's mainly dance music compilations; some Roger Sanchez, Faithless and Massive Attack here and there, but I couldn't name the artist of every track I listen to.

The beat and nature of the music relaxes me, and that's when everything falls into place mentally, because any nerves vanish with the sound and I get focused. I think about what might happen in the race and how I will deal with it. I am always reminded that I am there because I enjoy it and I want to have fun, and the other minor worries evaporate. The music thumping away also helps me think what I have done in the last six months building up to this moment and all the hard work I have put in, the countless hours spent in the gym, listening to the same sort of stuff. I remember the sacrifices and the dedication and then have no problem putting them to the back of my mind and appreciating them. This is the pay-off, the fun part; the reason why I am here.

I am quite an emotional person and when I am really pumped before a race, a lot of the time I feel on the verge of tears because I am in the zone and ready to give everything for the next forty minutes of my life. I often find it hard to look or speak to anybody beforehand for that reason! This profession is my life, and I have to live it every minute, whether I am watching what I eat, thinking of my fitness, checking a Lemsip so that it doesn't have any banned substances or merely thinking about what I can do to be better and faster. It gets tiring. You can easily get weary of the whole 110 per cent commitment day in, day out, and for sure there are some races that you enter as bright and breezy as you like. The GPs though are usually a serious full-on business because it's the top riders in the world, and there are normally fewer than fourteen or fifteen occasions in the season in which to prove you are the best. Music and a steely face is how I deal with the tension and seriousness.

Ten to fifteen minutes before the race, most of us are stamping and clearing the ground just behind the gate to flatten the earth in our slot. Getting rid of any stones and carving a line in which to put the wheels of the bike is a psychological thing as much as it has small practical worth. As the clock ticks down with five minutes to go, we start our engines and filter out of the waiting area and into the gate.

I had chosen to wear the number sixty-four this year, after liking the look of them when I was a kid. Unfortunately, I would not have the number one plate due to my class switch, and this might not have looked fantastic to sponsors and obviously wasn't in the same photogenic class as a number one, but the sixty-four was important to me. I don't regard myself as the superstitious type but the two digits existed from the early days and were a natural choice.

I eased my bike into the position I had chosen and the groove of mud I had made with my boots, and then kept revving the thing while I adjusted my googles and waited for all twenty-five other competitors to take their places. I was also looking at the track, using tunnel vision along the path I was going to take to that first corner and visualising myself out front and first as we start to brake and turn.

If I have learned anything from racing for over twenty years, then it's the sheer unpredictable nature of the sport. Favourites fall out of favour and the guy nobody was looking at before the action starts is suddenly the new star. It is not possible to win a Championship at the first race, but it's certainly possible to lose one; a DNF at the start is like being metaphorically stuck in the blocks. I was not afraid of any riders in that gate, what I was afraid of was the lack of a fair chance to show what I could do and prove my well-earned status as a World Champion.

I was stationed around four slots to the right of the first inside-left position, next to pole-position holder and Yamaha rider Fred Bolley on my right shoulder and Honda man Josh Coppins on my left. The race director, who was about fifty metres ahead of us, showed the fifteen-second board. This was it. I gripped the handlebars of the bike harder and when the five-second sign came up, I looked down at the gate. As soon as it even wavered a little bit, I was going. I primed the throttle got my left hand ready and paused.

The gate flew down and I whacked my right hand, jumped the clutch with my left and flew out down towards the turn with everyone else in an explosion of noise. The power surge was exhilarating and comforting at the same time, because at last the butterflies had eased and the race was underway. I worked my way through the gears of the bike and rushed onwards, trying to gain as many inches as possible over the riders to my right and left. The bike squirmed as the back wheel fought for traction in the flattened sand, and the front hardly touched the ground as I skimmed along. I had already lost a little ground to both Bolley and Pichon on my right side, while Coppins had also started well. I focused my vision on the first apex of the small, fast S-bend that flicked left and right, while keeping tabs on things out of the corners of my eyes to see where everybody was in relation to me and where I could fit into the turns. Unless you have the hole-shot and your front wheel in front of everybody else as you start to hit that opening bend, then you are looking to mark your own piece of track in the pack by searching any gaps or holes you can slip into. I wasn't leading, but had a good position and line.

By the time I encountered the ramp of the first jump, barely three hundred metres from the gate and the chicane, I was set for my race in fifth position and took to the air with Paul Cooper right beside me. I slotted into third less than a minute later, behind the two Frenchmen, Pichon and Bolley, and I could feel the adrenaline surging as I completed the first lap. Usually, I feel like I can make the opening circulation of race on pure buzz alone, going as hard as I can to gain any advantage at all, then after five minutes or so I start to settle down while still going like a madman, but trying to maintain a pattern to my riding.

I have never had a problem riding in the sand, whereas others simply can't last the pace; it's a strength-sapper for sure. It takes more out of you physically, because you are always fighting to keep the bike on a straight and narrow path. It's a technical terrain and requires a certain skill. I'm not what you would call a sand specialist like many of the Dutch riders who have grown up in the stuff and neither am I a hard-pack rider – I'm more of a mix and jack of all trades, I'm a good all-round rider and can go quickly on whatever type of dirt and conditions are in front of me. I guess experience makes you adapt to the different surfaces and how the bike behaves accordingly. Riding in the sand, I actually find quite fun and easy. The key is to formulate some sort of rhythm and not to fight where the bike wants to go too much or you will get worn out really quickly. On the soft sand, it will swivel and the wheels will be out of line virtually the whole time, but you have to try and relax and go with the flow of the surface and where it takes you. On some turns, you will have a rut or solid line to follow and that can be a good guide, but most of the time you have to follow the course which you feel to be the fastest.

After about three laps, I was surprised to see that I was losing the back of Pichon, while Bolley was several seconds ahead of both of us, having made the best start. I was told that I was three seconds in front of Pit Beirer. By the next lap, I had taken another second out of him, but I then had the feeling that I was not making any forward progress. I was still pushing the same, but Pichon was starting to get further away. The longer the race went on, the more problems I had with the bike and the set-up; my style didn't lend itself to the both of us lapping at a pace I would have liked and was capable of.

I was revving the engine, but having trouble shifting gear. I had to shut off the gas to go through the gearbox, and it was costing me a lot of time as well as wrecking any kind of rhythm I was trying to establish. The suspension was still doing me no favours either. By lap six, Beirer was right on my tail. It wasn't turning out to be an enjoyable race and became even worse when Beirer came past me to grab third place three laps later at about the halfway stage. I had no comeback to his superior speed and could only watch as he put some distance between us. Suddenly I was checking over my shoulder to see who was coming next. Fortunately, Coppins was nearly five seconds behind and not a lot faster, so I could keeping going and make sure of fourth.

I realised then that I needed to be in this situation, a race environment, when I was wringing the bike's neck, to learn the flaws we had mechanically. I tired towards the end of the GP, but I still tried to draw closer and pass Pit because it seemed as though he was also lagging. Pichon, in the meantime, had passed Bolley and recorded a simple victory unchallenged. I pushed as hard as I could for the whole race and I believe I got the best result the bike could manage; I was disheartened, but strangely content when I crossed the line because I had picked up fourth position somewhat against the odds. I had been aiming for top five, although the reaction of the team, a mediocre race result and the general air of foreboding present that weekend, left me pissed off when we started the drive back home. Upon reflection, I should have had at least third and my evaluation of the GP was one of frustration.

To finish some thirty or forty seconds behind Mickael was unacceptable. Apparently it was suggested that the reason the bike wasn't working at 100 per cent was my fault, and I begged to differ. I knew there was a lot of work to be done and I'm not sure others in the team shared my beliefs, despite me voicing my concerns. Some people's pride had taken a dent when I said the bike was not yet up to scratch, what with tinkering problems, breakages and all. Basically there is only enough room for so many egos in a pit box before the situation turns sour.

Over the next week, I thought about the weekend in Holland, and decided that I didn't like the atmosphere that was forming in the team. Very few people had their eyes open wide enough to see what was required on the bike, while others thought the disappointing results were the faults of the riders, which wasn't on (Gordon was a subdued ninth).

Pichon had taken first blood and looked very comfortable on the Suzuki, easily despatching the challenge of Bolley. I never said I could go out and beat Mickael Pichon in my first race, but what I have always said is that if I was given a bike capable of winning a World Championship, I'll put it up there, and I think I've proved my belief both times I've had that standard of machinery; in 2000, when I won three GPs and just lost to Langston, and then, of course, in 2001. I may be thirty years old, but I learned from that first GP in 2002. I rode to fourth, around the problems, and used my style and experience to guide an unfit World Champion on a spluttering machine to a respectable finish in their first 250 GP together; my frustration simmered, but my pride was undented.

Personally, I took the small positives from the whole episode and carried on, knowing that we would have to work on the engine characteristics and the suspension problems. Looking ahead and aside from the worries, it was still nice to be back racing again.

14 April 2002: Round Two
Spanish Grand Prix, Bellpuig, Catalonia

THE WEEK after Valkenswaard we had a meeting, and I said, 'Okay, guys, we have a problem here.' The trouble was the gears. This in itself was not an irreparable glitch but the powerband of the engine was in completely the wrong place according to the style of how I like to ride a bike. There was no power where I needed it to be, I was always over the top of the band. Where the technicians thought the spread should be and where I wanted it to be were completely different. For a guy wanting to ride through his local woods, the bike was probably great because the torque was low in the engine and would be easier to control. However, I like to race and push the machine at a high rpm, and the bike is harder to manage at that kind of 'grunt'. Changing gear was difficult because it was hindering my speed and race rhythm.

We tested again after Holland in the UK with some new configurations and I felt a definite improvement, especially when they slotted in the crankshaft that Gordon had been using for the last six weeks that I had not been able to try out. The gear change problem suddenly eased, and the power was twenty per cent better. However, where we gained in one area, there was still a lot to be done in another – the suspension. We continued working and moved onto another location apart from my practice area to try a different terrain. Fifteen minutes from my house is the Donington Park road-racing circuit, which also has a MX training course, and there were a few other riders also using it on the day we travelled over.

I tried to avoid a slower guy who had darted across the track in front of me, and crashed after losing the front end of the bike again. This time I was hitched over the bars rather than straight down onto my side, and while my almost-healed shoulder wasn't damaged any further, I did manage to snap the ligaments in my thumb. This latest crash happened a week before the Grand Prix of Spain, and I thought it would be difficult to race. I had a lot of pain in my hand and the suspension was still not working for me – hardly an ideal combination.

At this stage, I had two guys working on my shocks, both from suspension company, WP – Wilfred van Mil, a young Dutch guy who was keen to learn, and his older colleague, Ari Skog, who was very set in his ways. Ari was of the 'It worked three years ago, it will work now' school of thought. But it wasn't happening. I did not know the technical ins and outs of the fault, but I had real problems with cornering. I could not throw the bike into a turn with any kind of conviction. I could not enter a bend, hit a berm, line, rut or banking and bounce out like I could on the 125. The set-up is critical on a 250, and I found the bike was continually kicking me and the rear end would be in the air waving around.

We travelled out to Spain a few days before the GP and tried to test at a place in north Catalonia, but the session was not very productive and I had my hand heavily strapped up.

Italy and Spain are my favourite countries. I enjoy being in either place. I like the food! Give me a good paella any day, and the weather is ideal most of the time. The Spanish fans have always been pretty good to me, and I won at Bellpuig two years on the trot in 2000 and 2001. It's part of the deal – I'll put on a good show for them the more they cheer! Like the Italians, the Spanish have a large motorcycling culture and share a passion for most motorsports. At the races, they lean into the track to wave at you and can be very noisy, which all adds to the atmosphere of the event.

My parents have owned a villa in Spain for a few years now. It's about fifteen kilometres north of Murcia, and about twenty minutes south of Alicante; a nice townhouse near the beach and a perfect place to get away for a week or so.

Bellpuig is in the heart of the Catalan countryside, about an hour north-west of Barcelona, and is one of my favourite tracks. It's a technical circuit and constitutes real motocross in my eyes. It requires you to think and pick your lines, instead of just twisting the throttle and following a procession. The dirt is good and they rip it up well, so that it becomes very rough and challenging. There is a whoops section, some steep slopes and spectacular jumps; it's fun to ride.

I felt okay (ignoring the pain in my hand) in qualifying under some cool spring sunshine, and had no problem clocking a couple of quick laps to secure fifth choice in the gate again. Pichon had pole and grabbed the inside slot, because the first turn was a ninety-degree right-hander that led straight on to a low jump. Keeping the inside line, no matter how far back in the pack you are, can work well at some circuits, because everyone who has got a flyer out of the gate will run a little wide when trying to hit the apex, particularly on the flat, fast bend at Bellpuig, meaning that you can hug the shorter route around the turn. I chose the second gate, which meant that I was right next to him, and we would both be rushing along barely feet away from the bank of fans. My speed was okay in practice and qualifying, the thumb wasn't too much trouble with a mound of tape, and I was feeling okay about the race and semi-confident that I could get a top-three finish in some sunny conditions.

I made a bit of a dodgy start this time, and only my position on the inside of the turn saved me from being further back in the pack. Pichon rocketed into the lead and within two laps had several seconds on the rest of us – goodbye and goodnight. I was about fifth or sixth going around the outside of the second corner, a long left 'spoon bend', and picked off another two riders through the whoops. By the end of the first circulation, Pichon was just vanishing out of my sight as I pushed my way to second and was trying to fend off Bolley. I was like a moving roadblock. I was just able to hold my line and 'shut the door' on anyone when I needed to. Bolley briefly made the job easier on lap six when he crashed coming over the first jump on the circuit.

Within two laps, my breather had ended when Josh Coppins caught up and started sticking his front wheel alongside me. I found

I could drop him slightly after the first half of the lap, but he would bounce back with me on the faster section where I was having more suspension trouble. I did not deserve my speed for second place. Coppins on his factory Honda was faster than me, but I made sure that he could not get past and carried him for at least four laps. I rode a decent but difficult race, never breaking concentration. I had to fight for every second of the forty minutes to keep the bike on two wheels.

Then, towards the finish, my luck wavered from outstanding good fortune to the most miserable of race situations. Coppins was all over me with three laps to go, and I could hear his Honda right behind when he was close enough to touch me on some parts of the track. I was determined that there was no way he was coming through, and I was already thinking about and hoping for my first podium finish of the year. When I went past the pit lane and got the sign that Coppins was less than a second away and there were three laps remaining, I prayed that I could negotiate the next six-and-a-half minutes of my life without any mistakes.

When someone is right up your exhaust pipe, you tend to ride in a different way depending on how well you know the rider. Some will take cheap shots, while others will wait and size you up for a measured pass. I was trying to judge where Coppins would make his move as we came down to a tight right-hand corner that took us into the twenty-yard whoops section (the washboard-like set of small bumps that generally the fastest path through is to bounce on the top of with the throttle wide open and keep your balance, rather than trying to leap through in a coordination of jumps). Approaching this turn, I went around the outside and left of a lapped slower rider as he pulled up close to the inside bank of the track on the right.

Two corners later, and I noticed that the noise from Coppins' Honda had disappeared. I looked back and couldn't see him. I was alone in second and couldn't quite believe it. Looking at the videotape later, the Coppins incident was so freaky it was almost amusing. The backmarker had clipped the edge of one of the bagged hay bales at the side of the circuit and flipped the block straight onto the racing line in front of Coppins. He flew over the bars at slow speed and was now out of contention.

I would be suffering my own demons by the time I saw the tape, and I couldn't help but wonder which one of us had pissed off Lady Luck to such an extreme extent. Infuriatingly, my race finished with less than a lap-and-a-half to go when a stone went through the clutch cover, killing the engine and forcing me to stop in the middle of the steep step-up hills at Bellpuig. I was looking at a slope with such an incline that it was difficult to walk up, let alone push a 97kg bike up when its rider is truly knackered.

It pretty much meant my weekend's efforts turned out to be pointless, and I dropped my arms in despair when Chicco went one side of me to take second and the re-mounted Bolley leapt up the other to assume third. Other riders slowly filtered by as I seemed to pause for an age, breathing heavily and looking down at the bike in disbelief in between holding an audience to my own cursing. It was over. There was little point sitting there stationary; finally, the roadblock had stopped moving.

I pulled the dead bike around, slipped under the plastic fence and freewheeled down the hill and the other part of the track back to the pit. I handed the bike to my mechanic, Fred, and said that the engine had gone, not stopping to hear a reply, and walked straight out to find my scooter. The physical demands of motocross, and the effort it takes to race a bike at such intensity for one moto or several, means that any mechanical failure drives you to unparalleled frustration.

I was intensely pissed off in Spain and bolted straight back to the motorhome, which was obviously locked because Naomi was out on the circuit watching the race. Irritated still further, I went into the team truck, slammed the door as hard as I could and shouted a few expletives to try and calm myself down. When a rider falls off, makes a mistake or does not have the right condition to compete as best as he can, then he deservedly takes the post-race flak, often from lots of different angles. When a bike explodes, then everyone in the team starts to look at each other, and the blame can be shifted around and accusations made in the heat of the moment. A mechanical problem can really test the relationships in the team, and ours were already strained from our pre-season wobbles caused by the bike not being ready.

The guys knew to keep their distance from me for a little while, but I'm not the sort of person who carries baggage; the frustration and anger dies down quicker as I get older, but it still simmers for a day or two before I can forget about it and carry on. I knew everyone was under pressure and any mood swings from me were hardly going to be constructive. I was raging because I had wrestled that pig for forty minutes and left Spain on Sunday night with absolutely bugger all. Championships can be lost in the blink of an eye. I was in second place on the last lap and had not even gained a single point, so I felt like the fat lady was gargling and ready to go onstage as far as my title ambition was concerned. In a twelve-race series, you can hardly afford a bad result, let alone a DNF. My target for the year had been to keep within a single-digit point deficit to Pichon, and I failed at only the second GP.

We were suffering from being a prototype project. The carbon-fibre frame guards that are made for the factory in Belgium were not ready for Spain, and they had to fit 125cc components; the fact that they did not quite cover the necessary parts of the larger 250 engine may have had a part to play in that little rock wedging itself in the motor. The pre-production status and my role as guinea pig were emphasised the week after when the new frame guards arrived, as well as thicker clutch covers. We never had a similar problem after that; all good work for Mr Joe Public if he fancies buying a KTM 250 in the near future.

Gordon wasn't getting on the pace at all, and elevated my results to the forefront of the team and KTM even further. He had scraped a ninth in Holland and then crashed on the second turn in Bellpuig, in a little coming-together with Pit Beirer. He then had to retire a lap later with a broken rear brake. Beirer was ninth. Gordon was slightly swamped with trying to sort out his bike, and I think his frustration was already pushing him away from the team. It was a miserable weekend for everyone.

After Bellpuig and two wins from two races, Pichon was clearly flying on confidence. Everyone is nervous and unsure at the start of the year because there are usually surprises, either mechanical (positive or negative), an unexpected rider in the running, strange crashes or bad luck. But, after two consecutive winner's trophies, he was starting on the roll of confidence that only makes your riding and form better and better. The best, and virtually only, tactic to attack him with now was pressure.

If you apply pressure on the track with some close racing, and then in the actual Championship by keeping the points close, then suddenly that magical trail of winning form is harder to find and produce. Whether it's Pichon, or the Champion in any class, the way to sustain pressure is to keep at them, week in, week out, in practice, in qualifying and when you are chasing each other in the moto – that's how you break someone who is seemingly indestructible. It's not about doing it only in one GP; you have to make them feel threatened and not just at the weekend. He should be thinking about you all week. That's when the mistakes come and the mind wavers. If your rival leaves the track on Sunday thinking 'Fuck, I've really got to put some work in', then you know that you have a chance, and I guess the same is true in any sport when you are trying to gain the upper hand.

Pichon, I think, was glad to see that already there might not be any consistent threats for him in 2002. He had worked very hard developing the Suzuki, and it was one of the strongest bikes in the field. Fred Bolley had crashed and so had Beirer, the two podium finishers in round one. I picked up a fat zero and Coppins had also taken a lower score after his somersault. The Frenchman had already collected two handfuls of twenty-five points with relatively little hassle.

My weekend finished in complete contrast to how it had done in 2001. My World Championship year started in Bellpuig, and it had begun in the best way possible. Pre-season, I had been riding everyday and was getting faster and faster. Kurt always likes a bet and before the 125cc GP we set a little wager on how far in front I would win the race. I had myself down to clear off by fifteen seconds, and in the actual GP I was ahead of everyone by twenty seconds and slowed down to fifteen in the last couple of laps, just to screw 'em and take his money! I had that much confidence because I knew what I was doing and had a terrific bike.

In 2001, I was more than ready for the year ahead. I had changed my training and preparation to be set for the new one-moto GP format, which was more of a sprint rather than a case of preserving enough energy for a two-race affair.

Motocross is a sprint, it's not an endurance event. It shouldn't be about watching some guy just following another because he knows his third place from the first moto is good enough to give him an overall win. It should be about the fastest speeds, skill, and the top riders all going for it as hard as they can. All this, of course, also makes for better television, and this is the direction in which we had to head if the sport was going to grow and fulfil its potential as one of the best spectator motorsports.

Having one moto was tougher on the riders because it increased the tension. There was now only one chance to score points. Therefore, training programmes and mental attitudes had to change in order to produce a more explosive package; mistakes would also prove to be very costly. Technique and ability rather than pure strength were now the main criteria for a GP winner, and that was the level I wanted for the World Championships. It makes the racing better for everyone, most of all the fans. Having one moto means very little room for error, both on the track and in the garage, as highlighted by my Championship position of twelfth after two rounds of the 2002 season; this was thirty-two points away from Mickael, which meant he had a margin of over one race.

★ ★ ★

Obviously Bellpuig 2002 was not the first mechanical breakdown I had suffered nor the only one in such drastic circumstances. Riding the 500cc KTM at the 2000 Motocross of Nations in St Jean d' Angely, France, and leading until the last few turns was another disappointing moment. I had made a small mistake on my first competitive outing on a 500 and had slightly misjudged a jump towards the end of the race. I wasn't used to the firm suspension of the four-stroke, and as the front wheel landed in the soft top soil of the rutted start-finish straight, the rest of the bottom of the bike scraped the ground and a rock scratched through the base of the crank case. The bike seized as I approached the final bend, which was an uphill, banked corner. Luckily, I had just enough pull to get me to the top before the thing coughed. I pulled in the clutch quickly so I could roll down to the finish. I watched Ryan Hughes for Team USA come past to take my race, and they went on to win the contest.

There have been times when I have thrown the odd tantrum or two as a result of mechanical frustrations. In 1992, I was riding for Kawasaki in a difficult situation. Julian had put a deal together with the UK branch, and I signed to ride 250cc GPs on Friday 13 December, which should have been a warning sign really! As soon as we had inked the contract, we started to hear rumours that they were making cutbacks on the budget. This turned out to be true. We had to sell the truck, I got rid of my Mercedes and we had bog standard kit on the bike. I suppose the only good part of the deal was that we had quite a decent budget for spares.

The season was quite turbulent. Paul Malin, who was also with Kawasaki, had the factory engine and they kept swapping the bikes between us, with each section of the team building their own machines. Maler didn't win a race, and after the Swiss GP in which I managed to cross the line first, I had the factory bike.

It had a set-up which was completely different from my riding style, and I hated it. I switched back to my own engine for the Irish GP at Killinchy, just to the south of Belfast. In the first moto I was second, behind Donny Schmit, who caught and passed me for the lead. In the next race, my patience was tested when I had a flat front tyre. Then everything blew up in the last moto.

I took the hole-shot and was in front by around fifteen seconds when I jumped off a drop-down and the bike seized. I went absolutely ballistic, throwing the thing on the floor and lobbing my goggles as hard as I could at it. The crowd were going mental as they tend to do when something exciting develops at the front of a race. So I took off my helmet while I was walking back and threw it as far as possible with rage. The red mist lasted a little longer than usual when Kawasaki team director, Alec Wright, said to me afterwards, 'We've just got some new pistons through, be careful using the old ones because they can break'. Unbelievable.

The 1997 season was my first year back from America, and I was riding a privateer Suzuki with hardly enough budget for spare parts. At the British GP, the highlight of the World Championship calendar for obvious reasons, the bike's electrics packed up while I was in a hard-fought fifth position. Back in the paddock, I flipped out and managed to make quite a mess of the white plastic chairs we used to have outside the tent. Cheryl, the wife of the team boss Rob Hooper, still occasionally mentions that I owe her a garden set! I think it was the only time I have properly lost it because I had really pushed to get up to fifth and was possibly on for a podium. My brothers were equally as angry, and we ended up having a big row in the paddock. We can look back and laugh about it now, but it seemed quite dramatic at the time!

Throwing a petulant fit in some ways isn't very clever or mature, but then I feel that it does show my level of desire and effort, and I'd like to think that people would be more worried if I showed no reaction at all. It's like a kid who cries when he is playing football because the team loses or he has missed a goal; I'm no different in that 'this is the centre of my world and nothing else matters' mentality.

KTM is the finest team I have ever ridden for and make the best machinery I have thrown my leg over, but it has been a long trek to reach the Austrians. The Cagiva was a pain in the ass, and one hell of a way to mark my first year as a pro. I turned professional from the age of fifteen, my first year of competition in the 125cc British Championships, and only one full season before I signed with the Italians. I then had my sixteenth birthday, which meant that I could legally compete in the GPs.

The first factory contract I signed, back in 1988 with Cagiva, which is now Husqvarna, was at a period when a lot of people were speaking to me and other teams were interested. It was an exciting time. The firm were winning 125cc GPs, with people like Dave Strijbos riding for them, and I thought it was a good move. They said that I would have factory bikes in my first full year of GP racing. What could sound better to an ambitious sixteen-year-old kid? I had been 'smoking' people all over Europe, and I honestly believed that I would carry on doing well in the World Championships. A little naïve perhaps, but I was determined all the same.

The truth is, I didn't get half as much help and support as I thought I would, and the bike I was expected to ride was nowhere near what you would call a factory spec. machine; there were much better bikes out in the field, and mine seemed to be one of the oldest! It would barely last a moto, and a contractual obligation to keep my mouth shut meant that my reputation took a battering, and the label that I couldn't 'finish a forty-five-minute race' stuck unfairly for years. To be fair, when it wanted to work, the Cagiva was phenomenally fast, but sadly that happened far too infrequently. I remember one day when an old mechanic of five-times 125cc GP winner Italian Corrado Maddii took a look at our engines and managed to render us speechless when he said he recognised the serial number of our motor to be the same that Maddii had used in 1984!

Little things like silly crashes, mechanical problems and non-existent results meant that, mentall,y I finished the contract on a bit of a low. Nevertheless, as I mentioned, it was a good learning experience and toughened me up at a young age. In 1989, I was with Honda Britain and became the youngest-ever winner of the British 125 title at seventeen. Aside from KTM, one of the best teams I rode for was the Pro Circuit outfit over in America, headed up by an enigmatic guy called Mitch Payton, who owned the Pro Circuit performance-tuning company.

I had been with a privateer Kawasaki set-up in 1992 and was looking for a new deal in 1993. Nothing was really coming my way, and I was quite taken with the prospect of racing in America. I had been travelling across the Atlantic throughout my career, and people knew who I was because I had won some races in the US. It was still pretty unheard of for Europeans to take on the American guys, and Frenchman Jean Michel Bayle had paved the way with his success a few years previously.

Some American friends of ours, who were in England to import some pipes and other equipment, stayed with us in Derby at the end of 1992, and I sounded them out about getting a deal for 1993, possibly over the water. They suggested that I call Mitch at Pro Circuit and we went from there. I asked him if we could talk about a deal. Initially, it was a touch-and-go opportunity, because the team had just switched from Honda to Kawasaki and also had a new sponsor of Splitfire Hotwheels. Mitch made some calls to the sponsors and everybody concerned and they didn't have a problem.

Mitch sent me the confirmation fax offering me $500 a race and use of the Kawasaki, and I also got to keep a share of my winnings, minus my personal expenses getting to the track. The problem was that I didn't have a green card, so he taxed me almost forty per cent. I kept the fax and have it framed somewhere.

The day after Boxing Day, at the age of twenty-one, I flew out to the States to contest the lengthy racing season, with the SX indoor and MX outdoor competitions to look forward to. I got off to a bad start when I broke my arm in the first twelve weeks and had to have two plates and seventeen screws put into my ulna and radius. Another break later in the year didn't help.

Generally, Mitch was a real pain in the ass to ride for. I have never met anyone who hates to lose as much as him. He really takes no shit and works the hard-line approach to try and whip you into shape. It really transformed me as a rider because I had never really ridden under that pressure before, although at the time I didn't respond to the ass-kickings that well. I'm quite an emotional and sensitive person, and the bollockings didn't really get me fired up.

A good friend, Jeremy McGrath, would probably agree with me that Mitch can be the biggest asshole to work for, but when you were having a party he was at the top of the guest list because he was a real character. He certainly toughened my resolve. Mitch used to be a top desert rider in the US – the Baja-style chases they run out there in California. After a big accident, he was paralysed and confined to a wheelchair and then went on to create the Pro Circuit service.

Mitch, more often than not sporting an impressive mullet haircut, could have a temper sometimes. In other ways, he really helped me out and had a huge heart. When I was injured, he couldn't do enough for me. He used to lend me the old battered Pro Circuit truck so that I could get around. I would deliver some pipes and run some errands for him, and he gave me a lot of chances to build a comfortable life in America.

Without a doubt, the most miserable time I had with a team was Dave Thorpe's CAT Honda squad in 1998 at the age of twenty-six. I had returned from the American dream in 1997, and ran a season with Rob Hooper and his Suzuki team that year, finishing eighth in the 125cc World Championship. I thought I had made something of a dream move to Thorpe and Honda for 1998, how wrong I was.

Thorpe is arguably Britain's most famous motocrosser, winning three 500cc World Championships – in 1985, 1986 and 1989 – when the sport was going through its peak of popularity in Britain.

He was now the boss of the Honda marque he made famous, and the only thing I learned from him was that meeting your heroes is a very dangerous thing to do. He disappointed me in every way; as a team boss, a friend and a hero. The team was disorganised and lacked direction, and it was an episode of my life to forget.

The situation turned to shit when stuff started going wrong on the track and with the bike. Things went sour after a third of the season. In the first three or four GPs, I scored seventy-five points – I then finished the rest of the Championship with a total of 124, and this was in the days of two races, when it was possible to take twenty points for a win in each moto. The bike was not developed at all and just would not work. I started to get scared riding the thing. Thorpe had the audacity to start making noises that the poor results were my fault and that pissed me off.

Personally, I hold my hand up and accept some of the blame for not winning (when I finished) in 1998, because my physical preparation was wrong. I wasn't focusing on the right areas and was actually doing boxing training at one point. I was getting tired more easily, and that, combined with all the mechanical breakdowns, chewed away at my confidence. By the middle of the year, I was in a slump and didn't know whom to turn to in the team to help me out.

It got worse. For reasons unknown to most of the British motocross world, Thorpe decided to leave me out of the Motocross of Nations team. He was also the manager (and therefore selector) in charge of picking three riders. The tournament that year was even more important to all Brits since it was the first time the annual event, traditionally the international season closer, had been held on home turf since 1980. I have always given 100 per cent at the Nations races and, for some reason, it always gets the best out of me. He chose Paul Malin instead, who had only managed to beat me on three occasions in the entire year, as well as a young Carl Nunn.

This might well be my overreaction but, from what happened throughout 1998, Thorpe just didn't want me in the team through spite, and wasn't basing his judgement on form or ability, which he should have done. No disrespect to Paul and Carl, but I was angry and felt partially vindicated when both riders gained crap results. The way Thorpe handled the issue was all very petty and unnecessary. Understandably, 1998 was quite damaging to my career and I wouldn't blame people if they were beginning to think I was an underachiever. I was a bit of a mess after the experience, and luckily found some welcoming arms.

Going into 1999, I was riding for Rob and Suzuki once again. They were a great little team, and Rob helped me out immensely with the tiny budget he had; I had some of my best races outside of KTM with that set-up, although my dreams of being World Champion met a severe uphill test. Rob is a super guy and a very good friend but we literally had no money. There were no funds for testing and we couldn't even afford the fuel to get extra practice! The case was more or less the same as in 1997, and I also struggled then in the first races with a broken finger. The official Suzuki effort didn't help us much, as I had just come back from the US and wasn't seen as a decent enough rider. I was only paid £12,000 a year. From that I had to live, fork out for all my racing expenses like hotels, flights etc. and pay my mortgage on a house I had bought when I was eighteen in a suburb of Derby. My dad helped me out by letting me use my mum's car.

It was at that point in my career that I knew I really had to get serious about the whole World Championship business. If I couldn't win a title with Rob and Suzuki, I had to give absolutely everything I had to make sure I put myself in the frame for a factory ride in the future. I knew that if I had not succeeded because I didn't give it my best shot, then I'd have to live with the knowledge and regret that I was a lazy bastard for the rest of my life. No thanks. So I started knuckling down from more or less 1997 onwards.

As well as gaining eighth in the GPs that year, I also won five from seven British rounds and took the domestic title. Team GB also came third in the Motocross of Nations and I won the 125cc heat, which was a real honour. In 1999, we got a bit more help with suspension from Sylvain Geboers, who ran the official Suzuki squad, and there was slightly more money than the set-up in 1997. The Suzuki team was a really tight unit, and I loved and needed that. It was also very professional with the resources it had at its disposal.

On the track, we were never regularly going to fill the cabinet with trophies, but we nearly won a moto in Germany. However, a young lad called Grant Langston was amazing that day on a exceptional bike – a KTM. He passed me with two laps to go and wrapped up the overall victory. I took a creditable fifth in the Championship, after disappointingly losing fourth to Thomas Traversini at the last race in Croatia.

I'm extremely grateful that Kurt Nicoll gave me a chance with KTM – my first factory ride at the age of twenty-eight, and in a team in which I was allowed to develop as a rider. I had been speaking to Kurt a lot in 1999, and gently trying to get my name in the hat for a KTM seat. My friend, Craig Elwell, who runs a pipe company called DEP, was also forcing my case with the recently retired ex-GP winner and making sure that he didn't forget that I was looking for a ride. Initially, I didn't think that KTM wanted me, but Kurt pushed and told the factory that 'this guy can do it if we give him one of our bikes'. They trusted his opinion and I ended up in the team, feeling under quite a lot of pressure to justify my contract.

I think that's why he was pretty happy when I won my first race and GP for the factory in Bellpuig, Spain, the opener to the 2000 season. Maybe it's fair to say that I've given him his happiest times as a team boss! I've taken a fourth, second and a first in the last few years, and there aren't many people who have had those kinds of results.

Kurt was one of Britain's best-ever 500cc riders and, criminally, he never won a World Championship. He was runner-up no less than four times (Georges Jobe pipped him by only two points in 1992) and ruled the British series on seven occasions. He was forced to retire in 1998 because of injury and assumed a team-manager role with his last employers, KTM. Kurt is a real rider's team boss, largely because he has experienced all the highs, lows and most situations a pro MX rider will go through. He has an affiliation with his staff because he is still young enough to train and ride, which he does quite often, and even in the last few years carried out a lot of testing for the factory. Kurt doesn't really take any shit and can be an odd character if you do not know him very well. He was quite shy when he was a rider, but his lack of flamboyance masked an iron will and thirst for winning quite unlike anyone else I've met in the GP paddock – he still carries those traits as a team boss.

The thing that impressed me the most when I arrived at KTM was the bike and the level of professionalism of the team. The 125cc machine felt very fast, and I was almost overwhelmed by the amount of stuff there was to test in my first session. Frames, suspension, kits for the engine – there was a hell of a lot of work to do, but it felt fantastic to be part of this committed factory effort.

To my pleasure, the team soon gelled, and during the 2000 season, I had a magic little group of people in my corner. As the three classifications were not all at the same GPs at this stage, the 125 unit was again like another family gang – everybody used to pitch in. Jane, the girlfriend of engine technician Leighton, would come to the races and cook everyone food. Naomi also helped out with my boots, goggles and moral support. It was a great effort to be a part of, and it showed in my results.

In 2002, the immediate people around me from KTM were Leighton, looking after my engines, Wilfred from WP, taking care of the suspension, Kurt and Toby, as race managers, and finally Fred Kello, my personal mechanic, but we were only a little section of the vast KTM GP set-up. Working closely with numerous individuals towards a common goal really emphasises the word 'team' off the track. You have to trust your mechanic and it can be a double act. Fred is a good friend and I trust him wholeheartedly. He has always been there when I've needed him, listening to my frustrations and bitching. I think we are a pretty formidable duo, and it was an emotional time when we won the title together.

I wasn't World Champion until the age of twenty-nine, and that was just as much due to the bent politics of the sport as it was my poor decisions and badly-chosen paths. I'm not crying about this now, but if I had the right backing at a younger age, or had been fortunate enough to run into someone like Kurt Nicoll, then I might have a slightly longer trail than eleven GP wins and one World Championship in the record books. Still, it's not quite over yet.

28 April 2002: Round Three
European Grand Prix, Teutschenthal, Germany

IN BETWEEN GPs, I am already thinking about the next race. It's a matter of getting what work you can into the time you have available, which in my case with the KTM bike meant quite a hefty schedule. We were testing again after Bellpuig, and with the disappointment of Spain behind me, I was trying to get everything ready for the GP of Europe in Teutschenthal.

I went cycling with Julian on the weekend break, and he had checked out the 250 that was parked in my double garage on our return. He looked at it, mainly the suspension, and straightaway said, 'Tell me you're not racing with this?' He suggested a few things and we altered some settings. I then went riding, this time with the suspension guys from WP in tow. It was hard getting through to Ari, who had his own agenda – 'That won't work' were his first actual words.

We faffed around all day and, finally, as it was getting dark, with the last few laps we tried Julian's recommendations, and it started to feel better. It was a small step in the right direction. I'm a relaxed guy about many things, but with my racing I like everything to be organised in the build-up to a race, so that I can focus on what I have to commit, physically and mentally over the weekend. If I arrive at the track before I can switch my mind to what I have to do, I believe that it is too late.

Round three saw us travelling to the old East German state for the GP of Europe, which was in a small place called Teutschenthal. If ever there was a circuit 'off the beaten track' on the calendar, then Teutschenthal was it. Located in the rolling German countryside around a twenty-minute drive from Liepzig, it would be very easy to miss the track if there weren't signposts.

It wasn't so much tucked into the flattish landscape as virtually submerged. There is no hill or noticeable landmark to identify a MX venue (many places use a lofted feature of the countryside to constitute their course) until you drive up to the gate. The circuit itself is 'sunk' into the land, almost like an old quarry. The slopes generated by the sides of the marked-out track make for a decent set of viewing areas and may explain why, despite its remoteness, Teutschenthal is one of the highest-attended GPs.

I like the outlay of the Teutschenthal track. It has a little bit of everything and is very naturally situated. It flows and is fast, while being quite technical at the same time. There are some big, steep jumps, which make it quite spectacular, and it's also a decent place for passing.

Before 2001, it had been some time since the 250s had visited the former East Germany – 1971, in fact, was the last occasion, and the record holder for the most World Championships with six, Joel Robert, triumphed that day. The Teutschenthal venue was so untainted and natural that I doubted much had changed from Robert's era. Its flow and rhythm made Teutschenthal a popular track with the riders. It certainly was okay in my book and as Na, Gracie and I arrived at the paddock in a rental car, I had pleasant memories of my win in 2001.

In contrast to the sunny day twelve months ago, the whole weekend was pretty gloomy and was also very cold. During Saturday, the rain really came down hard, along with some big hailstones. I had already made sure of sixth position before the rain soaked the German countryside, and this slot was satisfactory for the race. I held the sixth spot in from the inside of the turn (like Bellpuig, a ninety-degree right-hander, but this time dropping down a slope), which once again pole-position man Mickael Pichon had made his own. Bolley was second and right alongside him.

Nowadays, that single second the gate takes to drop to start a race is the one of the most crucial periods of the moto. The depth of talent in the GPs has increased, and whereas before you could fluff your start and catch up because there were only a few riders running at the same pace at the front, now if you enter the first turn outside of the top ten and one of the good guys hole-shots, then you've virtually blown it and you are not going to catch him.

Starting is purely a reaction and an instinct. It's about hand-eye co-ordination that is as quick as snapping your fingers, and an area where a factory machine enjoys an obvious advantage. You need to know where to position yourself on the bike and where the power needs to be so, that when you grab the clutch and whack open the throttle, you are up and away as fast as possible. Confidence helps a lot. You have to anticipate the gate and you are looking for any little thing to move, like waiting for the gun in many ways. When the fifteen-second board goes up, then I think most of us really switch on to what is about to happen. I wait for the five-second sign, pause and then look at the gate, so that I'm staring at it for the minimum amount of time (too much, and your nerve and ability to anticipate starts to wobble), and just waiting for it to flinch slightly before I gas.

Once you are going, you then have to nudge up through the gears and try to elbow yourself some space if you need to, brake hard and scrub off some speed to line up for the turn, depending on the severity of the first bend, which can range from a 180-degree curve about five metres wide to a fast left-right flick like in Valkenswaard; it's an aggressive and decisive moment in the race, hesitate or bottle it and you can say goodbye to your podium. I'm booting the gear lever and leaning back if I need to get more traction with the back wheel on the approach to that first turn, where I am looking at the pack, the corner, and for any gaps to dart into. We are usually heading quite quickly into a narrow space, and it may seem like bedlam to a spectator, but you are reacting to what you see and where you are in relation to others.

There is quite a lot of banging going on most of the time. If someone is going to wipe you out, there is not really a lot you can do about it, as my shoulder scar from Sweden in 2001 will testify. It can become a bit dangerous if there is a big jump just after the first turn, because it's more or less one of the few times when you'll be taking to the air in a pack and can be unnerving for that reason.

I remember a time in 1992, at the Italian GP, when I got accused of jumping the gate. Harry Everts even came up to me after the race and accused me of cheating. I told him bluntly to 'Fuck off' because if he had the advantage I did, then he would have used it also. It was quite funny because all weekend this Italian guy had been walking around telling us that it was impossible to cheat at the start because they had a new button-operated electronic gate, which was foolproof. I lined up for the race taking the first inside position and, to my pleasant surprise, the goon of a race starter was standing right beside me, no more than a metre away, with the controller and button in his hand. That was it! I was off as soon as that thumb moved. I didn't even touch the gate, I went forward as it lowered. I was gone, you've never seen a start like it! They ended up calling us all back, mainly because there wasn't a Chesterfield Yamaha in the first five — they were sponsoring the event and Michèle Rinaldi went mental, so it was stopped.

This time, in Germany, the last rider I would have expected to cock it up made a huge mess of the start. The first corner at Teutschenthal is particularly tricky. After a sixty-yard sprint, thirty bikes then have to take a ninety-degree right-hand bend that is off-camber. The 250s were out first, so the track was machined and flat, no grooves, berms or ruts to hit in the first few laps. Grip was to be a precious commodity.

The weather was miserable. It was chilly and the sky was an unbroken ceiling of grey. It had been raining the night before and the circuit was very damp. I had a position four riders away from Pichon, and had a splendid view of the mayhem he caused within the first ten seconds of the race. He shot up the inside far too quickly without having the hole-shot. Bolley was right beside him on the outside of the turn, slightly ahead, and as he turned his Yamaha inwards and right to close the line and make the corner, Pichon rocketed into the side of him. Bolley was sent flying over the berm at the side of the track, along with Chiodi for company. The spill collected a number of riders and it was very chaotic. Luckily, I was behind Bolley before he was taken off the track and could turn the bike very tightly to avoid the crash; in fact, I had a good line down the hill and into the fast dip to be one of the leaders along the main straight. Overtaking Pit Beirer into a fast left-hand turn, which I nearly messed up completely, I was out front. Pichon, I discovered later, had worked his way back up to eighth from last with a damaged exhaust.

It just proves that even World Champions have their moments of madness. Pichon later claimed that Bolley cut him up. If there was any problem with Mickael in 2002, it was that he had lost respect for some of the other riders. When that happens, it can prompt some dangerous situations. If the guy behind you doesn't have a care in the world, if one of his passes throws you face-first in the dirt, then racing loses some of its fun. He had charged flat-out into Bolley, and while most of the incident was probably a mistake and a miscalculation on his part, it was still a reckless move to make on the first turn and in the pack. I knew that the Championship leader was down and effectively out of the race. No hat-trick on the cards for Pichon today.

Leading on the first lap, I felt nervous; suddenly the Championship wasn't quite over. This was a golden opportunity to get right back into the title chase. I was thinking too much and not concentrating enough. Suddenly, I had Kenneth Gundersen right with me, and the young Kawasaki rider, who was negotiating his first 250 season with a works bike, was proving to be a nuisance. He pulled alongside a few times, and we had a good little fight for a lap before I was able to make a pass stick and get a bit of breathing space. I found out that Bolley had remounted but crashed again after five minutes and was all but out of the GP.

Once I had settled down and made the small break from Gundersen, I knew that I could push and go a bit faster. On lap four, I was four seconds ahead and maintaining the distance. I was comfortable. Most of the time, except when you are in a scrap, riding on your own is all about rhythm and precision. You pick your lines on the track, and you ride as fast as you can through the sections that your mind breaks the circuit into. You usually know that you are quicker through certain parts than others, and linking the splits of the track together in the smoothest and most mistake-free manner conserves your energy and establishes the rhythm. When you try to push and increase the consistency in your low lap-times, then you hit particular sections harder. For less experienced riders, this can sometimes throw their rhythm and not have the desired effect. It can also lead to a mistake and a crash, especially if the track is changing throughout the moto due to weather or wear.

I had problems in that every time I tried to settle down and make some regular laps, the bike would chuck me off to one side and I'd have to correct and start again. The suspension was not helping. You don't think about a great deal when you are out on your own, and your mind can wander. Usually there is a high level of concentration and you are occupied with numerous little jobs. Positioning the bike correctly in that part of the corner to get more grip, looking at your lines and thinking about where to go on the track that might make you a bit faster, watching your lapboard to see how much time you have over the guy in second. These are things that you do when the race is going well. If your bike is not giving you a smooth and easy time, then you have that stuff to worry about as well as making sure you don't crash and having to take extra care of your riding while trying to go fast!

The thirty-five-minute duration can feel like an age, and a GP always disappears quicker when you are fighting for your position. Heading the pack and setting the pace is a skill on its own, and there are many who cannot hold it out until the flag. Sometimes you do notice things around you. You look at the clock that is counting down the race time as you ride past, you see flags and people leaning inside the circuit cheering you on, and you can easily have a good look around when you have some decent airtime over a jump.

I held a gap of a few seconds over Gundersen after ten minutes. On the fourth lap, I crushed my exhaust and almost lost control in an incident that would act as a prelude to disaster. The third corner of the circuit was a 180-degree hairpin at the highest point of the landscape, and you had to hurry up a fifteen-metre slope that was at such an angle it was almost vertical. I threw the bike into the banking that lined the outside of the hairpin but, instead of rebounding off and away, the soft mud and sawdust they had packed into the end of the four-foot wall of mud gave way slightly, and I squashed the end of the bike. Usually, I held my gear in this turn and revved out and over the lip as we dropped back down the slope in the other direction. With the pipe slightly damaged, I lost power going over the edge and almost 'endo-ed', launching myself over the top of the bike. I stayed onboard but wrenched my weak thumb back trying to hold on. For the remainder of the race, I was constantly distracted by the pain from my hand, and literally had to grit my teeth on some parts of the track where I needed to tug on the bars.

At about the midway stage, for almost ten minutes I wanted to try and push, but I was actually going slower – I had to back off. With the 250 suspension set-up and my throbbing thumb, I was trying harder to establish a winning margin over Gundersen, but the thing was not responding to my efforts. The rear end of the bike felt too low – when I wound the power on, it would 'sit down', then when I hit a bump, it would kick off, making it unstable and at times almost unrideable. I didn't know where it would go or what it would do under acceleration on bumpy ground or hitting holes in the ruts. To be honest, I thought it might have been a problem with the front forks, because of the way it was moving around and bucking me.

I was concerned, but still concentrating fully, and I was determined that I would not lose this now because of dodgy thumb ligaments, I was the one in control here. Only I could lose this race and I almost did several times, holding onto the bike and hoping I wouldn't fall.

On the last lap, my lead was down to two seconds and I was halfway to the chequered flag when I committed the mostly basic and costly error of my fifteen-year career. It was a nightmare scenario that I had never ever experienced before, not even as a kid. I had lost count of the moments I had saved the bike beforehand but, as I approached a banked hairpin right-hander and took the grooved racing line at the top of the curve, I tried to hit the berm but the front wheel lost grip – I had no more strength, my thumb folded and down I went. The bike was higher than me as I rolled down the hill, keeping hold of the thing with my left hand. I had crashed on the worst part of the track.

The 250 was upside down and on a slope, and it took me longer to stand the thing up and get it going than if I had rolled off on a flat turn. If the mistake had happened somewhere else, then I would have been able to jump back up, kick-start it and at least have taken second, if not fought Gundersen for each remaining inch of the race. As it turned out, I heard the crowd squeal with surprise/shock/delight at the late moto development, and saw Gundersen, Coppins and Pit Beirer go past before I could re-enter the race. I had to fend off Paul Cooper and Jussi Vehvilainen for the last minute-and-a-half before I coasted across the line fourth and rode straight back to the team tent, pissed off with my stupidity.

I had the worst feeling in my stomach, like nausea mixed with deep disappointment and anger. My thumb was killing me and, for a moment, it took my attention away from what had actually happened in the GP of Europe. It had swelled up like a tennis ball and I hoped there was no serious damage.

Kurt was pissed off. In fact, there was a revealing television image from the moment of my crash when he saw the episode on the monitor screen in the pits and promptly kicked the side of the pit box in frustration. I think it admirably summed up the feelings of everyone that day.

It was a bad day for KTM as Gundersen won the 250s for Kawasaki, Everts took the 500s for Yamaha and Mickael Maschio collected the 125cc GP for Kawasaki. Inside the team, nobody was more annoyed at the day's outcome than me. KTM wanted to prove that their 250 two-stroke could be a success and, while we were slowly, slowly getting close to a potent bike, there was still pressure to justify the investment and give the motorcycle a win by all means possible. The firm may have lost the two other GPs in Germany, but I'm sure a debut 250 victory (no matter if it was ill-timed in comparison with its development) would have softened the blow. I couldn't quite swallow the fact that I had missed the podium again on the last lap.

I went to get the thumb X-rayed when I arrived home, because I really thought I had fractured it and wanted some clarification. It turned out that I had pulled what was already a weak ligament and basically the injury had just re-occurred.

Unusually for me, I kept re-living the crash in my mind over the next week. As I rode up the banked turn, I wanted to cut in sharp and square the corner off, but the front wheel just lost grip in the uphill groove that was hardly a rut at all. As soon as I couldn't grip the bike with my hand and started to fall down the slope sideways off the bike, I was screwed. It was a horrendous feeling that filled me the millisecond after it happened; one of panic and blind rage. From a professional racer with my level of experience it was unacceptable, and I'd go as far to say it was the most embarrassing moment of my life.

People were cracking jokes, thinking (more often than not correctly, but not this time) that I was over the GP and I could have a chuckle about it. This was much worse than then the disappointment of Spain, and I was ready to rip people's ears off if they tried to take the piss. I started to watch the race again on television and I felt like squirming in my seat. I felt sick and couldn't face the whole programme; to this day, I have only seen parts of the GP. It must be the only one of my races that I have not sat down to view afterwards. The thought of that simple, but ever-so-costly, blunder was doing my head in.

Looking back over the years, I have never committed an error of that size and intensity at such a late stage in the race. I think that is what made the Teutschenthal crash even worse to bear. Even at thirty years of age, I was still experiencing first-time occurrences in my career. Of course, last-ap mistakes happen across the whole spectrum of the motorsport world. Like missing an open goal or letting the ball through your legs in the final minute, it is an excruciating and painful last word.

★ ★ ★

Like most sportsmen, I have gone through some dark periods in my career, and the disadvantage of having raced from the age of five is that I have lived a fairly competition-heavy childhood; meaning those horrible moments when I've wanted to throw out my boots and hand the helmet to someone else were inevitably frequent.

A disappointing time was the 1996 SX season when I was battling with Kevin Windham for the Championship. There was nothing between us that year, and I was riding the indoor circuits better than I had ever done. At a round earlier in the campaign at Houston, Windham and I were tied on points and I was rounding the circuit in practice and approached a triple. I built my speed up ready to launch, and two kids in front of me hit the brakes. I was just behind and between them, and tried to slow down, but ended up crashing in between the second and third jump and smashing my chin. I chopped the end of my tongue off, lost three teeth and had to have twenty-five stitches. I then broke a foot peg at another round later on, which confimred the end of my title aspirations.

I have been a motocross professional since the age of sixteen and have experienced the highs of a World Championship and SX success to the lows of injury, team feuds, bad form and total demotivation. In 1991, at the age of nineteen, I signed another supposed factory contract with Yamaha. The team boss was a guy called Gary Benn, and he used the former 500cc GP winner Swede Hakan Carlqvist as a rider/coach, although the latter would be largely running the show. Carlqvist's pre-season regime was like an army camp. I'd have to test for five days and then I'd be allowed a day off, before another day of making timed practice sessions. In these sessions, he would have a cut-off lap time, and if we didn't beat it then he'd say that he had a prize for us. Predictably, we did not break the time barrier, and the prize was to complete a long run while he sat there with the mechanics, laughing and having a beer. That managerial style really did not work for me, and it soon built a wall of resentment.

We used to test at a public track near Lommel and one day, as I hit a step-down after a kid on a mini-bike had veered onto my line, I crashed and broke my collarbone quite badly. Naturally, being out and injured, I returned home and found the social life I was missing out on with my friends. It was a hard time for me professionally because I was feeling low, and I was getting distracted by going out drinking and chatting up girls. I also suffered with a method of man management from Carlqvist that served to piss me off rather than help my self-esteem. More than anything, I needed my hand held rather than to be screamed and shouted at. When I recovered from the collarbone, I still wanted to be a success in motocross but I was also torn in the direction of wanting to go to clubs and meet girls. I got out of Yamaha at the end of the year.

1996 represented my last year racing in the States and another low point – I was fed up with my career and motocross at the end of that season. I rode a factory Suzuki in the SX and a private bike in the Motocross Nationals, where I was still the top rider for the firm, despite the fact I was spending $1,500 a week from my own pocket on spares and my racing budget. I had gained second in the 125cc West Coast series, my best-ever SX Championship placing, and managed to win a 250cc MX National, even though I was taking parts from other riders that were semi-knackered and that had already been used in the last race.

I was fired before the final round where I had a chance of making third or fourth overall in the outdoor Nationals. I had been having problems with the Suzuki and asked Roger De Coster, who was the co-ordinator at the time, if I could use factory rider Tim Ferry's bike because he was injured and would miss the last race. He said he didn't have a problem, but he would first have to ask my sponsors, Performance Engineering. The same week I received a letter from PE, saying I was out of a ride because I had not given them sufficient publicity and return on their (minor) investment and had been slagging off the team. This largely stemmed from my National win, when in the post-race press conference on television I was so tired I could hardly move and was trying to remember everybody I had to thank, and referred to the firm as PE, as they were widely known in the industry. It turned out that this was not enough, and my voiced annoyance about having to shell out so much of my own money to go racing, I think, was the straw that broke the camel's back, after my chasing of De Coster for more support. Roger did not want to get involved, and I left America disillusioned and pissed off.

My family has always helped me through the low times, and we are a close bunch. At the end of 1996, I started to find my own immediate little family and, true to cliché, I knew from the moment I saw Naomi in a nightclub in Stoke that I was on to a winner and, at that time, I had just the angle with which to get her.

As my enthusiasm for MX waned towards the end of the season, I had started taking up another profession: modelling! I was introduced to a friend of stunt rider Mike Jones, who was a top male model from New York. His name was Phil Bickett, and he had a portfolio that was amazing, working for Armani and basically making moves at the top of the fashion ladder. A few people had suggested that I should try a bit of modelling because I was obviously in good physical condition and could put on a decent pout when required! I was single at this time, and thought it would be a fantastic way to pick up some girls and have a bit of a party.

In March of that year, I gave Phil a call in New York and managed to get some assignments in the Big Apple. I also knew his wife quite well; a woman called Mally Roncal, who is one of the top make-up artists and now works for people like Jennifer Lopez, Beyoncé Knowles and the Osbournes. I used to stay with them when I was in New York, and they helped me find some work. I had some castings and was set to do a commercial at the end of 1996, but I still had racing obligations to O'Neil and ended up missing the shoot. I believe I could have made a go of a career in New York as I certainly had the right contacts and there was plenty of money to be made, but I still had the nagging belief that I could achieve something in motocross. It never turned out to be a serious option and was only a bit of fun.

In autumn, on one of my trips home (soon to be a permanent return), I went to Prestige nightclub in Stoke where a friend of mine, Pete, used to host an evening. Back in those days, I was high on confidence after all the modelling fraternisation, and used to walk around talking to all the girls and trying it on big-style. The very first time I saw Naomi, handing out her flyers in a skimpy outfit as part of a promotional campaign that got her free entry into the clubs, I was impressed. She had a guy with his arms around her, so I waited, figuring that he was going to leave her at some point. As soon as he disappeared, I walked over and said 'Hi, is that your boyfriend?' Her reply was, 'No, and I don't do boyfriends.' A 'bugger off' line if ever there was one, but it was like music to my slightly drunk ears at the time. We started talking and soon had a bit of a kiss. Now to be fair, she has a version of the story whereby she says she had to hide in the toilets because she thought I was stalking her. That is a slight distortion of the truth, but I was indeed smitten and reluctantly went home with only a phone number.

A week or two later, I had to go back to LA to meet my fate with PE and De Coster, but I kept calling Naomi to meet up, only to be rebuffed by the 'I'm washing my hair' kind of excuse. The chase was great – when I really want something, I've got to have it! I wrote her a letter from the States and included some photos that Phil Bickett had taken of me that looked fantastic. It didn't actually matter who was in the shots they were that good, and Phil was a dab hand behind the camera, just as he was in front of it. When Naomi's mum (bless her) saw the photos, she said to her daughter, 'I think you need to see him.'

We started going out when I came home to ride for Rob Hooper, and she started studying sports science at Middlesex University shortly after we met. Naomi is everything I ever wanted and was looking for in a partner. We have similar characters and the same outlook on life. We have immense trust between us, which had frequently been a problem with my relationships in the past. I would find that girls would get jealous, either of my lifestyle or the rewards that it can bring – stuff like travelling a lot, having fans and attention, particularly from other females. Naomi is my best friend and she knew from early on that my family were a close bunch and she didn't freak out or feel excluded in the way some others girls had done.

After the Grand Prix of Italy in 1998, I asked her to marry me under the leaning Tower of Pisa. We were with my parents because it was their twenty-first wedding anniversary, and it was a very romantic time. In 1999, she moved to Derby with me, and completed her final year by commuting to London by train. We tied the knot with a great party on 14 October 2000.

★ ★ ★

Like Bellpuig, Teutschenthal 2002 was again the complete opposite to what I had experienced exactly one year previously on the 125. I had won, but it was a hard race. My back brake failed with six laps to go, so I had to keep pumping the foot lever and ran off the track on a few occasions. I took my time and rode the circuit. It was a fairly straightforward GP, but it was a good win, my third in a row and fourth from five. I had a cold going into the weekend and felt a bit weak, so to win as comprehensively as I did was encouraging. Erik Eggens was on the podium again and took second. Erik would always fight tooth and nail to keep the gap to within about four seconds, but as soon as I broke that barrier, he just faded. Watching Fred hanging out the pit board, I could see the difference going up to seven seconds, then ten, then eleven. I won by sixteen at the flag, and was proving to be unstoppable with a fifty-five point lead.

Of course it's all 'ifs and buts', although if I had taken the points from Spain in 2002, I would have arrived at round four in France only four behind Pichon. If I had actually sealed the German victory, then I would have been eight points in front. I would have been bubbling over the win and Pichon would know that 2002 wasn't going to be all his show. Pichon is an exceptional talent on a motorcycle, and it was already clear after three rounds – despite his German excursion – that it would take somebody truly on top of their game to beat him.

Looking back, my season was lost in Teutschenthal. The Championship swerved into Pichon's hands, especially with his home GP next on the calendar. To some extent, the pressure was on the Frenchman, because he had to resurrect his winning ways and he would have to do this in front of 20,000 cheering countrymen, desperate to see him win. His crash in Germany was perhaps not the best preparation. However, because of my mistake, he wasn't under the cosh in the way that he should have been. He was still leading the series and nobody had really emerged to take advantage of his Teutschenthal slip. Gundersen, while fast, was a rookie in the 250s, and was as likely to crash one week as he was capable of making a podium the next. The same was true of Beirer, who with his aggressive and cavalier style was completely unpredictable, even if he'd had seven years in the 250 class – this was easy to see in the first three races. He had beaten me to third in Holland, then crashed on the first lap in Spain, and then was gifted another podium at his home GP.

Josh Coppins was the dark horse. Coppins struggled to get his speed up to a level that could win the race from the start. He often made a hole-shot or was right up among the leaders, but then could not force a break from the pack (a skill that Pichon had already mastered and that I had also done in 2001, but was struggling to apply so far). Coppins' strength lay in his consistency, and his second place in Germany, his first trophy with Honda, was a warning sign to the rest of us that he was starting to up his game. While I regarded Coppins as a fast and capable rider, I did not personally see him as a threat to my 2002 aspirations of victory. I knew I could beat him. He had not won a GP in his career, despite numerous close calls, and the first one is usually the trickiest to get under your belt. After that initial view from the top step of the rostrum, if you are a smart rider then you remember how it's done, and hopefully the floodgates open. Coppins was also the closest to Pichon in the points table, and Mickael knew that he would have to start to put Josh behind him at every race to try to forge a cushion.

In the break after Teutschenthal, I was doing an interview and wheeled out my catchphrase that you never stop learning and never learn so much as from your mistakes. The journalist asked me what I had learned from the disaster of Germany, I paused to think and could only reply 'Don't fucking do it again.'

12 May 2002: Round Four
French Grand Prix, St Jean d'Angely

DUE TO KTM's commitment solely to the World Championships, I have had to limit my racing appearances in Britain in recent years. It is always a pleasure to race in front of your fans and my decision to stop contesting the British Championships at the end of 2000 was very hard in one respect, but I also saw it as a necessary sacrifice if I wanted to concentrate fully on achieving my world title dream. I also have an issue with the way that the Auto-Cycle Union run the whole series. They have never wanted to try to help any successful British riders, and their philosophy concerning motocross is inefficient and old-fashioned.

The British competition is still very backward and is not progressing as a commercial entity (which most sports need to be these days) in terms of its appearance, backing and organisation. The standards are not improving fast enough, in my opinion, with regard to things like the circuits, safety and the facilities. I have clashed with the ACU a few times over the years, and what largely finished my participation on the British scene came down to one meeting at Wakes Colne in 2000.

I went off the start and into the first corner in fourth place and couldn't even see my front mudguard – the dust was that bad because they hadn't watered the track. I did one lap, pulled in and said that we could not ride because it was too dangerous. Dave Smith, an ACU official, said to me at the time, 'We don't give a fuck who you are, we've never stopped a race before and we are not going to fucking stop one now, especially for you.' That sealed it for me and basically summed up the sad state of affairs. It's the kids and young guys I feel sorry for. The ACU boast of having sponsorship from Maxxis and a large amount of cash available for the winner of that cup, but they are missing the point. The riders who are likely to clinch the series are already bringing home good money. There should be a privateer fund or a financial plan that stretches right out into the grass roots.

The race format is another problem. How can young talent come through and progress up to single-moto GP level when a British Championship still has three races on one day? Two thirty-minute motos is a better idea, then at least they are getting a taste of what they will have to face when they eventually step up. My suggestion for the future of British MX would be to have a three-round open cup, where all the top GP riders could make time to attend, boost crowds, raise profiles etc., and then have the traditional British 125 and open classes as a ten-round championship through the year, where all the kids and emerging talent could show off their stuff without being blasted away by stressed-out GP riders every other weekend. If the right people with commercial sense are behind both projects then, in theory, it should work.

Along with all the negatives concerning the British Championships, there is also the fact that I am at a stage in my career when I am no longer rushing out of my front door to race. I have won a British pro title four times. My motivation for racking up the same award has dipped a little with age and with my GP career finally bearing fruit. The main reason to race at home these days is to make an appearance for the fans and supporters, and if we badly need some more testing mileage with the GP bikes.

In the week after Teutschenthal, I had an offer from the new breakaway Future West British International series that sounded like a decent idea and had some financial clout behind it. The brainchild of Ken Winstanley, I was intrigued to see if somebody could really eclipse the ACU and I thought it was a bold attempt. He adopted the two thirty-minute moto scheme, and had juniors and amateurs altogether at the same location. The meeting on the bank holiday Monday was based at a circuit all of fifteen minutes away from my house within the Donington Park road-racing track. Along with the cash, the organisers persuaded me to lend my name to the event. I knew that the positives (valuable testing) outweighed the possible negatives of injury or mishap. My sore hand had enjoyed some time off as I had kept my midweek riding to a minimum after the X-ray showed that there was no serious damage. I did a lot of television and press work that week as the Future West organisers used me to spearhead the publicity for the launch of their new MX Championship, and I was doing interviews with the local television and newspapers.

I was thoroughly frustrated by my start to the season that had been as dramatic as it had been disastrous; and it seemed, judging by his behaviour at the Donington national round, that Gordon was feeling the same way. We were both out front in the two motos and it was looking like it was very much going to be a KTM fight, with nobody else able to get close. The Future West people had hoped for a good show and, by God, they got one. I think Gordon's performance was the dirtiest by any rider I've shared the track with.

I won, and beat him, in the first moto, then during the second we were fighting for the lead and I made a clean pass; Gordon retaliated by hitting me and pushing me off the track. Luckily, there was no fencing on that section and I could run wide onto the grass. By the next lap, I was right behind him again, and he tried a similar move that was very close to putting me in the mud. It must have looked like great racing from the outside, but I wasn't at all happy. Gordon was going at it like we were fighting for the lead in a GP, and I would have been totally pissed off if he had caused either of us to fall and get hurt for nothing. It was so strange to be in a race with him like that, because off the track he is the politest and friendliest guy. You can be hard without being dangerous, and sometimes I see Gordon falling a little bit into the latter category.

The second Donington race hadn't finished. I grabbed the lead again and he followed me for a while, then towards the end of the moto, he jumped over the tapes at the side of the track and slammed into my right side as I took my usual inside line. He knocked me so hard that he snapped part of my foot peg clean off. His front wheel locked together with my bike briefly, I elbowed him to get away and he slipped to the ground. Post-race, Gordon was immensely pissed off and so was I, to a lesser extent. Nothing was really said because I'm not one for confrontations and didn't want to make a big deal of it, and he couldn't be bothered either, but the atmosphere was thick and heavy.

We were both in the same boat in that we were scratching our heads trying to work out the puzzle of the KTM, and he was not helpful with any positive criticism, but to be fair to him it was hard to find something to rave about in the early days of the season. Gordon gives the air of being very relaxed and easy going, but with his racing he is almost over-the-top serious and looks deeply into every little thing; he's a complex character, who needs to have everything right in his head to get going.

Three days after the Donington victories, we travelled out to France for the fourth round of the World Championships at St Jean d'Angely. France usually has a fantastic crowd and they love their motocross out there; it helps, of course, if you have a couple of home riders pushing for the various Championships. The French were flush with heroes. Pichon and Bolley needed no introduction, while Demaria was back in action in the 500cc class and Mickael Maschio had surprised many with his success in the 125s. The GP of France represented the only meeting on the calendar in which all three races could theoretically be won by a native rider, and a noisy and appreciative crowd filled the huge banked slope that sat opposite, and ran the length of, the track in anticipation of victory.

St Jean is similar in a few ways to Ernée, the GP circuit we used in 2001. It has that same setting whereby the start straight is situated at the flat bottom of a gully, with all the spectators on one slope and the track lining its way back and forward on the other, giving some generous views of the track and providing some very tight corners, with the course constantly doubling back on itself, roving up and down one side of the valley. When we arrived at St Jean, it was raining. Nevertheless, the French race had the potential for the highest attendance of the year despite the gloomy weather, which was forecast to cover the whole weekend.

The Grand Prix tracks have been getting a lot better in recent years. The layouts themselves are okay, even though the terrain could generally do with some more work. Off the track, the paddocks have been getting bigger and bigger every season, and there always seem to be a couple of new semis starting the year, which is a positive thing. Of course, the look of the paddock is very important for the image of the sport, and shows a good face to any sponsors who want be a part.

I believe motocross is becoming a big deal. It's obviously not as huge as something like Moto GP and it probably never will be, but then again the American SX series has taken off in a huge way, with audiences around the 50-70,000 mark every week, a lot of media exposure and, of course, the money. I am pleased to see that the Motocross GP scene is evolving and getting better, but we still have some way to go and I think the modernisation of the sport is over-due. Dorna, a new Spanish media company that owns the rights to the road-racing World Championships and who took the Moto GP series to a high level, got involved in motocross in 2001 and changed the sport to have all three classifications racing on the same weekend, with one moto for each category. Putting us all together was the right move, as was switching to the one-moto format. We had to make sure that the Motocross Grand Prix package was the best way of promoting the sport and appealing to the demands of television, where we badly needed the extra exposure. Dorna suffered many complaints with the changes they wanted to enforce. We knew they had experience in promoting races worldwide, but what kind of experience they had in motocross was another story.

Dorna had a steep learning curve to climb, and maybe the mistake they made initially was wanting too much, too quickly. Money and instant elevation will not arrive overnight in motocross, because it does not have an infrastructure where the dealings and rules for road-racing events can be applied. In short, there is neither the cash nor backing nor fan attendances for motocross to become an instant mainstream hit — the sport needs good, clever marketing, and this is the biggest transformation somebody needs to come in and implement. The way that Dorna tend to ignore the teams and voices inside the sport, I fear they will not succeed because they have their own priorities, which, from the look of things in 2002, was trying to limit financial losses rather than pumping up GP motocross. 'Speculate to accumulate', as the saying goes — I'm sad that I can't see it happening at the moment.

One of the problems is that MX is a sport in which the GPs are hosted by local clubs and circuits, and those same tracks and organisers could not afford the sanction fee being asked by Dorna. I do worry when some very good motocross circuits are ignored simply because of financial reasons, and instead we end up in places like St Jean, where after a few practice sessions, rock starts to come through the mud. When the racing has to take a back seat to cash demands, then there are problems. On the other hand, personally I'm not sad to see some of the old-style and ill-equipped tracks disappear. The sport is moving on and trying to adapt to a new television-friendly corporate image. If we look good and motocross looks good, then that's okay in my book because I'm thinking about the future.

One problem area is that the riders and teams have no representative body. There used to be a time when the bosses would announce proposals and say they would take effect in one year or two. Now the FIM and Dorna dream up what they like, and suddenly it's part of the rulebook without any consultation or anything. It's a lack of communication that is stopping us from finding the right path and heading down it together for the benefit of motocross. The single-moto format is something I agree with because it is a recipe for excitement and only really annoys the 'old school'.

I love the racing in America, there are so many passing moves and so much action because everybody is racing as fast as they can. This attitude never really caught on in Europe in the past, because people were racing around the old two-moto strategy. There seemed to be a lot more of the ancient cat-and-mouse tactics, where one rider would sit there waiting for the other to go. It's another form of motocross, and I do not want to disrespect the riders of the bygone days, but to me that is not racing. As soon as that gate drops, you go as hard and fast as you possibly can for the entire duration; this delivers action and excitement, from which everybody wins – sponsors, fans, television audiences and the riders have more fun.

We are content to take the money, so we must make sure that the service and entertainment is good enough with a view to the future. Motocross now has to compete with a lot of other sports (many that are less visual) that have changed and adapted to a snappy all-action package that people want to see, whether on the television or as a new first-time spectator. People have been slating the layout of the tracks this year, and I haven't generally had a problem with them. They are not too short and not too supercrossy, which seems to be the common cry from the older riders. This is motocross. We have eighteen inches of travel on the suspensions for a reason. Spectators do not want to see us doing 140kph across dirt. If they want out-and-out straight-line speed, then they can go and watch road racing. They want us up in the air, they want thrills, they want crashes – that's racing and that's the appeal.

The atmosphere and the buzz around the track and paddock is the main draw of GPs for riders. A Grand Prix is the top annual motocross meeting in the respective country, and for me it is always nice to get inside that environment. In St Jean, the problems I was having on the track clouded the euphoria surrounding the event, as the French lapped up their only chance to see and get near to their off-road heroes. I always enjoy the autographs, the meeting-and-greeting, the photos and the signings much more when I don't have to direct my thoughts elsewhere. If I was slow on the second split on the track, why? What can I do on the bike to make it behave better in turn six? What if I hit a different line between turns eight and eleven – will I pick up a second? How do I feel on the bike? Am I able to push? Do I feel safe? All this stuff and more is swimming around in your head at a GP, and it can be hard to enjoy the peripheral activity which can be flattering and good fun. I noticed that some British fans that had caught the ferry over to France, and it's always great to see a Union Jack waved when you are abroad.

Due to the rain and constant drizzle, the track was a nightmare throughout practice and qualifying. It was turning into a worn and stony mess. I ended up with seventh pick in the gate after a cautious session. In terms of the bike, we had one or two worries about the acceleration and getting up the long hills in St Jean. The power transfer to the back wheel didn't feel so good and was lighting up straight away as soon as I got on the gas, meaning that the traction was suffering as a result; again, more head scratching for the engine guys and the suspension people and a less-than-ideal machine for me to try and race with.

After so many years, I'm not often one to walk and ponder a track before the action begins. I like to look at it when I arrive, just to see any changes, but then I'll just ride it in practice. Walking a track, it is possible to see little things and details about a corner, but it can also be a bit pointless because after a practice session or two then it will change a lot and not necessarily be the same curve for the race. I prefer to have a good look on the sighting lap, fifteen minutes before the GP moto. I usually go round very slowly and check out any areas that I'm interested in, to see if there have been any repairs by the machines or if a new line has started to appear after the free practice. I've always looked for the shortest way around a racetrack – that means mostly using the inside line, which can get very rough, but it is also the quickest. If you can ride the roughest line as hard as you can for forty minutes, then you are already doing part of what you need to in order to win.

A GP weekend can sometimes pass slowly. As it is now, on Saturday we get two free practice sessions of twenty minutes, and a qualifying session of thirty minutes and that's it until warm-up on Sunday morning. We don't need a vast amount of time to set up the bikes according to the track. There is not a lot you can change or try on the motorcycle that is going to make a great deal of difference, unlike with road racing.

On race day in France, once more the weather was pretty horrible. It was cold and breezy, and the rain overnight had turned the track into slush, especially at the base of the hill on the straight and flat sections. Racing in heavy mud can be grim. It gets everywhere, and if you have to come through the pack, there is likely to be a time where your visor canister will run out or it will break and your goggles will become useless. Riding without eye protection is hazardous in case someone roosters a bucketful of stones at your face, and those things come at you like bullets. Even if you avoid the stones, after the GP your vision is all blurry for up to a few days later because of all the crap that has hit your face. It's one part of the sport where you have to grit your teeth and do what you have to do; a result in the mud can act as a measurement of how much you actually are willing to push yourself to win.

I knew Mickael Pichon would be feeling tense at his home race, but he was too experienced to let it affect him. There are two ways a home GP can work. The first is that you can let the pressure get on top of you and crumble. You become too nervous, too uptight and watch the race run away from you or crash, giving a performance that is nothing like you would normally do. The second is to enjoy it and realise that ninety per cent of those people are there to see and cheer for you, providing a lift and a buzz that no other rider of a different nationality can hope to match. For the good riders, the World Champions, the second situation usually applies, and I suspected Mickael might be unbeatable today. Pichon had pole, and I counted seven spaces in from his slot on the far right of the gate, ready to try and take that inside line on the first turn.

In contrast to Teutschenthal, I got a shit jump out of the gate this time, and as we sloshed out way down to the first turn, I was in the middle of the pack and trying to keep as far to the right and the inside of the corner as possible. For at least half of the first lap, I was awful. My timing was wrong and I wasn't reading the muddy terrain very well. I lost time and ground in numerous corners, when I should have been trying to barge my way past the Kawasakis of Gundersen and Andrew McFarlane.

Mickael had timed his start almost perfectly, and within half a lap he had overtaken Pit Beirer and was off on his own, enjoying the race with only his screaming fans for company. At almost two-thirds of the way through the first lap, Gundersen rammed me on the inside of a left turn. We call it a 'T-bone' because I was horizontal to the apex of the corner, having already entered the bend, and he had shot up the inside line too fast and physically used me to stop himself from running wide. The impact was a bit of a shock, even though I saw him coming out of the corner of my eye. His front wheel whacked my engine and bent the gearshift pedal under the ignition cover, making a complete mess of it. As I tried to correct myself in the turn, I couldn't find the lever with my foot. It was all covered in mud, hidden under the bike and I was stuck in one gear and couldn't shift. I spent the best part of two to three laps at the back of a four-rider group vying for fourth, kicking at the side of the bike and slowly getting the lever out into a position where I could use the gears. I wasted a lot of time as I pinned the throttle in whatever gear I could find in an effort to keep going. I was hovering around eighth position, with

Gundersen just in front and a Finnish rider Marko Kovalainen just behind.

Eventually, I prised the pedal out from under the bike and was able to get the bit between my teeth. I started to make some progress and pulled up three places in five laps. I hit fifth spot at the halfway stage by having a good little tussle with Paul Cooper, and made an overtaking move stick by sliding past into a corner and having enough power and speed to climb the subsequent steep uphill rise and put him behind me for good. Fifth position meant that I was just over four seconds away from the Hondas of Josh and Pit in front, and I actually was managing to close the gap. Like Pichon, Bolley was racing himself in second; a perfect one-two for the home fans.

Unlike most motorsports, where a single racing line is the fastest way around a track and is hardly ever deviated from unless for a pass, motocross relies more on an individual's preference and tactics; it's about where you can see a line and how you can make it work in terms of going faster than everybody else. This means that time gaps between riders can vary greatly, but also be squashed in a matter of laps. A few errors or somebody else finding a new line or a good rhythm can destroy what seems an unbreakable time advantage or deficit.

Motocross can depend on the state of the circuit and, perhaps more so, a higher level of timing on the rider's part because of the jumps. Half a metre longer off a jump on one lap could cost you half a second or a second. People can run wide or out-brake themselves in road racing, but generally it won't happen more than once in a race. In MX we are running for forty minutes at extreme energy-sapping intensity, and there are usually more mistakes than most people realise.

The only moment when MX can get processional is when everybody is riding as hard as they can without any troubles or mistakes, in a supremely professional way. That is why race-starts can often be the very small difference between winning and losing, because the standard in GPs is so high. Road racers have often said to me how they think MX is more fun for racing because you have more freedom to implement a strategy and skill, and it's true; you will not witness any action more exciting in the world of motorsport than two world-class motocrossers on a decent track, fighting it out over jumps and switching lines all over the place to squabble over a position.

There are circuits, of course, that are worse than others, where there is only really one decent line to follow otherwise you will be losing time. St Jean was like that in many sections, so I was only slightly chipping away at the four-second margin because the Hondas were taking the same route and keeping the same speed. Then, for maybe three consecutive laps, I made a few mistakes on the first section of the circuit through a combination of eagerness and being caught out by a shit track surface that dropped me off the chase. It was the fastest part of the course, but also the hardest, because the long curve at the bottom of the slope hardly contained any mud on the racing line. We were bombing along on stone. It was easy to see as it wore through and was slippery like you wouldn't believe because of the rain. The track had been horrible throughout the weekend. It was technical but like riding trails, and now, in the latter stages of the race, it was getting worse.

I did not have enough faith in the bike and its unsettled suspension to hang my balls on the line, and did not attack the stretch like I would have done normally. I lapped for a while on my own. Riding is very much a natural instinct, and while I do think about what I am doing, sometimes my head just wanders off because my body is working and reacting without pause to the job in hand, be it during one lap, one corner or one second.

In all of the races so far this season, something had been amiss or out of the ordinary, so my mind wasn't disappearing that much. In 2001, it was quite the opposite because I was riding so well, feeling so strong and I didn't hear a peep from the bike. It was like I was on cruise control, and I was leading and winning races.

When you are in front by twenty seconds and firmly inside your rhythm, then that is when the concentration can start to creep away and catch out the inexperienced. I have thought about some strange stuff in a race, like what Naomi is doing or what my friends are up to. I think it's a result of being completely in sync with the bike, your confidence, the track and current situation. When your mind starts to go, it can even be a reassuring thing because you have reached a certain zone of comfort in the race; you have, or you are doing, everything you wanted to achieve that day. This time in France, I was focused on keeping the bike up.

For some unknown reason, with three laps remaining, I was on my own, bored and just shut off and stopped trying. Nine times out of ten, I would always push right until the end, just because of the sheer unpredictable nature of the sport. If Josh and Pit had clashed and taken each other out briefly, then my continued effort might have been rewarded by catching up to only a second behind them both with all to play for, or even a gift of a podium like Gundersen had received in Germany. I confess that, on this occasion, I just gave up. There were five minutes left in the GP, I was in no danger and unlikely to improve my place; uncharacteristically, I just accepted the position.

It fucked me off when I thought about the race later, and there haven't been many times when I have behaved the same. 'Why did I do it?' I kept asking myself. Josh was the perfect example of why you should never chuck it in. He pushed Pit right until the last lap, and as the pair clattered into each other, Coppins came off better and gained a podium for his efforts. I was right behind Josh until my slip-ups. I put it down to a lack of confidence and paranoia. In the last two races, I had reached the final stages, only for something to go wrong and end up with nothing (fourth place was hardly a consolation in Teutschenthal). In St Jean, I had a position, not one that I really wanted, but it at least was a finish. I guess I was scared of more bad luck rearing its head and just wanted to cross the line.

I later thought giving up in France was unforgiveable, and I didn't dare tell anyone that I was just coasting at the end of the GP, mostly because of a pang of shame. I felt that I just didn't have that extra bit of belief in myself and the performance to just GO! I had negative thoughts going through my mind and it translated into a flimsy throttle hand. It could well have been one of the most miserable GPs of my career for the whole non-event and shambolic finish. It was imperative in my mind that the GP of France would not finish badly, and when that happens you are not racing anymore.

★ ★ ★

In 2001, a solid second place in Ernée was enough to set my Championship quest back on track after the brief interlude of the collarbone break in Sweden. The GP of France had come slightly later in the year, at round eight of fourteen, so it was an important time as I had won five, taken a runner's-up place to Eggens in Valkenswaard and then scored a zero in Sweden. People were keen to see if my Championship campaign would now go off the rails and someone else could step into the breech.

I wanted to let everyone know right away that I was racing fresh from an operation and I was here to stay. I really pushed in the first practice and got the best time. Predictably, in a bit of reverse psychology, everyone started saying that I hadn't broken the arm but I wasn't rising to it and I think my plan had the desired effect because it fazed a few people, judging by the race performances. My fitness for the race would be the question mark, and after Saturday I felt so tired that I went to the circuit doctor and asked why I felt so woozy. He said the anaesthetic was still in my system and would take around a month to clear.

I was surprised and relieved that the race was reasonably straightforward. Gundersen repeated his Swedish performance by blasting away at the front, and I was happy enough to settle into a lonely second away from his roost. It was a solid but uneventful moto. I concentrated hard on the track and riding my own race. Eggens crashed twice, the second time hurting his ankle and forcing a retirement. Steve Ramon on the Kawasaki (third place in the standings) also had problems and finished outside the points. Aside from me not winning, it was the dream scenario.

When I got the good news that I had increased my point advantage by twenty, I enjoyed the podium ceremony immensely, and I'm not sure I have ever been more content with a second place. I still have a photo somewhere of me that day, sitting on the back of the podium, and you can see all over my face that I knew it wasn't over and I was thinking 'I've got this'. It was a rollercoaster of a ride. In the space of two weeks, the Championship had gone from looking like it might be under threat to my new-found confidence that it was only mine to lose; nobody else was going to interfere, all I had to do was get out on that track.

Motocross is a test of your fitness, without a doubt. Now, with one moto, it is also a test of your motorcycle handling skill at the fastest speed possible. I was fifteen when I first started to ride in the senior British Championships, and then had to begin honing my physical shape. Physical preparation was a very different scene when I was a youth compared to how it is nowadays. I was largely on my own and left to my own devices regarding training. I did not have anybody driving me. The lack of guidance didn't hinder my on-track education, but neither did it push me forward and make me progress at a successful rate in the GPs.

One thing I would advise any kids wanting to become a motocross racer is to find the right kind of help, because to become exceptionally fit is not something that can happen in one month, or two or six. It takes years to reach a decent standard. Ricky Carmichael has been training since he was thirteen or fourteen. At that age, it's a big step for a teenager to take. It may sound dramatic, but it's a bit like the end of your childhood.

The start of your life as a professional means most things you do/eat/drink have to fall in line with the parameters of countless training programmes, weight guidelines and diet. I spent a lot of my younger years in minor conflict because I was a happy kid and liked to hang out with my friends and have some fun, instead of sweating away every day in the gym, which I was required to do. On the other hand, I also wanted to succeed as a motocross racer, and I put in the effort from the ages of sixteen to twenty-four, virtually as much as I do now, if not more, but the difference was that my heart was not really in it back then. The desire has to be there, you cannot simply go through the motions in the gym.

The sport has changed over the years and the pot of gold has grown a lot bigger. Arriving at the top back in the late 1980s and early 1990s, there was a good living to be made from GP racing. Now, a lot of people in the World Championship field have a comfortable life, with the winners in particular rightfully gaining the lucrative prizes. There are more incentives for riders' careers and off-track lifestyle if they post good results and get a factory bike – the training has now become a very scientific and serious business because of that factor. Riders are no longer guys who gather for some scrambling every weekend. They are self-employed businessmen, and that means they have to invest in their 'business interests'; aside from riding every waking minute, the next easiest way to improve is to hire a trainer and get their physical condition to its peak.

There must have been hundreds of motos where I have faded at the end because I was not as fit as I should have been. In the last few years, that hasn't been a problem, but there have been many times when I haven't been able to ride any longer through fatigue. Of course, in motocross you can be knee-deep in mud one week and then in the forty-degree sunshine of South America the next, so the conditions are there to test you and catch you out.

America was a long curve of adjustment for me. Initially, I struggled to get used to racing regularly in the heat and used to fade in quite a few events when I moved over (much to Mitch's annoyance). The 125cc GP in Portugal in 1999 was one time when I succumbed to the heat, and it turned out to be quite a funny story actually. The thermometer must have been in the low forties that day. I couldn't push anymore towards the end of the second moto and dropped from third to fifth. Steve Hendersen, my mechanic while I was at Suzuki, went mental. In the pits he threw the lapboard down in disgust and stormed back to the paddock effing and blinding, until he got back into the van and passed out! They put him on a drip and took him to hospital; he was a bit more forgiving about my result after that.

Wet and clumpy mud can be equally as tough conditionsas warm temperatures. Unless you grab a hole-shot and disappear, then it is a real endurance test as the stuff sticks to you and the bike, making everything heavier and more tiring. It does sort the men from the boys. I have tended to get good results in the mud because I did put in the hard work away from the track – this was especially true in the 2000 season, when my training was really paying off. Determination also plays its part. I believe that I have had more ups and downs than most people, and have been around on GP bikes longer than anybody else, except maybe Marnicq Bervoets who started a year earlier. No one's career is a bed of roses all the way through, and I try to make all memories of the knocks and negatives work in my favour. Determination is an undervalued and now clichéd commodity, but while everybody claims to have it, only a few are prepared to show what they are really made of.

It took many years, a lot of hard work and several attempts for me to get out of the pigeon-hole that I was an under-achiever, and that's what made people's words (even in my own team) that I was lazy and not trying in 2002 so hurtful. For years I have been trying little variations of training, from pure strength to solely cardiovascular, sometimes experimenting with the regimes of other sports, such as boxing, to find something that worked for me, both on the bike and inside my head. I made an error in 1998 because I focused on boxing exercises and practically drove myself into the ground. Looking back now, it was totally wrong for motocross. I was training very hard for two or three hours every single day, doing rounds and exercises in the ring, skipping for an hour and using the punch bags. It seemed more interesting at the time but, with hindsight, I was mistaken. I ended up getting burnt out and was tired in the races. I learned then that everything I do has to be very carefully adjusted and related to my sport.

Every fitness coach I have worked with has their own little ideas and methods, and I have had some people barking orders at me and others who seemed pretty clueless about what I should be doing. I had been looking for a good trainer all my life who was based in Derby, and, towards the end of 1999, I bumped into a friend (Dave Parkinson, who worked as editor of the local *Telegraph* newspaper) at the David Lloyd gym one afternoon and we got talking about trainers, because I had just landed the contract with KTM and really wanted to push myself physically like I hadn't done before. Parky knew of Kirk because he had covered his boxing matches in the paper, and also was aware that I was on the lookout for a fitness expert. He suggested a meeting and, even though Kirk was quite busy at the time, we started working together immediately.

Kirk used to be one of the best amateur boxers in England. He never made the jump to professional because an eye operation meant that he could never fight as a pro. He's a competitive guy like me and is now well into his X-training tournaments. Kirk set up his own personal training business based around circuits, spinning and classes like 'boxercise'. Kirk admitted that he had seen me around the gym before and thought I looked like a bit of a star, which made me laugh. He also thought I seemed like a lazy trainer, which made me laugh even more.

He had trouble making space for me in his schedule, so I suggested training 'with' him, rather than 'for' him. It was a good way to break the ice because he was hitting the circuit and working out for his competitions and I was trying to catch up. It was tough, but different. In the early days, through the build-up to the 2000 season and onwards, Kirk and I really put the miles in at the gym. I would join him as he used to work out for three hours every morning, Monday to Friday, on different areas of his body. We would have Saturday free, but I would join him for circuit classes on Sundays, as well as Wednesday and Friday evenings. He used to be particularly heavy on the legs with steps, curls and cycling. Sometimes we used to literally crawl down the set of stairs that led up to the fitness room. I was really motivated for the 2000 season and worked harder than ever. I even went training on Christmas Day. Kirk had to learn about motocross, but that also meant he brought a few fresh ideas and approaches to my workout.

I now do a lot of leg-squat exercises to resemble the load and impact that my limbs endure when doing the jumps and controlling the direction of the bike. The arms and shoulders do a hell of a lot of work constantly throughout the race. Absorbing bumps and terrain and holding onto the bike alone require vast amounts of strength, never mind the basic requirement of having to guide and steer the motorcycle around a rough track. I do weights and drills to help my arms cope with these stresses.

Aside from broken bones and ligament damage, arm pump is probably the most common motocross complaint. When I have not been 100 per cent prepared, I have suffered from time to time, but if I have done all my work in the week, which is often the case, then the race passes by without any arm trouble. I haven't had any problems since 1998, when I was affected quite badly with low confidence and having the wrong physical condition. 'Pumped arms' is a horrible sensation. It is like becoming as stiff as a board and it is impossible to control the bike. It takes a supreme effort to brake and just keep hold of the bars. It feels a bit like cramp, or if you imagine taking one of those springy wrist-grip exercisers and squeezing it until you possibly cannot do it anymore before trying to ride.

It can depend on the state of the track in relation to your fitness, and is also a mental thing. If you are riding too tensely, then your arms will lock up after some time. People have changed training programmes, altered their handlebars, had operations and tried numerous other solutions to fix the problem. When you are in a position of searching for a cure, however, then that is when it is most likely to be a psychological thing of stress and worry; whether it's about the bike, your own fitness or the fact that you are losing two seconds a lap on the leader.

Kirk has me doing a lot of aerobic and circuit training. The main area of focus is strength endurance. The plan is not to make me a bulging powerhouse, but to create a form that is as light and strong as possible – to have a guy that is twelve stone, but with the power of a thirteen- or fourteen-stone person. Isometric exercises, with weights and movement to develop strength in the joints and not just the muscle, are the main tasks in the gym. Everything I do is high intensity, with hard and fast sets of reps. At low intensity, I could probably train forever. It takes a lot of effort to build up a firm aerobic base, and that is the platform of fitness on which to build.

For the 2001 campaign, I trained like a madman. Kirk, well before this time, had devised a 'motocross circuit' that was my routine once the season drew near and got underway. I explained to him the rule changes for the Championship, and said that I wanted a programme that would let me push as hard as I could in a single race for forty minutes. He tuned my training to the specific needs and demands of motocross and the one-moto format – stuff that would help prevent arm pump, work my legs and let me charge as hard as I could for the length of one race.

People like British commentator Jack Burnicle reckon real motocross men are those who can put in two motos of forty-five minutes, and he was pretty condescending about my world title at the end of 2001. Those two motos are okay if the riders are capable of going flat-out and producing some exciting racing to the flag, rather than a procession of riders, gassing for ten minutes then backing off and having a look, then going for it once again. While Burnicle may call it proper motocross, I call it boredom. To this day, the World Championships still has to get out of its two-moto hangover and start producing the action that the format change prompts and is designed to deliver. Actually riding the bike is a big part of training aside from just the gym and the exercise. If I were completing two motos in the World Championships, then I would practice two race distances. As it is, I now ride alone and compete against the clock for forty minutes.

In 2001, I had the same agenda that I follow now – I rode or tested in the mornings, then cycled the four miles to Wilmorton College, did my circuit and rode back home. I was in the best condition of my life that season, and Kirk is quite right when he said that the strong mental and physical state that I was in when I broke both my collarbones was a vital ingredient to being able to continue and win the World Championship. We are a good double-act and he has a lot riding on my success, because my physical condition is a reflection of his work. He cares a lot about my endeavours in the sport, and I know he feels bad when things are not going so well.

The 'motocross circuit' is not complicated and has to be completed rapidly without a break, in between the drills involving weights and aerobic resistance work, basically meaning that the harder I push, the tougher it gets. Then there is the abdominal work, with sit-ups and lower-back exercises. Kirk has a 'motocross press' in the circuit that involves standing astride a bench and lifting and lowering a bar with a weight to resemble the arm-pumping motion of holding a set of handle bars.

Music is another big part of the gym existence for me. I listen to the same dance stuff that I put into my minidisc player while preparing for a race, and it tunes me straight into what I have to do. It helps me slide into a zone of concentration. While at the race, I also remember the times when I have struggled to walk out of the gym hearing the same track, and I remind myself of the reason for the aches and pains.

The high intensity of the MX circuit is the key. It has to be of a level whereby you feel like being sick after you have just finished. An average person who went to the gym for a workout every week would not be able to get even halfway round. I also have to take care of my aerobic side and fat burning, and this can be a slog in pre-season. I do this by running and cycling, sometimes in the gym, sometimes outside, just for a change. There are some nice scenic routes just outside of Derby!

Kirk has my total respect because he trains almost twice as hard as I do. If he says to me 'do five more', I know that he could also do five more. I find a 'partnership' more of an effective tool than an instructor-pupil relationship. In the beginning, I explained this to him and he was more than happy to push me and come along for the ride. From the start of our association, and the subsequent results that came on the track, Kirk really got me into thinking that my peak physical condition is connected with my confidence, and he works a lot on the mental side of things.

Quite often, when I am having to dig deep on the rower, bicycle or the treadmill, he leans over and says stuff like 'Pichon and Everts are making this distance ...' or he tries to make me imagine I am in the last two laps of a race . His method is effective because he tries to take me away from the fact that I am on a machine; instead, I am battling with someone at the end of a GP or charging to try and make a podium position inside the last five minutes of a moto. It's the carrot-on-a-stick effect, and him telling me that my last 400 metres on the rower is also the last 400 metres in a race, is something I find quite useful.

I tend to do a lot of mental practice, which I hear is scientifically proven to aid sport performance on the morning of the race, and my music really helps me focus and concentrate. I often try to visualise the perfect start (an important element because it is all down to reflex), and if I have not made the 'virtual hole-shot' then I have to cut it off in my mind and begin again, until I can follow it all the way through. Concentration is another issue and a valuable skill to learn. It's hard to stay in the zone 100 per cent over forty minutes, and the level does fluctuate. It partially deserted me at a crucial moment in Teutschenthal.

One area that I know Kirk disagrees with me on is my diet. I like to mostly keep a low-carbohydrate food agenda. Any kind of diet is difficult for me because I love food! I eat carbs – mainly stuff like rice, pasta and potatoes – as little as possible but do have some, mostly in the evenings. He believes that I should be feasting on a high-carb programme because it is important for energy and hard training. Unfortunately, however, carbohydrates carry water, which also means weight gain, and I want to keep my body mass at a minimum. It's all to do with my build really, and I do eat things from the carb food group, but don't like to munch as much as he recommends. I eat protein-based foods, such as vegetables, and do my best to stay off the cakes and biscuits in the house.

I can't say that I am a fan of training. I don't especially enjoy it (in contrast to quite a few other riders) and can think of other things to do with my time, but I know how incredibly important it is. When I switch on, which is nine times out of ten, I really go for it and could put anyone's workrate to shame. If I had to identify one area of preference, then it would have to be cardiovascular exercise because I can disappear into my own world of thought. Things like cycling, hard rowing, stepping or running; these are activities that I have been doing since a young age and I almost switch into robotic mode when tackling the job in hand.

My shoulders are probably the weakest area. I have broken them on several occasions now, and once I seem to get them strong again, something else happens to set me back, and it takes months to let them heal and get up to 100 per cent again. For the last two seasons, I have suffered at some stage with my upper body. I take the view that every part can always be a bit better or stronger, and that helps with the daily motivation of getting down the gym.

Training is always easier when you are winning on the track. Period. Motocross is a difficult sport and also a lonely one. You are practising on your own and often training with just yourself for company, and for that reason (and why I use Kirk a lot) it's important to keep your own personal drive and impetus. Many people ask me how I can be in the gym so much and not get bored. The answer is that I think about my racing every time I'm on a machine. It is a well-accustomed mood and mindset. If I do start to lag, then that is when the trainer really helps out. My dad has always said 'You get out of life what you put into it', and I've always believed that to be very true. I'm more afraid of failure than I am of whatever ordeal awaits me in the gym.

26 May 2002: Round Five
Italian Grand Prix, Castiglione Del Lago

ASIDE FROM the motocross tracks, I love everything about Italy. Like Spain it has elements such as the food, the weather and the people, who are fantastic. I would really like to try to learn another language someday, and Italian would be the one to go for; I'll certainly encourage Gracie to be bilingual, because I have seen in the paddock how important and useful it can be.

Castiglione Del Lago was the host of the 2002 race and seems to keep on popping up in my career. It was the scene of my GP debut and also the 'skating rink' where I wrecked my 2002 pre-season with the crash and shoulder injury. I missed the 2001 GP, and this was to be my first racing appearance since 1992, when I rode the 250 Kawasaki.

Set in amazingly beautiful countryside in the north, near Perugia, the 'Castle by the Lake' has been a steady, if infrequent, venue over the years for all three classifications, mainly because it is one of the better tracks of a bad bunch. Castiglione is a quaint town just down the road from the circuit, dwarfed by the big castle fortification on the hill with plenty of old-style streets running through and around it, adjacent to a quite stunning lakeside setting smack bang in the middle, which looks fantastic on a slow Italian summer evening.

It's not a bad track, as Italian circuits go, usually they are awful, very hard-packed and hardly maintained. More often than not, they can resemble a road, having no bumps at all. The place sadly does not have the viewing structures or space to accommodate a great deal of people. Castigilione hasn't changed that much from all those years ago. It's a fast circuit and used to be quicker until they slotted in some chicane elements and extra jumps. It's also the only track that includes an uphill start for something a little different, and that makes those first two or three seconds getting out of the gate all the more vital.

Needless to say, it was a different prospect on the eve of Saturday practice than when we had come here earlier in the year to test. They had actually managed to do some grading with the dirt, and there were little modifications and alterations that had been made to several corners to prepare it for a weekend of wear and tear.

The Italian Grand Prix represented my lowest point of the year. It was hideous. I had everyone in the team against me. I was fed-up with saying 'Do you honestly think this bike is good enough?' and having a response along the lines of 'Yes, we do', which to me was almost like saying, 'You're a prick, the bike's fine. It's you, you're crap.'

As a team, we have to pull together and strive for the same goal. I sensed that some were losing sight of that fact and only cared about their individual tasks. I can understand self-interest and giving priority to your part of the job, but it was that attitude that was causing all the trouble. I was stupid and also getting selfishly affected by it. I thought 'If Leighton doesn't care, then it's costing me', or, 'If Wilfred can't be arsed, then I'm going to suffer', when I should have just been focusing on my personal performance instead of fretting about what I might be missing out on. From the first moment that we wheeled out the bike, the whole weekend was set to be a disaster.

In practice, the bike had been shaking with severe vibration. After five laps, I was struggling to hang onto the thing; it felt like the engine was going to shake itself out of the frame, as well as losing power. I came into the pits during practice, and Leighton had a long face and was pissed off, while I found, once again, that fingers were jabbed in my direction. My treatment of the bike and estimation of it were apparently the issue.

It was, without a doubt, my worst qualifying of the year, thanks to the bike finally deciding to stop shaking and spit its guts. I was in third or fourth with about ten to fifteen minutes to go, and the track was starting to get better and rougher. I am more dialled in towards the end of the thirty-minute period, and make any changes in the first half of the session that will set me up for a late and final flyer.

The bike went bang as we were going into the latter half of qualifying, and I crawled back to the pits with it gurgling. The mechanics quickly checked it over and actually thought that the main bearings had gone, so they said, 'Don't even bother thinking about using this one again.'

The spare bike was in the pit box, but it only *looked* like it was ready to ride. It had the wrong tyres, the wrong jetting, and was only there in an emergency, just in case the first machine had broken in the first five minutes and I needed to get a lap, any lap, just to break the top thirty and get in the gate. So I lost half of the qualifying because the bike was not ready to go.

The reason for the failure was that a carbon-fibre engine-mounting bracket that held the cylinder head to the frame had come loose. The titanium screw holding the two parts together had snapped and that explained the vibration problem we had been having. The reason for the breakage was that we had been testing the week before with a new head, and they didn't quite get it lined up because all the parts were pre-production and man-made and it wasn't symmetrical. Coupled with the misalignment, the eventual wear, extra natural vibration and punishment the bike was experiencing had caused it to weaken and break. So, having worked out the problem and made a few token efforts on the spare bike, I ended up dropping down to ninth and we put the session behind us and started to talk about the race. Fred and Leighton went about fixing the failed parts on the first bike, and the spare one was prepped in case of a similar emergency the next day.

Morning warm-up on Sunday went well under some wonderful clear sunshine and blue skies, but my optimism wasn't quite so bright. I entered the gate five slots from the inside, again from the right, as the first bend turned away ninety degrees in that direction. Coppins was to my left and Pichon was further along, on pole position again and this time choosing a space located more centrally on the line. I would have to veer across to my left slightly coming out of the gate so that I could hit the apex, but it wasn't a bad position and I hoped I could get a decent lift and traction to carry as much speed as possible up the hill.

The first corner was a tough one, with the outside of the turn an unforgiving bank of mud that had the pit wall located roughly two metres on top of it. After about ten yards coming out of the bend, we hit the steep face of a large tabletop that could be quite dangerous with a closely-grouped pack of thirty riders fighting for space in the air. I gated well and slid around the inside of the turn in about fifth, with Colin Dugmore ahead of me, the two Hondas and Pichon right alongside. Thankfully, I got over the tabletop with no problems and hurried along the fastest part of the track, a hefty straight at the end of which was a tight hairpin. We were sideways into that turn like supermoto riders, and I passed both Dugmore and Coppins in the following section of corners. The track had been thoroughly watered overnight, probably to cope with the quota of dust that would rise up through the day's activities, and I was sloshing mud everywhere as I passed through a few puddles that remained on the surface of the terrain making it quite slippery. Pichon was now just ahead of me in second, and Pit Beirer had taken the hole-shot once more and led the way.

On the first lap, it seemed as though Pichon was in his strange stupidity mode again. The talent he has is unbelievable, and he was riding on a tidal wave of confidence by this stage, but he did not give any respect where it was due. He believed that everybody should move out of his way. I had a great view of the tight right turn where he tried to plough straight into Beirer and where he slipped off himself. The turn was uphill and the slowest on the track, so as I passed him, he had lost only two or three positions by the time he had quickly picked up the bike, which was still running so he didn't have to kick-start it, and got going. Beirer had wobbled but recovered from the near miss, and I had him squarely in my sights for the lead.

Pichon was engaging in his usual 'attack like a maniac at the start of the race' ploy, so that he could get to the front as soon as possible and ride his own race with a superior speed, often meaning that he pulled away from everyone as long as he wasn't disturbed. He is the best in the world at reeling off a set of quick laps, and it explains why he has taken so many pole positions, sometimes with a time two seconds faster than the nearest rider. On this occasion, though, he pushed the limit too far in his impetuousness, and could have easily have punted Beirer off the bike at the same time in a moment of rash inconsideration. The incident obviously riled him because as he caught back up into third, he came at me with venom in the next few laps, and I loved every minute of it.

I felt like I was going to have a good race. I was second and shaping Pit up for a pass by showing him my wheel in a couple of corners. Mickael caught us both up within half a lap, and his attack resulted in an entertaining battle that people tell me was some of the most exciting action of the year. There are two ways to have a decent scrap, very hard and very dirty. Pichon and I, in my opinion, were racing very hard. I'd block him and he'd block me; that was what it was all about. Finally, I was giving Mickael a taste of what he should be having every GP, he was in a race and knew it.

I was looking over my shoulder a lot at him as he went over the jumps and hung in the air, simply because I did not trust him. We were fighting more or less for the duration of one lap, and I knew the longer I frustrated him by holding my line and passing him as aggressively as he was doing to m, then he would get more and more uptight. That was partly my goal because he was riding like a desperate man and was on the pace without a doubt, but the situation did make me feel uneasy as much as I was enjoying the struggle. Mickael is an unpredictable rider, and the incident with Beirer only two laps previously was evidence enough. I block-passed him once and he slammed into me a couple of times, and it must have looked pretty tasty from the outside.

That's what people pay to come and see. It was not malicious and I didn't think it was dangerous; if he is going to open the door then I am coming to take advantage and vice versa. I had a good look at him going over a long tabletop that dropped down into a gully because on the previous jump we had taken together, I had had to move from my line otherwise he would have veered over and crashed into me. I cut him off going into the next sharp corner and then wanted to see what he was up to as we hit the tabletop.

At the bottom of the gully was a very sharp left curve that then headed uphill for about ten metres before going into the tight right corner, where Pichon had clashed with Beirer. I took a wide line going into the left and Mickael came up the inside. He was going a little faster, and we both took a different radius in the bend. I braked and steered quickly to go back up, while he turned later because of his extra speed, and his bike had slightly better traction going up and left, so he had the inside as we swung right. I went close into the corner and we touched again, as he tried to squeeze by with barely enough space to fit a bike between me and the wall of dirt bordering the turn. He was on the inside and had less track to cover, so emerged from the corner slightly ahead. We crested a jump that then led downhill about thirty metres to a hairpin right. It was a pretty good place to try and pass because you were carrying a lot of speed from the downhill and could glide up the inside, if you timed your braking properly and there was a bit of room.

Mickael and I bolted down the slope and I moved slightly to the right, planning to take the inside line in the hairpin and continue letting Mickael know that I was still there and wasn't going to roll over. I got on the brakes and slid right up close to the inside of the corner to hit the apex at barely walking speed. Pichon, just in front, had already started to make the turn in and cut off the line as I got my front wheel turning. We clattered each other again, but his momentum took him out of the corner first. Over the next jump, he started waving at me and pointing to his head. My feeling was, 'What am I supposed to do? Let you by?'

Heading around the next few sequences of turns, I hit trouble and knew the fun was over. The titanium screw had been replaced, but on the fourth lap the carbon-fibre bracket snapped altogether, and the engine started jumping around in the frame again. It was the worst vibration I had ever felt on a bike, and I just could not hold on going through some parts of the track, let alone think about pushing any harder. I lost the back of Pichon in the space of three corners, and he pulled out a two-second gap and right up to the wheel of Pit, who barely put up half of the resistance that I had managed and his lead was gone.

I was going backwards from that stage. The bike wobbled, rattled and shuddered, and I could not make any forward progress. If the bike hadn't broken, then I might have been able to run with Mickael and our lap-and-a-half fight might have extended to the whole race. The 250 was not yet in a condition or state of readiness to keep up with Pichon and the Hondas. Like Kurt said later in the year, 'We were just a little bit off what we needed, but that little bit means a great deal when racing for the lead of a Grand Prix'. With someone like Mickael on his Suzuki, that means you are a long way off.

My hands had gone numb with the vibration. I knew from Fred's signals that Andrew McFarlane on the Kawasaki was catching me; ten laps into the race he passed me to take third – I could not force the bike to go quicker without chucking it into the mud. On the eleventh lap, going into a turn, I held a tight line and just clipped the inside of the front tyre on the shallow bank of the track-edge and the contact made me lose balance and crash at slow speed. Coppins, Gundersen, Johnny Aubert and Paul Cooper went by before I could get the bike started, into gear and begin following them. I was not too far away from Cooper and held eighth position right behind him for four laps until a small piece of luck fell my way and he pulled into the pit with a broken Honda. With only five circulations to go, Gundersen was out of reach in sixth and I was badly fading in the last three laps with my shaking mess of a race bike, so much so that an Italian privateer called Cristian Beggi started to get very close, and I had to find some reserves on the last lap to make sure of a limp seventh.

The long faces were back by the time the race was over and everybody was back in the tent. The debrief was a moody one, and the accusation hung in the air that I was giving excuses for a lousy ride when I was trying to explain that the bike had broken again. That was the worst point; having to justify my innocence to my own crew. I can take criticism from most quarters, but from my own team was too much. I was having enough trouble sorting out my head and confidence, without having pointless accusations that the bike's mechanical glitches were my fault. I had doubts and insecurity flying from all directions at me, even Naomi was beginning to think it was my riding, and went to speak to the mechanics and Kurt to say 'What's going on here?'.

Leighton, the engine technician, is a lovely guy and the incident in Italy wasn't his fault because how can you predict that sort of occurrence? Yet, he was one of the people who were getting on my case. It was a time when maybe he needed to stand up and admit that there had been a failure on the bike, but like several other occasions that season, he seemed beyond criticism and just couldn't face up to telling me or anybody else that there had been a problem in his part of the package; it was too easy to blame me again.

Everyone was bull-headed about their ideas with the 250. I was not doing a good enough job of persuading people that the suspension wasn't up to scratch or the engine was not configured properly for the racetrack. In the end, after being ignored, I had started to sulk and had a 'Well, if they won't work for me, then fuck 'em' approach.

Everybody was pissed off with a poor weekend's racing, but back then I had to deal with mechanics in the tent looking at me like I was some kind of idiot, and it all got a bit fiery! Finally, with Neil and Kurt hanging around and being less than positive, I flipped. That weekend, I had had enough. Hearing comments that I 'just gave up' or 'got tired after four laps' riled me, and I called Kurt aside into my camper for a crisis meeting, and said, 'I cannot take this any more.' I was almost in tears trying to explain that I was tired of him and everybody else saying that I was not fit or not confident or not trying. I said 'Get the 125cc bike ready, it's the 250 and the attitude around me that's the problem here, not my riding.' From that moment on, I was competing in two races at the next GP in Austria.

I explained that I had ridden maybe forty to forty-five times so far in the year in practice and qualifying, and I could count on one hand the amount of times I did not have some sort of a problem. People were just not hearing me, or they were listening and not doing anything about my mechanical grievances. I also said that, in my eyes, one of the drawbacks was that there was no team manager this year. Kurt had a series of meetings from when he arrived at the track until he went to the hotel, or he was always on the phone. The only time he went up to the pit area was for the race. I missed Kurt being around because I trust him implicitly. I think also that he was unaware of what was going on because he heard things second-hand and was never really there to witness it for himself. So he was partially missing out on the racing side of things, and Toby was also skipping around the place because he had twice as many riders as usual.

Kurt and I started talking about the troubles, and he correctly pointed out that I had a part to play in the problem. My negativity concerning the need for mechanical development and the relationship with Gordon was not helping. I also had to deal with the fact that as World Champion, I would be struggling to win a race in 2002, and this disappointing realisation wasn't making me the easiest guy to work with. I said that I felt the team was fragmented and not as supportive. The unit was being pulled in various different directions, with people having their own agendas or priorities instead of trying to make Jamie Dobb and Gordon Crockard GP winners. I recognised during the meeting that, as much as the team needed sort out the communication, I needed to grow up a bit and accept the structure for what it was.

He rightly said that everybody was trying to do all they could to make the bike a success, and I knew very well that people were making the effort, it just wasn't in the right directions. Importantly, Kurt believed me when I explained that the bike was still not able to win, as evidenced by the faults. Maybe even he was a bit deluded or misinformed about the first few races of the season and still believed his convictions, but, finally, I felt like I was getting through to him, or somebody at least.

Like I said to the team on numerous occasions, every Japanese manufacturer in the class has put maybe two, three, four or even five years' development into their motorcycles; KTM have produced a bike and slotted it straight into the World Championships within a period of eight months. The first test with the 250 occurred in August 2001, and here we were in May 2002 trying to beat Pichon, who had been evolving the Suzuki since 1999.

When the finished article arrives, I have no doubt that it will be one of the best bikes on the track and importantly one of the top two-stroke 250s available to buy. KTM is one of the world's biggest manufacturers of off-road motorcycles, and when they sell a bike it is virtually exactly the same as what we race, whereas in my experience with the Japanese machines, there is a hefty difference between what the customer wheels out of the shop and what the mechanic pulls out of the van every weekend. I believe KTM are ahead of everybody when it comes to making race-replica production motorcycles, but after the Grand Prix of Italy, I think they realised that on the racetrack we were actually playing catch-up to the major players of the 250cc field with the new project .

Despite my concerns and frustrations, I wasn't going to stand up publicly and blame the lack of trophies or my sinking confidence on the motorcycle. That wasn't my style and besides, I believed that the 250 I was riding was not a bad machine, we were just plagued with rotten luck and the kind of small glitches that arrive with a prototype – the stone in Spain, the gear shifter in France, and now the bracket in Italy. The meeting worked and highlighted the vast communication problem we had been having up until then. After explaining my views, he said that we obviously needed some more options, and over the next few weeks there was an increased level of activity, with more new things to try out.

He told me just to go out riding and testing, and made plans for me to stay in Italy that week with Fred and Vincent. The idea was to show the team that I was ready to make the effort away from the GPs, and at the same time have some fun; just to ride and not think too much about everything. The first time I enjoyed myself on the KTM during the whole year was the week after the race; I just took my time at the places we stopped at and concentrated on feeling the positive elements of the bike.

Kurt now knew the feelings of everybody and the situation was like an expanding balloon that had finally popped. At least everyone's emotions were now out in the open and we could work from here. I had also secured a 125cc ride for Austria, and was beginning to look forward to wearing the number one and proving I still had the golden touch.

We drove to several tracks in the region, planning to end the week by parking the camper at Mugello for the Italian Moto GP, which was quite exciting. I had already met Marco Melandri, the factory Aprilia rider, who was one of the favourites for the 250cc title, and this time we got talking more and swapped numbers to stay in touch. He was a motocross fan and I was a racing fan, and we hit it off right away because he's a nice guy and easy to talk to. I also knew Valentino Rossi after meeting him at a supercross race in Genoa in 1996, and was hanging out with him a little bit on Thursday and Friday.

I've been to many road-race GPs over the years, and even I was a little surprised at how the paddock is now a showground of big money and big technology. It totally looked the part of wealth and professionalism, with huge rigs and motorhomes everywhere.

Up until Saturday night, the weekend was going perfectly. I had forgotten about Castiglione and was happily distracted. Sadly though, I was disappointed that I couldn't stick around for the races. Dorna were nice enough to give us passes for the event, but wouldn't let me park my camper anywhere near the track, so we were up on the hill with the fans and it was like a war-zone. I had never been to the Italian GP, and while the atmosphere and the enthusiasm of the fans was electrifying, it was also scary and dangerous. In the campsite, people were racing flat out across the fields and car parks, slamming into each other and some guys had engines on the back of low-loaders and were revving the shit out of them until they blew up. An ambulance was permanently circling the area. I made the decision that we should leave so that the camper didn't become an object of unwanted attention, and also because I had to be at a press day in Austria on Monday.

With the Moto GP experience and riding in Italy, I did not get too much time to reflect on the Italian GP and probably did not want to either. When I saw a video of the race on the television in the week leading up to Austria, the scrap between Pichon and me did look quite exciting, and it was great to see a decent advertisement of the sport like that.

★ ★ ★

Mickael surprised me a lot in 2002 with his intelligence to pick lines. In Italy, for example, I was lagging in the moto and being caught by McFarlane almost two seconds a lap. I then tried a different line around a downhill turn that seemed slippery, but when I kept using it, I actually started to stabilise the margin. Looking at the video of the GP, I noticed that Mickael had been taking it all race long.

Mickael's a nice kid and I lived next door to him for over a year in the States. He can be a strange character, but is usually up for a laugh. In America, we were still in the European minority (nothing like it is now with every other rider being from France), and we used to hang out and screw around, boxing and generally messing about. We got some proper gloves once and his girlfriend Stephanie did not like it too much. Mickael would turn a bit serious sometimes and start getting a bit carried away, and he was losing a few kilos to me! So one day I said to him, 'Lie down on the floor for a minute and

I'll go and get Stephanie.' So he lies down and I run into the other room and shout, 'Stephanie, come quick there's been an accident.' She belts it into the room and starts screaming, seeing him prostrate on the floor with these big gloves, until we both begin cracking up. I don't recall doing much sparring after that little gag.

We have always got on well, but competing against each other naturally carries some tensions. We've had some good races in the past and we both want to win, but like Alessio 'Chicco' Chiodi, I have a relationship with him whereby we can bang bars, and if he wins I'm okay with it and vice versa. I don't associate confidence with arrogance, but Mickael is very confident! He's won enough over the last few years and he is still only twenty-six. His temperament has made him a controversial figure, and a few altercations with the authorities in the past have helped fashion an edge of aloofness. Mickael was certainly better at SX than me and benefited from doing it a lot as he grew up. I stopped for almost five years before I took it up again in the US.

A natural comparison to Pichon would now be Ricky Carmichael, who is winning everything in American SX and MX, and is ushering in a new era of super-hard attacking racing. I always joke with Ricky by saying, 'You've won a lot of things on a 125 mate, but you never beat me!' We faced up at the Nations in Brazil. We had a good scrap in the heat race and he crashed, so I had the win. You have to do a serious amount of work if you want to beat him now, and I don't mean just for one season, I'm talking years. The man is a motocross animal. The intensity and workrate that RC puts into his riding is amazing.

I know Ricky quite well and he's a good guy. He's a chubby little kid and has to work hard to keep the weight off! He's very down to earth, and if you need an example of somebody who has made sacrifices for their sport, then look no further than Carmichael. A lot of people have the wrong idea about him and perceive him to be arrogant, when he is just immensely focused and serious about his profession. At only twenty-three, Ricky gets a hard time from the fans sometimes in the States, and that's quite rare because they love their winners. He takes the sport very seriously and that may be why he doesn't enjoy the same level of adoration as Jeremy McGrath.

If I had to race Ricky now, the only way I would be sure of winning is if I locked myself away for six months and trained like never before. At the end of the day, you have to want it more than he does.

Sooner or later somebody was going to move MX/SX onwards in the same way that McGrath did. Ricky is an example of how the line between outdoor motocross and indoor supercross is becoming very blurred. Previously, there were outdoor specialists like Stanton and LaRocco, and then indoor untouchables like McGrath. People like Ricky, James Stewart and the latest young sensations, the Alessi kids, have seen this divide and know what they have to do in order to cross it.

They all have their own SX track and they practise, practise, practise and then do it some more. The skills come naturally at a young age, and before you know it every young motocrosser is proficient in both disciplines. Ricky is probably a bit better outdoors than indoors, but his speciality lies in being able to reel off twenty scorching laps.

Current teenage American sensation James Stewar, will lift our sport to another level, maybe even beyond Carmichael. What he can do on a motorcycle is a pleasure to watch. The way he handles the bike seems to defy physics. On a SX track he is more or less hitting the same lap-times as Carmichael, but on a 125. If I had to name the five best riders in the world today, then would be: Carmichael, Stewart, Pichon, Chad Reed and Stefan Everts. If I were to talk about the best riders ever then Carmichael would still be in my list. Rick Johnson was so skilful, while David Bailey was beauty on a bike. He was fluid, never made a mistake and made it look so effortless and easy. Bob Hannah was also another of the early pioneers. You then have to look at Championships and count De Coster, Robert and Everts. At this moment, I can confidently say that, in terms of natural ability, Stewart is the best motocross rider in the world.

Carmichael, Stewart and people like Pichon make the sport exciting to watch because it's like seeing a forty-minute series of qualifying laps. They are a little bit out of control, power-wheeling everywhere, attacking every inch of the track and riding the edge. Compare it to the old days when a race time would be something like five or six seconds slower than qualifying and it doesn't even compare as a spectacle. Nobody wants to watch someone just cruising around anymore. Motocross will progress in the American style and be all the better for it.

As a racer, I don't believe you can allow yourself to accept mentally that anyone is as good as you or can beat you. I think I can beat anyone in this world: Carmichael, Stewart, Everts. Line them up. If I sat here and said 'I can't defeat Pichon,' then he's won already.

Paul Malin and I came through the ranks together, and he was probably my longest-running rival and the first rider that I really had to work to beat. We would always be racing each other for the win, all the way up through the junior levels to British Championships. We would then be fighting in the GPs as well. It put strain on a lengthy relationship at times, but we never really had any clashes. I only developed a problem with Paul after 1996. He had finished second in the world that year, and everybody had been telling him how he was the best thing on the planet. I had been through a tough and financially costly season in the US and when we met up at the Nations that year, I thought he had become quite arrogant.

I try to be as honest as I can with my racing and if I lose to a better rider then I will give credit where it is due, but Paul was not like that. In 1997 and '98 we fought in the British Championships and he was always full of excuses, about the bike, the track, the weather, anything. When Paul switches the button he is an unbelievable talent, and I should know because I have raced him since I was five years old and we are from the same town, but he was just not a sporting rider at times. Our relationship is okay now and he called to wish me luck before Gaildorf in 2001, which was a nice gesture. Like he said, with the talent between us, and the dominance we enjoyed through the amateurs in Europe, it would have been a crying shame if one of us hadn't won a World Championship. When we were kids, we could go anywhere in the world and nobody could get close to us.

Rob Herring was my major rival as a pro and we had some good races together. Rob is a really good guy and perhaps even too nice. Herring and I would swap classes in the British Championships. I won the 125 title in 1989 and he took the 250. The following year, we claimed each other's crown! Outside of the 500 class, with Thorpe and Nicoll, we must have been among the very top riders in the UK at that point. Rob's weakness lay in his dedication – he suffered a little with his weight – although, like Malin, he was a very strong rider, who was capable of absolutely anything if he had his mind engaged. It's a little sad that he never took a World Championship with the ability he had. With the right backing and greater self-discipline, he would have been in the elite club without a doubt.

When I competed with Brown and Langston in 2000, we used to really attack the racetrack (and sometimes each other!) but it was thrilling stuff. Mike Brown has speed like you would not believe, but he would sometimes freeze or it would come in fits and spurts. He is definitely better on a 125 than a 250, and on his day he can't be caught. He suffered in 2000 because, compared to Langston and me, his bike was a pile of shit, and it is credit to his abilities that he won races and kept up with both of us when the odds were against him. Brown was the classic case of contrasting personalities: he was friendly and unassuming off the track, but so fired up about his racing that he would become a proper hard bastard on it!

We have had our comings together. I remember bumping into him during practice at a race in Daytona for the 'Bike Week' supercross. I had passed him going through the whoops and into the start straight where, at the end of it, you swing out a little to turn and double jump. I moved into position, not realising he had come back around, and unintentionally cut off his line. The next thing I know, he slams into me and starts screaming 'Motherfucker!', over and over. I rode off the side of the track and he jumped on me and started swinging away! We were both riding for the 125 factory Honda team and there was no way I was getting involved in a scrap. He swore some more and rode off. A few hours later, I was speaking with him as normal! We had a couple of run-ins when he was trying the GPs and racing in Britain and we'd slam into each other – he is similar to me in that he hates to lose, but different in that he can go over the top.

I learn quite quickly about my opponents by watching them closely. You soon find out where they are faster and slower on the circuit. Also, watching their bikes and actions sometimes can give clues if they are struggling with their set-up or a tyre. Body language on the bike is a good tell-tale sign and it's easy to spot if a rider is really on it, tiring or not having fun and riding tight. I try to find the weaknesses of my rivals and sometimes it can be easy to spot.

Emotions do run high and sometimes in motocross, riders go for the same line. I'm a big guy and will fight for every inch that I and get. Often that brings out confrontations. With Grant Langston, things got a bit silly. We were both quite arrogant that season, and he especially so. He was a good rider and had a lot of confidence, but he was also petulant and up-his-own-arse so that set us apart. We generally didn't see eye to eye on things and frequently it flared up.

At Spa in 2000 for the second moto, he drifted out wide on the second corner and our lines came together, he went for it and I went for it. We collided and he ended up crashing. I won the race and afterwards he came up to me all guns blazing, wanting a fight and tried to throw some punches. I felt embarrassed because we were both riding for KTM, all the bosses were there and the owner of KTM as well. Kurt was standing near and saying to me, 'Don't you even dare.' I just stood there and thought 'I'm not going to fight back', I was a grown man and the whole thing seemed appropriate for the playground with this eighteen-year-old kid trying to give me a load of attitude and calling me a 'pussy'.

I remember saying to his dad that year that Grant should thank me because he'd hole-shot and go backwards or win the odd race. I'd put some fire in his belly and he would come from way back and finish third just to chase me. He was also quite shit in the mud and that aspect of his riding got better. I like to think I unwillingly helped Grant progress as a rider.

9 June 2002: Round Six
Austrian Grand Prix, Kärntenring

AUSTRIA IS more or less how it is often depicted in the movies – very green, mountainous and picturesque country, it is a real pleasure to visit and feels very clean and untouched. It reminds me of England in some ways, but also gives the sensation of more space, less pollution and can seem more spectacular in terms of its landscape. Austria is also the home of my employers.

The KTM factory is based just north of Salzburg, about two-and-a-half hours away from the new Kärntenring circuit where the GP was being held for the second year in a row. The HQ is where we stayed in Austria all week after coming up from Mugello and then travelled to the circuit on Friday. That night in the camper we watched a fantastic performance by England against Argentina in the World Cup, and it got me feeling very patriotic and fired up to do well that weekend.

A big itinerary came through from KTM HQ with the times we had to be places for things like signings and appearances. It was no more than usual for me, and I am always happy to pose for a photo or sign an autograph because I am also a sporting fan and wouldn't hesitate to ask someone like Lennox Lewis or Rio Ferdinand for a moment of their time.

It was my first outing at the Kärntenring. The track had taken its bow as a GP circuit in 2001 for the final race of the season, and I was out injured and didn't even bother making the trip. My first reaction was that it seemed an odd location in which to place a track. Surrounded by hills and spoilt for choice in terms of mountainous landscape, the circuit was laid on a stretch of ground that was so flat it would have put a Dutch venue to shame. The course, jumps and obstacles were 100 per cent man-made and, upon initial viewing, it resembled a supercross track due to its sheer artificiality.

I was interested to try it, and it was clear that the ability of the track builders would come under particularly close scrutiny here. The main advantage of the Kärntenring was that a big new driving school complex lay adjacent to the track and its roads acted as the paddock, which meant that everybody was happy on flat asphalt and had plenty of space. Around the edges of the course were some slopes that provided decent spectator banking, and the greenness of the immediate area created quite a scenic picture in which to race motocross. The track wound its way back and forth like a scalextric on a part-grass, part-mud surface, and what it lacked in exciting drops and step-ups, it seemed to make up for with several technical sections that might produce some decent racing.

After first practice, my impression of the track was not a favourable one and it should have been of a better standard. For example, there was a 'rail section' where you could go inside or outside over a sequence of jumps and the track was split in two. A loop at each end meant that if you took the inside for the first turn then you would hit the jumps before having to go around the outside of the next corner. The idea was good and it certainly looked quite different, but it didn't work because the first turn into the section was too narrow and didn't allow any kind of overtaking to try beat another rider into one specific route or force him to accept a line he didn't want. One path was always a bit faster than the other, you just had to be experienced in tackling the jump section slotted into the short straight linking the hairpins. You could do it in two or three different ways, but the fastest method (although initially longer) was to go outside and quicker on the bank into the first corner, so you would be carrying enough speed before slowing up and punching out of the next hairpin on the slow inside to get away. If you had to choose the inside line on the first bend, then you didn't have the momentum to get a good run at the jumps before reaching the fast bank on the outside of the second turn.

Generally, the take-offs and landings of most of the jumps were crap; they were either too short or too steep. It detracted from the spectacle of the sport because nobody was going to try to whip their bike and really show off; if you got it slightly wrong on those landings, you were going to crash. It's a little bit of a shame because I applaud what the organisers had tried to create with Kärntenring.

I like to think I am not one of these riders who picks a fault with every little thing on a circuit or one who wants to return to the old-style tracks where we are doing 100mph up and down hills. We need to have big jumps and things like whoops – it's the future direction of the sport and what the bikes are made for these days. The SX flavour of the modern motocross circuit is not everyone's speciality and may divide the field, but it can only breed a more skilful element of motocross riders in as little as five years' time, when maybe we will be producing our own versions of James Stewart. The fastest guy is always going to win. The best ones will always be at the front, whether the tracks are made thirty seconds or three minutes long. In time, the playing field will narrow and that is what the public want to see – good, close racing.

In terms of getting a 125cc factory bike, the situation was perfect for me because Erik Eggens (Steve Ramon's team-mate) had been out injured with a nasty broken leg and ankle since May, and would be lucky to make it back before the end of the season. Austria was also the right time for me to try a 125cc GP. I would not be affecting the Championship too much, because there were still six races remaining, and I did not want to get in the way of the factory's chances of winning three years in a row. I would not have to worry about things like team orders or having to let Ramon or Patrick Caps, also on a KTM, go past.

As the proceedings started, I was under no illusions as to how tiring the whole thing was going to be. I would come back from one practice and have to go straight out into another. The 250 was still the priority, although underneath I was raring to go for my 125 comeback. The 125 was still a beautiful bike to ride and sweet to handle. I felt like I was really having fun on it, and several people remarked how much more comfortable I looked on the track. I hardly had to change anything to get it set up and ready; it was like falling back into an old routine.

Swapping the bikes during the afternoon meant I was best placed to comment on the immediate difference between riding the different motorcycles. Obviously, the first area is in the power. My 125 had about 41 bhp, the 250 had somewhere between 55 and 58. You really notice the increase. I can't gas the 250 as much as the 125. On most circuits, I could pin the throttle a great deal of the time on the 125, whereas on the bigger bike you need to be more measured with when and how much gas you have to use.

The second aspect was the weight. My height (six foot) and weight (thirteen stone) are disadvantages on the 125. I was losing performance compared to someone like Eggens, who is smaller and leaner. I used my strength over the years to pull the 125 around the track. The 250 was heavier and, combined with its extra power, made it slightly more tiring to ride.

The overall packages felt quite different. The 125cc is a pure race machine that was gagging to be revved and pushed as hard as it would go. The screaming two-stroke engine, responsive handling and little weight meant it was a perfect MX tool. The 250 at this stage didn't give me a secure basis on which to judge, because of the problems we were having with the suspension, but the bigger engine and extra weight requires perhaps more precision and a little bit more thought about how you place the bike on the circuit to gain the faster times. I didn't really have to adapt my style all that much, but I was more aware of my riding when I was on the 250.

Importantly, riding and clocking fast times on the 125 started to massage my confidence and, all of a sudden, I felt like a motocross racer again and not as a test rider who was doing his work in the GPs. My speed on the 125 made me realise the depth of the struggles I had been having on the 250 this season.

Alloy had given me some new kit with a big number one on the back, and Fred had also made up some gold front and side plates printed with my status in the class to tie on to Erik's bike. It was another small confidence booster to circle the track on Saturday in my new livery. I was the 125cc World Champion and it had been a lifetime dream to race with the number one plate.

A lengthy Saturday started brightly with the 125cc free practice. It felt reassuring to be back, and my shiny gold number one plate couldn't have given me more impetus to rush out and prove that I truly was the World Champion and still the best in the class. I made about seven laps and felt fast on the bike as I got a good look at the track. On the sixth circulation, I went for a quick time and grabbed the top slot in the classification – a perfect way to let everybody know I meant business. I then immediately swapped bikes in the awning and rode down to the pit for the 250 free practice where I got the third-best lap.

The 250 was like riding the big, ugly brother of the 125, and I could already sense in some parts of the circuit that I didn't feel like letting it hang out – the 125 had been better behaved. I had all of a twenty-minute break before putting my helmet on again. I was out of the blocks straight away in the 125 pre-qualifying practice and set the fastest time by over half a second from Marco Dorsch. This meant that I would have first choice in the gate for the initial heat race.

Again, it was a straight swap for the 250, and I toured for several laps, just feeling the adjustment and slightly different places to hit on the circuit. Thankfully, there was then time to take off my boots and grab a bit of food over the lunch break before the qualifying race.

The twenty-five minute heat went like clockwork. I made the hole-shot and held off Trampas Parker for enough time to create a decent so that I could just cruise around for the win. I was not in the top ten of the World Championship standings, so after those riders had made their own timed session, I would be going into the gate eleventh and that was fine by me. Unlike in Italy, 250cc qualifying went off without a hitch. I was there or thereabouts in and around third or fourth position before finally taking the latter when the thirty-minute time limit ran down in the pits.

From a 9 a.m. start, the day finished at 4 p.m. and I had ridden for most of it. I felt slightly re-energised after having a shower in the camper. We went for dinner in the KTM hospitality area and I signed some autographs before my next appointment. That evening, all three World Champions had a photo call for the press, and I felt even more a part of what I had achieved in 2001. It was a nice tangible reminder of the level I had reached in the sport.

I lined up with Mickael and Stefan Everts in the gate fully dressed up with all three bikes arranged to provide some pictures for the television and newspapers. We posed and chatted for a while, and I was happy to do some promotion work purely for the sport; it was an overdue and far too infrequent provision from Dorna. On Saturday evening, I lazed knackered on the sofa, watching television and knowing that I had done a days' work.

The next morning the sun broke early, and warm temperatures meant that the weather was going to be fine once again. After a quick cruise around the twenty-minute warm-up just to have a look at the track, the 250 race was the first order of the day. There was slightly more pressure than usual to get a good result because of all the KTM staff, not to mention fans, wandering around the circuit. This was the nearest I would get to a home GP. The bosses were keen to see how their 250 two-stroke project was coming on, and that put more eyes than normal on both Gordon and me.

The start straight shrank and narrowed to a ninety-degree left-hand turn that went into a fast kink and up to a slightly banked left loop. I took the inside place to the far left of the gate and had Paul Cooper next to me on the right. If I went straight ahead off the line, I would end up in the fence. I would have to get up and move slightly to the right to get a good position on the inside of the corner.

My jump was sluggish, and I had to slow down far earlier than I would have liked to turn in. There were a lot of riders in front of me as the pack threaded left, and I couldn't attack the bend like I wanted because I was maybe five or six metres further back than I imagined in my perfect start. I held my ground going through the kink and cut inside going into the left loop. Through the next section, I made a position or two to hover in seventh or eighth. The rail section was quite busy and for the first lap I elected to go safely on the inside. I could see Gordon ahead in about fourth or fifth, having forced his best start of the season so far. I was seventh at the end of the first lap and was quite surprised when I looked behind me to see Pichon.

I knew Coppins had taken the hole-shot and was leading, but Mickael, like myself, had made a mess of the first corner and was having to move through from slightly further back than normal. For about a quarter of a lap, I tried to make myself as wide as possible, but it was fairly pointless. I half expected to see fire burning out of the Suzuki's exhaust as it slipped by me, going down into a rutted hairpin. I focused on staying as close as possible to the back of the Frenchman. He rode the bike like it was a perfect extension of his body, and he let it buck and bounce to his heart's content while getting heavily on the gas. I only wished to be able to punish my bike in the same way without being in danger of it throwing me off.

Pichon gained space quickly and then attacked Bolley, who was just in front, on his path to the leaders. I looked on in envy as he affected the race. Coppins had better be setting a severe pace because Mickael was on the charge. Gordon, in third place, looked as though he might be next for the treatment.

Andrew McFarlane on the Kawasaki came past to drop me back to seventh again as we both glided past Frederic Vialle. McFarlane was riding aggressively but not consistently, and was holding me up in some sections. By the end of the second lap, I was about seven seconds away from Josh at the front. I could see Mickael had passed Gordon and was after the Hondas of Beirer and Coppins.

It took me another three laps wasting time behind McFarlane before I could make an overtaking move that kept me firmly in sixth. An empty track awaited me because Bolley was about six seconds ahead, and I could see him going through the following collection of corners. For two laps I pushed to try and reduce the gap and was handed some luck when Fred suddenly slowed up and I was right on top of him. He must have made an error or maybe suffered a mechanical problem, because I motored by without any opposition.

I was now up to fifth and could see Mickael leading by some way from Gordon, who had surprisingly despatched Beirer and then Coppins. I was a long way from the tail of Beirer in fourth and would need further fortune akin to the Bolley incident to make any more positions, despite being only halfway through the race. With Pit and me recording more or less the same times, I could only chip away at the space between us.

As I settled into forging a lonely rhythm, I faced a fresh challenge from Paul Cooper who, I learned from the pit boards, was catching me. I took a few chances in the following laps to increase the gap and earned enough of a margin not to have to worry about the front wheel of the Honda appearing alongside me. After about five laps Cooper backed off, either from the pace or from a few mistakes, and the distance climbed to just over seven seconds around four laps from the end.

I eased halfway through the last lap because I was suddenly aware I would have to do this all over again in less than two hours. I was still charging as hard as I could up until that point because Pit could have already backed off and lost maybe two or three seconds. From a five-second gap, that reduction means you suddenly have a race and it certainly would be much harder for him to pick up again having called it a day, in comparison to my speed and momentum because I was still pushing. Halfway through that last lap, Pit was still roughly five seconds away, and I knew the chances of me rising higher than fifth were slim.

I crossed the line and saw the guys heading over to the podium, where Gordon had deservedly scored the first top three result for the team (behind Pichon again). Contrary to what some might think, I was okay with the situation. After the drama of the year so far, it was an overdue performance and it was an important podium result for

KTM. I knew Gordon had been getting as frustrated as me over the last few GPs. He had signed for the team with the impression that he was going to fight for the title, and up until Austria, his best results had been two seventh positions. It was a relief for him, and also for Kurt and the KTM guys in some ways. To see some smiles in the tent was worth it, even if I should have delivered the first silverware long ago.

I missed the 500 GP, instead electing to lie in the camper and get some rest and fluids. I was able to scoff some fruit and relaxed watching the sport coming into the big television via the satellite dish on top of the camper. A member of the KTM crew later relayed the whole 500cc event to me, because the moto had been a classic and easy contender for best race of the season, so they said. Watching the race on television the next week, I had to agree.

Demaria had made a flyer for KTM, and Stefan Everts spent most of the race trying to catch him up. The Frenchman dramatically faded towards the end, and Everts consistently made ground going into the last lap. On the final corner, Demaria went wide and bottled the turn while Everts cut in tight and got the gas on earlier. The Yamaha weaved across and relegated the KTM to second with barely ten metres until the line. It was an exciting finish and the images of Kurt throwing stones at the track in frustration and the Rinaldi brothers hugging each other in celebration made the spectacle a perfect moment for television.

The three hours between the end of the 250s and the moment when the 125s were being warmed up in the paddock passed a lot quicker than usual. With Pichon taking his third win in a row (and five from six for Suzuki) and Everts rudely dumping KTM off the 500cc top step in view of the chequered flag, the 125cc GP was the last chance for the firm to get a victory at their home GP. The stakes were raised slightly, and that number one plate, while being a badge of honour, began to feel a little heavy.

I changed into my other Alloy kit, complete with onboard television camera. I didn't really notice the difference that much, and because the track wasn't muddy I did not have to worry about the lid collecting more weight. This would be my only outing in the 125s all season and I was keen to generate any little bit of extra publicity from my appearance. The stage was set.

By the time of the last moto of the day, it was the middle of the afternoon and turning out to be hottest race of the year so far. I could see on the parade lap that the 500s had cut the track up a hell of a lot, making it incredibly rough. This wasn't a bad thing, but made it an all-the-more tiring prospect. The top ten 125 guys were as fresh as daisies. They didn't have to worry about the qualifying heats, they had only ridden a twenty-minute free practice, thirty-minute timed session and a twenty minute warm-up on Sunday.

For the second time, I lined up in the gate. I took my eleventh position pick to the left of Ramon, who was stationed adjacent to the box that housed the gate mechanism. The little black crate in which the race starter hid to drop the metal barrier was in the middle of the gate. I had Maschio on my left, and directly ahead was a line just to the right of the apex of the first turn. I had made a slight error in the 250 GP by picking the inside slot. It had worked well for me in the 125 heat race, but if I messed up again then I would be shoved into the throng of a busy 125 pack where anything could happen, and it would be far more frantic than a 250 gathering.

So, this time I banked on pure straight-line speed and hoped that I would have a better track position by moving along the gate by about eight slots. My reaction to the fall was sharp and the 125cc power slightly easier to manage from a standing start. I beat and cut across Maschio and also had a yard on Ramon. Alex Puzar had the hole-shot, but I was in about fifth place and a good position.

I was quite impressed with the onboard television images of the start when watching the video later on (even if that sort of first-person perspective stuff does, ironically, make me feel a little sick), and the super slow-motion camera the Dorna production crew use also showed a great shot of my exit from the gate. They may certainly have their faults, but the guys at Dorna really put a lot of effort into their television coverage, which is probably the best quality the GPs have ever seen.

I made sure of third position halfway round the course, with Philippe Dupasquier and Puzar ahead. I turned my attention onto Dupasquier and lined him up for a pass by taking the outside line in the split section. I gained more momentum through the jumps and exited the second loop just ahead. He retaliated and tried to come through on several of the following corners, but I was a little stronger and wouldn't let him get into a position whereby he could attempt an attack. Puzar was no more than three seconds ahead, and I pushed hard to drop Dupasquier.

At the end of the third lap, I saw that Ramon was some way behind, maybe in fifth or sixth. I was slightly clear in second position from Dupasquier by a second or two and bided my time for four laps, slowly reeling in former World Champ and veteran Puzar on the Husqvarna. Alex was riding quite well and I imagine it must have been some time since he last looked so strong at the front of a GP, but I was taking pieces out of him in various places and was pulling closer and closer. The 125 was like putting on an old favourite pair of shoes that are still in fashion, and we gelled. It felt a pleasure to ride, and I sensed the confidence to play and push the bike coming back to me.

On lap seven, I was right with the Italian and lined him up going through the whoops. We went left after the bumps and headed up to the 'Everts–Demaria' hairpin–right final turn. I braked later as Puzar took a high line and block-passed him. I slid the bike across his path and approached the finish-line tabletop, leading the 125cc GP of Austria.

Strangely, as soon as I saw the vacant track, I started to feel tired. It was about fifteen to twenty minutes into the race, and my concentration and effort to catch Puzar had taken some doing. Johnny O'Mara once told me 'If you feel tired and like you can't keep on going, push for one more lap because it could be the one that breaks them'. I adopted the strategy and it worked, because I continued to ride strongly and stretched away from Puzar right at the crucial time when he would have been expecting to tail me and re-pass.

I charged for two laps until the end of my energy when I got the sign that I had a three-second margin with eight laps remaining, and from there I knew I could ease off a little and keep the rhythm to the flag. I had been doing 2m 8s laps to catch Puzar. I overtook him at the start of lap eight and by the tenth my time had slowed to 2m 10s. With three laps remaining, it dragged to 2m 11s, and I knew I had the race from that point because there was no way he was going to make up the five-second deficit and, with this bike, there was also no chance of a mistake from me.

The pace must have surprised Puzar because he dropped back some more in the last few circulations; the final classification had the time gap down to just under five seconds, but my last lap was a 2m 15s because I was truly knackered.

I made a special point of taking notice of the applause and cheers on the nineteenth and final lap and, as I approached the line, I punched the air with satisfaction, relief and vindication. I was too tired to whip the bike over the jump and just trundled past the waving chequered flag that was a welcome sight after what felt like a long absence. I removed my goggles and savoured the victory lap, even though I could have done with getting off the bike! As I came down the only rise on the track to the pit lane, I saw Kurt smiling away at the bottom and I patted the number one on the front of the bike, just to remind him who had given KTM a victory today. Halfway round the track, I stopped to get a big Union Jack flag and toured back to the podium area.

I was dead on my feet after the race and barely felt I had the energy to talk to anyone. Naomi, Fred, Toby and Kurt were with me near the podium and were ecstatic. The podium ceremony and television interview, which had been such a familiar procedure in 2001, now felt like a novelty. I remember thinking at the time that I wished I had more life inside me to enjoy it. In the small interview,

I took my moment of live airtime to express that it had been a hard year for me and that I was happy to show I was a worthy World Champion. I then just about managed to remember to list all my sponsors who hadn't been getting the same exposure as they had done in 2001.

Up on the steps afterwards, it was special to hear the British national anthem again, the first time it had been played this season in any of the GPs. I was presented with flowers and a golden tyre, as well as a cup big enough to put Gracie inside. Standing isolated on the top step is a reminder of what you alone have personally sacrificed and given to achieve the honour.

The champagne is quite fun and you'll be surprised how far that stuff actually goes when you shake it up. I always make a point of giving the girls a good soaking. In the press conference, I spoke to Alex and he confessed that he was thinking what I had suspected; that when I passed him I would be tired, having already done one moto, and he only had to wait for me to fade. I believe the effort to break away caught him off guard and finished the race. I looked at the lap analysis back in the tent; I had been recording 2m 8s to catch Alex, while his best was a low 2m 9s. After taking the lead, I was still a second a lap faster than him for two circulations before we hit near enough the same pace. The extra charge had been effective.

I explained to the press my exact feelings at the time. I wasn't part of the 125 Championship, but I had more pressure in that GP than anybody. KTM had paid for the event and had not won a moto. I was riding for the first time with the number one plate, which was like hanging a huge target on your back. I felt like I had absolved my title. I was the fastest 125 rider in the world and I beat everyone, having already raced one moto. I also had to show the team that the problems in the 250 GPs were not the result of my riding, and I was just the same guy who had been World Champion ten months previously.

I had to then go up to race control and perform a dope test, which was quite funny because it usually takes a long time to be in a position when you are ready to be able to piss. Ben Townley and Patrick Caps had already been hanging about for thirty minutes while the podium stuff and press conference was going on, and I walked straight in and asked for the bottle. They were sitting there looking at me as if to say 'What are you doing?'. I filled it up, signed the paper and left them to it! Josh Coppins also gave a urine sample that day that would go on to have serious implications.

We got packed up and left fairly soon after the race. On Monday morning, I felt a little more tired than usual, but nothing out of the ordinary. The trophy found a home in the spare room along with my Championship-winning bike and so many other shiny metal pots and plates that Naomi says she is reluctant to dust!

★ ★ ★

Needless to say, the moment of victory is always the ultimate payoff. When I am fifty metres away from the finish line and leading, when I pass the chequered flag, I am bursting at the seams. I pass the mechanics and my heart is beating faster than ever. You feel like screaming 'YES!' as loud as you can.

On the victory lap, I tend to calm down a little bit more. I'm very laid back and not the sort of person who gets so wound up that they run around hugging everyone and throwing all their kit into the crowd. After a race, the sense of satisfaction on the podium is enormous. All the sacrifices with regards to your social life, energy, state of your body, money and so on all seem worth it. You have dedicated a big part of your life to win a GP and now in return you can have this sense of wellbeing. In a way, it shows in this life that 'for nothing you get nothing'. Put in the work and you'll receive the reward. As the anthem plays, I am a little numb and try to take it all in and remember the good feeling because for me it wears away quickly, sometimes even in minutes, and I think, 'Right, let's get to the next race.'

I wish I could enjoy it more. Some people go mental when they win, and the sacrifices they have made come pouring out. I think my reaction is maybe to do with my age. The way I have progressed in the sport and the mistakes I have made make me think 'Why wasn't I doing this ten years ago?' I want to get going and grab another one, to collect as many wins as possible in the time I have left in my career and accumulate all the good feelings that I can and should have been experiencing at an earlier age.

Namur in 2001 counts as my finest-ever race. Two broken collarbones, slippery muddy conditions, and no goggles from the first lap onwards; my speed to win that day brought me closer to the World Championship than ever before.

My first GP moto victory in Switzerland during 1990 was special and very emotional. I crossed the line before everyone else in the first race, completely covered in mud, to be met by Julian and my dad weeping. There was a deep and special feeling of having finally 'made it'. Reaching the top and marking yourself as one of the fastest in the world is a truly enriching experience, and I was only eighteen at the time.

Foxhill in 2000 was another big win. Over two motos in the worst mud, I took the overall victory and drew within three points of Langston in the Championship. It was the British GP and to win a race as big as that in front of your fans, who had camped out in the rain, was an emotional and unforgettable moment. Going into the GP, I was fighting at the top of the Championship, so while I was unsure if I could win, I knew that I *should*. The rain that week had turned the track into a swamp, and I suspected that I would have an advantage over the rest if we were ploughing through the mud. In the first moto, I made a great start but then I froze slightly instead of trying to push straightaway. Brownie dived past and I followed him, but couldn't find room to overtake. After a few laps I slipped past, but on the next circulation I'm not sure what happened going into the face of a jump, but the bike twisted and threw me off. I quickly got up and recovered the thing, adrenaline firmly flowing and I dropped to about sixth place. Along with the bike, I was covered from head to toe in mud and it really weighed me down. I got back to second place.

In the second moto, I wasn't going to make the same mistake again. I charged as hard as I could into the first corner. There is a great photograph of the pack in that initial turn where I am leaning slightly on Alex Puzar, who has his elbow raised trying to block himself as I'm coming through on the inside. I didn't want to take him out, so I hit underneath him and got to the front. It was such a good race. I was just yanking them and had pulled a lead of something like a minute. Everything felt so easy until about twenty-five minutes from the end. My front mudguard decided to snap under the weight of the mud. I was then getting 100 per cent roosted by my front wheel. Mud and stones were being flicked up into my face. I waited as long as I could before ditching the goggles which had become useless. I couldn't see much, but held on to win the moto and the GP.

Foxhill was crammed full of British fans and they were so loud. I was nervous but really determined at that meeting, and felt immensely proud. The weather had been so bad that they called off the 250 and 500 races on the Sunday because the track was becoming unsafe.

It was insane to win my home GP. It had been a dream since I was a kid. I imagine it to be bigger than scoring the winner in the FA Cup or something like that. It's the closest thing you can get to the experience of taking a World Championship.

Bellpuig 2000 wasn't a spectacular GP, but it was an important one. I marked a new era with KTM in the best way possible and removed some of the pressure Kurt and I had been carrying because I was on the team and an unproven GP winner. It was a long, hard race and I had the shits all weekend, but it set the tone for two years of high-flying results mingled with the occasional dip; in the past, the situation had been mainly the reverse.

The victory in Unadilla got me noticed in the States when I became the first British rider to win a National Motocross round in

1993. Unadilla is perhaps the most famous track in the USA and has a fine tradition. It really used to be a crazy atmosphere at the circuit. Fans from different towns used to sit on either side of the hill and chant stuff back and forth. One year, someone put a load of dynamite in the toilets and blew them sky-high. It was the heart of the US National calendar. I have always been a fan of American motocross, and to be there and taking part in the Unadilla round was a big thing for me.

I scored a 1-4 over two motos for the overall win. It was wide-open racing for both races, and I had people like McGrath, Emig, Henry and Lusk chasing me. It was a hot and dusty day, and I followed Lusk for some time in the first moto but he was just berm-bashing everywhere. I reeled him in and his bike seized from all the punishment it was taking. I was squaring off the corners, and while his method was faster, it turned out to be costly. I had the lead and pulled away.

I got up the next morning and felt on top of the world. I was only twenty-one years old and had gone out to the States as a relative unknown, only to beat the Americans. I was in California as a nobody but had risen to the task and made an impression that I believe was the first chink of light through the door that led to it being swung open, for many other Europeans to invade the US scene. People who had doubts back in Europe saw my result and thought, 'We might as well get across there'.

Aside from the Championship-winning year, 2000 must count as my best season. It started fantastically when I cleaned up in Bellpuig. The title then progressed into a three-way chase between me, Grant Langston and Mike Brown. I showed my capabilities in the mud that season, also taking wins at Foxhill in England and Grobbendonk, Belgium.

Grant eventually beat both of us, but the one GP where I thought I was head and shoulders above him and everybody else was again at Spa for the European round (and why I was happy to go there again in 2001). Launching off pole position, I was taken out in the first turn and fought back from dead last to fourth place in six laps. I was passing people and still catching Langston, who was leading by three seconds. Then a rock smashed my clutch, a completely freak thing that has never happened to me before. I ended up hanging on to fourteenth when realistically I should have won the race, but instead I had to watch Langston win and add eighteen more points to his Championship standing.

The second moto that day was easy. I even stopped halfway through to pick up some more goggles, went back out there, caught them up and took the chequered flag without even a second glance. Prior to Spa, I was trailing Langston by one point (with Brownie also up there), and after he grabbed a third behind me, I was looking at a deficit of fourteen points. What should have been a great day turned into a nightmare and set the tone for the rest of the year. Instead of me leading the series and him having the pressure to make results and catch up, the roles were reversed. He started to eke out more of an advantage and the onus was on me not to make a mistake and gain as many points as possible. Another clutch failure in Luxembourg wrecked the Championship, as Grant rode well and took the title. It was a bittersweet year because I had been so close. After finally losing to Grant, the penny well and truly dropped about what was required to win, so I knew that 2001 had to be the season.

★ ★ ★

Back in 2002, the old cliché of being only as good as your last race sometimes isn't always applicable to just one result. So far, I had discovered a rapid low after achieving an all-time high in 2001, and my 125 win in Austria was a loud reminder of the performances of which I was capable. Entering the second half of the season, there was hope yet that the Kärntenring trophy might not be my last.

23 June 2002: Round Seven
Bulgarian Grand Prix, Sevlievo

THE SEVENTH GP of the year took us to the first of two brand new locations on the 2002 calendar. It is very important to go to countries like Bulgaria to increase the breadth of appeal of the World Championships. In 2001 we had something like five races in the Benelux region, which doesn't really give the series a large enough scope on a global scale.

I got my travel details through from Alan Skirving at Pickfords travel agency. This was the first race without Naomi and Gracie, and I was flying out with the mechanics. I have been with Pickfords since 1997 after getting a recommendation saying that they were helping out Dougie Lampkin and some of the trial guys. It's far easier than sorting out all the details and arrangements myself; Alan usually takes care of the hotels, planes, cars and everything. I think most of the British riders going to the GPs now also use the same agency after I passed the word around.

In the week before the race, I worked really hard in the gym with Kirk and felt good about my physical condition – it put me in a positive frame of mind for the GP. After a relatively short flight, I landed in Sofia, the capital city towards the west of Bulgaria and faced a two-hour drive east to Sevlievo, on what seemed like the only main road heading to the centre of the country.

It's unsettling to go to a place where the lifestyle is so different. The people you meet don't speak any language apart from their own, and the whole place seemed very poor and insular. The warning from the girl at the car-hire desk about leaving stuff in the vehicle, and her matter-of-fact attitude that the car would probably be trashed or broken into anyway, did not make me feel any more comfortable. I bundled in with some of the mechanics and we set off.

The Bulgarian scenery struck me as being very rural and open. We passed through hardly any towns and were constantly weaving through green hills and valleys on a fast A-road, on which everybody else felt the need to drive like a lunatic. There was little in the way of urbanisation. We drove past roadside 'commercial areas' that extended to a quarter of a mile and consisted of tiny bars and stalls with people selling their wares. What really enforced the culture difference was seeing things like an old man sitting on a horse-drawn wagon bursting at the seams with hay, trotting away on one side of the road like he had fallen out of a painting. It was like travelling back in time by fifty years.

When we finally reached Sevlievo, it seemed very quiet and tucked away. It was a reasonably big town based around a ceramic and materials factory, but over the three days I stayed, it barely got busier than a small English village and felt eerie in its desertedness. Accommodation and housing verged on poverty in places, and the huge modern hotel in the main square looked very out of place. A gloss was put on the whole scene by the amazing weather of blue skies, sunshine and high temperatures. The people I encountered were friendly enough and were excited about the GP circus rolling over the hill.

There must have only been two places to stay in Sevlievo because the KTM guys were an hour's drive away in another town, which was far too much, and I was also down to share with them. I approached the guy who was in charge of the travel with Dorna and asked him if he could sort me out with a room because I did not fancy an hour's drive first thing on the morning of the race. Luckily, they had one spare in the smaller hotel on the other side of the main square. It was pretty basic and I realised how spoiled I had been all year with the camper and its comforts.

People had been grumbling about the cost and risk of the travel, but arriving and seeing the actual circuit took away the edge of the negativity. The course sprawled across a dugout hillside. The track was very wide and appeared fast and natural. It had technical elements with the positioning of some jumps, while numerous turns looked as though they would offer various lines. Standing at the bottom on the flat apron that was the start straight, I could look from one end of the circuit to the other on the hill and see practically everything.

In practice, it was fantastic; fun, challenging and scenic. The facilities were also decent – a floodlit, stony, level paddock that was immediately adjacent to the track, a new pressroom and mini grandstand, and decent showers and washing blocks. It was a sign of how Dorna were trying to carry the sport into the future, and I have to admit I was impressed. Looking back, it was definitely the best circuit of the year. However, Bulgaria became the worst race at which not to have the camper because it was easily forty degrees and we had nowhere to hang out with air conditioning.

The KTM factory set-up at the races involves two semis, each with their own awning rig erected around the truck. One truck/tent area is for the 250 and 500 effort, which holds the bikes, large work and presentation area, compartment for autograph signings and changing space for the riders – inside the truck is the living and sleeping space for the mechanics. All the tools, spares, equipment and bikes are stored in the back. The other semi is the hospitality. We only had the main truck in Bulgaria and the trip was a throw back to 2001 (where the 125 factory team had its own unit) in terms of relying on hotel food, trying to keep amused and having to hang around a lot.

Naomi and Gracie stayed at home, primarily because of the accommodation decision. Considering the heat, it was a wise move but make me miss them any less. The KTM tent was like a sauna under the sun. I couldn't be in there for more than fifteen minutes without leaking sweat. The heat was relentless, and when I wasn't practising or sorting out what I needed to with the bike, I walked around the paddock talking to people and trying to keep myself occupied until it was time to get a lift back to the hotel. I kept popping in to see Andrea, the Italian helmet technician from Airoh who cooks an amazing lasagne, eating his pasta and hanging out in his motorhome.

The timetable factor is usually the problem with GPs in the further reaches of Europe. It becomes harder to relax and involves a lot more waiting for the moment when you can leave the track. Usually, I'm a good boy when I'm away. I'll go out for dinner and then hit the sack to get some rest. I usually carry a laptop to the fly-aways, and it's handy to watch DVDs to kill time — I always have to find a way to get my television! GPs are an early start, so it's not uncommon for me to be asleep by 10.30 p.m.

Travelling is one of the more tiring parts of the job, odd as that may sound. People assume that it's a lovely life to visit all around the world, but in truth you get little time to see places and cities. Motocross circuits are rarely based in tourist spots anyway. Everyone knows how knackered you can feel when you've arrived back from a holiday; well, that tends to happen every week! In 2000, I raced the 125 GPs and the British Championship; it was more or less every weekend for seven months, a lot of time on the road with the cramped little camper we had back then. I think most professional riders or drivers in the motorsport world would agree the novelty of travelling to all these exotic locations wears off sooner than you'd expect; mostly it's a series of tracks and hotels. To be honest though, I would not swap the lifestyle, because I love getting to the races and visiting the variety of different places and countries that make every GP individual in its own special way.

Practice was a complicated affair, due mainly to the 250's mannerisms. It's fair to ask why a rider in a factory team is still having suspension trouble seven races into the season, and my answer to that is the same reason why I have problems with it even to this very day — namely, that WP weren't prepared to experiment fully and regarded their own ideas as gospel. It's their units on the bikes and there was another cracked line of communication between what I kept telling them I wanted or would like to try and what they would actually tweak. I was not in an engineering position or with sufficient specialist knowledge to be telling them their job. I had a minor gripe with the fact that they didn't seem to listen to my feedback correctly, although to defend them partially, it's a very delicate and complicated area to get spot on.

We started the season heading left with the suspension, got to a different circuit and then went right. That didn't work, so we went left again and so on. On a 125 you can ride around things and get away with stuff. A four-stroke has a very different power delivery and needs a completely different suspension for that reason. The 250, though, brings out everything. If you have a problem in the chassis or the springs, a 250 is going to suffer because of the extra power and speed combined with the lighter weight.

With engines, I believe I have an instinct about what I want and how to get it. Concerning the suspension, I have slightly more difficulty translating back what I feel or I need the technicians to do to make it better. The suspension was an old issue that wasn't going to disappear until we got some fresh input and a different perspective while testing. Instead, the engine was now also starting to play up once again.

I had a problem with the clutch slipping in the two practice sessions, and Leighton gave me the usual spiel about it being my fault or my imagination. I was getting used to it now – it was almost like a routine. Later, after examination, they found out that the clutch bearing had broken up; Leighton still couldn't tell me. I was angry because I was having a tough enough time and didn't need to think that I was going mad and screwing up the engine. There was tension between us all year, he was not being truthful with me and was therefore also being stupid, because it's not as if I wouldn't have found out.

By Saturday's end, we weren't very happy because qualifying had generally been shite. The track was fun to ride, but I was not producing any decent times — I finished the session in sixth. The clutch failure was another worry, and I hoped it would not strike again.

Sunday morning was another scorcher, which meant that the race (due to start at 11.05 a.m. as per usual) would be a test of fitness unlike any other GP so far this year. Mickael again had pole and took his inside position this time on the very left of the gate. I counted six along and slotted in next to Josh Coppins on my left, and Chicco moved into the space on my right. The first turn was a left-right kink into an open, uphill hairpin right.

After trying the onboard helmet camera and breaking a jinx that I often associated with it in the 125cc Austrian GP, I was asked to run with it again in Sevlievo. I reluctantly agreed and was alarmed to find that as I put my goggles into place and got ready for the fifteen-second board, I could feel somebody pulling at the cable on the back of my lid. I tried to swat the person away because I was afraid that it might screw up my start. I didn't turn around because I was trying to focus, which later on the video looked like I was trying to get rid of an annoying fly from the distant television camera showing us all on the line. Finally, the guy let go of my helmet when the five-second warning came up, and I looked at the gate, ready to gas. I later found out that it was one of the Dorna television technicians trying to replug the cable that linked the carbon-fibre camera casing to the battery because I had disconnected it when I had put my goggles on. Cheeky as his intervention was, I was glad that I wasn't carrying the extra weight for nothing.

The incident didn't help because I got hardly anything coming out over the gate, and both Chicco and Coppins cut in front of me, as we rode up left and into the elongated first right turn. Gordon slid into view and I must have been just outside the top ten as I held a tighter line than my team-mate and put him behind me. I counted my position back to eleventh as we all climbed and then descended the first part of the circuit on the hillside. I had a British rider called Justin Morris in front of me, but knew the situation wouldn't stay like that for long. Before the end of the first lap, Pichon had already rushed to the front and begun another disappearing act.

It really was looking like nobody would be able to do anything about Mickael this season. He knew that as soon as he was leading, nobody would be able to match his speed and the race was over – that confidence and belief is a powerful weapon in itself. I had exactly the same sensation in 2001, and I knew how indestructible it made him feel.

So, barring a mistake from the Suzuki rider, which tends to only happen once a season these days (and we had already seen the farce in Teutschenthal), I knew another chance to win was gone.

With Pichon out and away and taking Bolley with him, third place was there to fight for, as I moved into seventh on the second lap past Morris. I felt pretty good, was riding well within myself and keeping a decent speed. Coppins was less than a second away from me in sixth. Josh was always pretty slow in the first few laps of a race. By the end he was flying, but initially, if you could overtake him and pull away, you could build up some valuable time before his pace improved. On this occasion, I could not get by. He had just enough power to keep in front the few times that I managed to pull alongside.

As we hurtled up a hill on lap five, I tried a different line on a step-up to try to cut a path past him. The bike kicked out a little bit off the ledge as I caught some air – not so much that the wheels were vastly out of line, but as I landed and hit the entry to the corner, I went sailing over the bars and the people watching on television got a nice view of the dirt. I had no idea why or how it happened, but I smacked the ground just over the crest of the hill, at the apex of the corner, with my chest. I trudged, slightly shocked, back to the bike as everyone buzzed by, and looked back down the hill. I must have been in the last group of seven or eight riders as the stragglers came up over the jump. I kick-started the KTM, swung it around to the left and set off.

From that moment on, I was trying to rescue my race and going for whatever points I could get. Instead of fretting about Coppins and the disappearing podium, I just concentrated on picking off the riders in front of me. Some laps I had a lot of action, with a group of two or three riders to get past, while at other times, I just had to work on reducing the distance to the next position.

The temperature was stifling, something like forty-one degrees. It was hot and I was working hard. I certainly knew I was in a motocross race and was happy that I had been putting in the time at the gym. I kept going and plugging onwards, and quite enjoyed the challenge of making up positions because I felt like I was at least being competitive. I was gaining ground instead of losing it.

Finally, I crossed the line in tenth, after making my way back from twenty-first. I had notched eleven places in ten laps and was four seconds behind Gundersen, who was ninth. My clothing was soaked with sweat and I was gagging for a drink. The race had been another disaster really, but I felt quite content with my riding, and in many ways it was my best performance of the season, although there was not much to compare it against so far in the 250s. According to the timing sheets, I was catching everyone behind Coppins, who ended the race in third. It was a solid outing while also being a missed opportunity.

The video of the race did not help with the cause of my crash, although they had been taping the footage from my camera. All I could see on the replay was a fuzzy image of the apex of the turn, before very quickly getting a close-up of the mud and a stranded KTM. I described the fall to the team and we couldn't decide on a reason. I did not think it was rider error. Personally, it felt to me like the suspension did not absorb the impact from my leap up onto the hill, and it may have been the jolt that pitched me onto the ground. The incident was not without repercussions. A few hours later, I started to feel a pain in the side of my chest where I had hit the ground. Assuming it to be bruising, I ignored it, but made a mental note to get it checked out when I was at home, just in case.

The Championship goal had been binned before we got to Bulgaria, but it was certainly squashed now, especially as Pichon had won his fourth race in a row. The change in the scoring system to bring everybody closer together meant that he only led Beirer by thirty-eight points, but the way he was riding, it might as well have been three figures for the rest of the field. The gap stood at sixty-eight points for me, back in sixth place overall, and it was almost a position from which to wave the white flag.

When I got home, I had an X-ray and further examination revealed two stress fractures on my ribs. It meant more rest and back to square one with my fitness, just when I had been making real progress and feeling very strong the week before. I kept having to build my condition up when I could, and the races were coming around too fast for me to be physically clear of small injuries in order to be able to do that.

I was taking my forced relaxation at home when I received a call with the news about Josh Coppins. The dope test he took in Austria showed up positive. I could not believe it. According to the press release on the motocross websites, Coppins' urine sample exceeded the FIM rules, containing 157 ml of pseudo-ephedrine (cut-off level 25) and a concentration of 7.4 ml of cathine (cut-off level 5). I'm sure our sport is not completely clean, but for someone as high profile as Coppins to get caught out was quite amazing. The level of pseudo-ephedrine, a substance that is linked to performance enhancement, was enormously high.

His story revolved around running out of medication for hayfever tablets while training at his team's base in Italy. He allegedly asked the pharmacist if the tablets were safe and then ingested most of the packet before coming to the Kärntenring. Josh is a friendly guy and I have never had a problem with him, but it seemed like everybody in the media was very quick to jump to his defence. I am not disputing his story, and if it is the truth then I feel very sorry that he has had to go through this kind of ordeal when having the best season of his life and lying second to Pichon in the Championship. My point regarding the issue is that maybe he meant it, maybe he didn't. Who knows? People close to me would not necessarily know if I was injecting myself. It's not the kind of thing you broadcast.

I don't believe that Josh is stupid enough to make a mistake like that. If you are going to ingest some medication, you know that you have to speak with your boss or seek some advice from someone that you trust because you cannot afford to take a chance. I know exactly what kind of Lemsips I can drink if I have a cold and the energy drinks that I have to avoid. Somebody told me his doctor in Belgium was the same guy who was in trouble for supplying banned substances to the Tour cyclists. In the wide paddock gossip circles, it did not look too good for him.

There was also the curious matter of how he suddenly became so strong in the latter half of the races. From two podiums as Pichon's team-mate in 2001 to a serial trophy winner in 2002, the leap to Championship pretender (five podiums from seven races) seemed a hefty and swift one. Josh was in the unfortunate position of being partially implicated by his success.

The phone calls were doing the rounds, with people both supporting him and condemning him. Like everybody, I was not sure, but the fact remained that he had been racing against us with a banned chemical in his body and had been caught. I was disappointed, but also interested to see what would happen. Josh did not have a history of this kind of behaviour and seemed to enjoy quite a lot of support outside the majority of riders. I hoped the FIM would deal with the case efficiently and I could see him facing a ban.

Things got worse for Josh in the next day or two after the FIM press release. His Italian Honda team suspended him in a hasty and ill-advised move, which showed a total lack of support for their rider. Talk about guilty until proven innocent. Coppins was set to face a hearing a few days before the GP of Sweden.

Again, I agreed to race for Ken Winstanley and his Future West series, this time down at Foxhills, which I found out on arrival has slumped to become one of the worst and most dangerous high-profile tracks in the UK. I knew that the circuit was a bit of a state, but I was quite shocked to turn up early on Sunday morning, after staying the night at the Hilton just down the road in Swindon, and see the unkempt stony mess that used to be a GP track. Not a 'plus' for the Future West boys, but almost forgiveable in their first year.

This time I was riding my 125 practice bike and using the meeting to make a public appearance to the 5,000 fans or so, and also get a bit of training done. Had I known the condition of the circuit and how much of a survival exercise the two motos would turn out to be, I probably wouldn't have risked it, in spite of a decent remuneration from Ken.

Stephen Sword took two fantastic starts that day, and although I tried to catch him, I opted for a sensible safe second in both races instead of a crash, which would surely have meant a hard and damaging landing. My ribs were grateful for the relief. Stephen is part of Britain's bright future in the GPs. He's yet to deliver the goods in the World Championships but now, with the Albion UK KTM team, he is in good hands and has the right equipment to make a sizeable mark in the 125s.

Stephen has a few things in his favour. He's very clean-cut and always presents himself very well, which is an important thing in this day and age. He looks like he trains hard and takes good care of himself. Apart from yours truly, he is the best 125 rider in the UK and now has to get his head around the fact that it is possible to further his success on an international scale.

Carl Nunn cleaned up in the UK and he scored a reputation-earning 125 GP win in France during 2000, but he has been a bit quiet since and now regularly haunts the top ten of the 250s. Carl is another one of those guys who is fast in Britain but hasn't yet found the knack of reproducing the speed in the GPs. Sword is only twenty-three and Nunn is twenty-four, so I think that with a bit of experience they should be able to nudge their careers higher up the ladder; once you know how to win, then everything becomes just a little easier, but the pressure also starts to mount.

Carl Nunn has an amazing amount of natural talent on a motorcycle, but at the moment he is missing the complete range of attributes needed to be a GP winner. He doesn't seem to be mentally tough enough when it comes to the World Championships and is beaten before he even starts. I think he could have done with a few more years in the 125s as he has the right physical build for that class. Carl's technique is wonderful and he really looks as if he is making hardly any effort riding the bike.

In contrast, there is Billy Mackenzie – another of Britain's prospects for the future. Billy is still a teenager but is a hard and tough rider. What he lacks in style, he certainly makes up for in determination and confidence. I think if you combined Carl and Billy, you would easily have another World Champion. While Nunn has the finesse, Mackenzie has a big heart and a real 'I don't give a fuck' attitude that can be as useful as it is harmful sometimes. I remember going to my first GP as a rider and running excitedly around, peering into tents and trying to collect autographs. Billy has been more or less deadly serious about his racing from the word go and doesn't give respect easily.

I think he has to slow down and be a bit more patient, as he is still quite low down on the learning curve.

If I had to put my last hundred pounds on the next British rider to hit the big time between those two, then I'd have to go for Billy. He doesn't have the natural ability of Carl, but I think his attitude would win it.

★ ★ ★

Watching the Bulgarian race on *Men and Motors* that week made me think about Sevlievo, and then all the places, countries and continents I have seen over the years. Obviously the biggest cultural experience for me was leaving my life in England and moving to America. There were ups and downs in the United States, but my time living there was what I needed as a human being. I had to work hard and I experienced the harsh end of the professional spectrum many times in terms of having next-to-no finances and having my ambitions curtailed by injury.

The physical damage I incurred in my initial years were mainly because of inexperience. Like most things in America, the pressure to learn fast was huge. The change in maturity and character America would force upon me at the age of twenty-one was clear from as early as the second day. A friend, Jamie Sterns, picked me up from the airport and I stayed with him the first night. He then dropped me off the next morning with all my bags at Pro Circuit's race shop in Corona. I walked in, said, 'Hi, I'm Jamie Dobb' and introduced myself to everyone. After the pleasantries, I was told, 'There's the bike and your helmet. When do you want to go and ride?' 'Well,' I answered, somewhat surprised, 'I've got to find a place to live first.' Mike Hooker, the team manager at the time, threw me the yellow pages and said, 'We ain't no babysitters, look through there.'

A little disturbed, I found an apartment as soon as I could, and a few days later I practically snapped my arm in two during my very first test. Talk about a tough welcome. My $500-a-race basic wage covered the rent and living expenses, but my eyes almost popped out of my head when the first phone bill arrived. $1,200 was the price of trying to maintain a three-year relationship over that distance and missing my friends and family.

I hung around with a lot of people inside the sport, mainly with Mike LaRocco because he lived in the same block. My accommodation was a humble two-bedroom place, and I rented all the time while I was out there. I did not have the cash to put down on an apartment and could not get credit. I had bought a house in the suburbs of Derby when I was nineteen so I could move out of the family home. I purchased the contents of a show home to go inside and finally managed to rent it out, but I had spent all of my savings living in America and paying the mortgage until, luckily, my dad arranged for a tenant to move in.

I bought the house in 1991, when I was injured, and maybe I was in need of a break, having raced since the age of five; the broken collarbone gave me a forced vacation that I savoured just a little too much. I had come back to England and was going out and enjoying myself. I would usually meet up with friends and have a laugh on a Thursday night (without really drinking), and travel to a race meeting on Friday. At one stage, I did not think the weekly habit was a bad thing because I had won a GP in Austria. I was living at my parents' house at the time and used to gas the car down the road to the house and then cut the engine and lights, so that I could roll into the drive quietly without waking anybody up. That was the routine for a month or two. Then, one night, I was creeping through the living room to the stairs to go up to my room and 'click!', the light came on and my dad was sitting poised in an armchair. 'What time do you call this?' he said. 'Time I was getting my own place', I thought.

I found our current house in a new estate and have more or less regretted buying it ever since! I was a law unto myself back then. I missed home and little things like not being able to play my music full blast. Most of the time, I used to hang out at my parents' house, eat there and only drive back to my place to sleep.

Around 1992 I was completely into dance music. I liked to DJ and was sucked into that 'everyone loves a DJ' image. I used to have a session at the Progress Club in my local town, which was a way of making a little money. I was on the decks at the opening night, and it was one of the top ten clubs in the country at one point. It takes so much skill to DJ properly, you almost have to be a musician and need to put in hours and hours of practice.

I frustrated my dad when I was younger, because he always believed that I had the ability to win GPs and make a big name for myself, but I just didn't want to work at it. He is completely the opposite when it comes to graft. In some ways, I was a lazy bastard, but then I was also just a kid. I wanted to be with my friends. I was only nineteen or twenty and missed the social scene. I guess I felt lonely, and needed to know what else was going on apart from motocross.

I still do not like being on my own. The house is always full of people, sometimes to Naomi's annoyance. If I'm on a plane alone, I'll wander around to find someone to talk with, and my mobile phone always needs to be on charge because of the constant use. So, the first few months in America were very hard because I did feel homesick. To get over it, I kept thinking of the great things that lay ahead of me. While the broken arm was mending, I was training like nutcase with a bicycle and a stepper. I got friendly with some of the kids around the area and used to go out front to play football or baseball with them.

I struggled with cash initially. I was living quite basically and did not have the money to hang out with people. Before the first race came up, there were a few weeks when I had the phone bill, mortgage, rent etc. to pay and I was dry. My savings just ran out. I already had a water dispenser in the flat, so I was okay for drink and when we used to test I would go along and raid the box they brought along full of sandwiches. I ended up buying these pots called 'Top Roman Noodles' (you could get a pack of six for a dollar) and living off those for a few weeks. Thankfully the season soon started and Mitch gave me my $500 a race despite the busted arm.

For 1994 and 1995, I moved house becuse I wanted to find something a bit bigger, but I stayed in Corona because it was so handy for riding with all the SX tracks in the region. Mike LaRocco and I were the first riders to live in the town and now it's like 'MX HQ'. Corona is near Ontario Airport (which is good for internal flights) and also next to Freeways 15 and 91. Anaheim is twenty-five minutes away, while San Diego is only an hour. I fitted in quite quickly ,and while things like the weather and lifestyle were a little different, none of it was in a bad way. I'd move back there tomorrow. I would miss England and I would need to come back, but I do like the American culture.

Most of the complaints people have about American culture are the things that you end up missing after you have lived there. Their attitudes feel fresh, positive and cheerful. The sports events have all the glitz, glamour and show that you can see on the television. SX has become more spectacular and wealthier since my US days, but there were still all sorts of activities going on in the nineties, including fireworks, freestyle, cheer leaders – the whole works.

It is quite something to walk into an arena filled to capacity with 60,000 people, all cheering and making a racket. The hum of all those spectators and the camera flashes going off everywhere sends a shiver down your spine. My first few times as a rider, I thought I had a fraction of the sensation of what it must be like to be a rock star or walk out on the pitch at Wembley. The atmosphere was usually highly charged, and it made you more aware of your role as a showman as well as a professional racer.

I blended in with the fashion and even picked up some of the accent and dialect, although I only got into the party scene in 1996. At that time, I was getting to the point where I was getting tired of racing and motocross and was seeking a more rounded life. Mainly I went out and got bladdered that season. We partied a bit more after the SX had finished at the start of the summer and I was single then, so it was a new lease of life.

Monday night was always a big one. Everybody would get back from the Nationals and we'd call a limo for about ten people and meet up at my place, which was quite central for everyone. McGrath, Emig, myself and a few others would head into Newport to a place called Club Rubber, where they had a stripper night. We knew the owner of the establishment and, of course, he recognised all of us. In turn, we got to be friendly with all the girls working there and used to hang out with them. I recall on one occasion waking up on my sofa and taking off my jeans to find lots of ten and twenty dollar bills – I had got pissed and danced for the girls, who had obviously rewarded my efforts.

Having been in the racing world for sixteen years, I have seen many people come and go. Within motorcycling, all the different disciplines cross over, and many road-racers like motocross. I count Marco Melandri and Valentino Rossi as friends, and have dialogue with Carl Fogarty, Dougie Lampkin and Neil Hodgson, amongst others. I did a supermoto race with Foggy back in 1989, when we were both with Honda and before we had both won anything, so we've known each other since then and he's quite a cool bloke who definitely doesn't have a problem speaking his mind.

Neil Hodgson is a super-nice guy. In the past, he has been too nice and I think it has affected his racing, but with experience and age, he has been getting better and better. I hope he can win a world title. Neil and his wife, Kathryn, are good people and they deserve the success. I used to race against him in schoolboy motocross. In 1995, we met again when he came out to the Daytona 200, and I was also out there riding on the dirt. He likes to blame me for the time he broke his knee when he crashed my bike a few years ago, but I had nothing to do with it!

I'm a huge racing fan. I love watching the top guys and I'm always a little in awe of being with Valentino, Ricky or some kid full of natural talent like James Stewart.

I am very close to Paul Edmonson and have known him since he brought his dirt bike round to the house when we were kids. At the second farmhouse, we had a quarry in which to ride, but to get there we had to go through some woodland. The family who owned the stretch of trees used to ride three-wheelers and quads, and built a track running through the undergrowth. That's where 'Eddy' did a lot of his training. The course would be only slightly wider than a set of handlebars, but we used to have races round there, being able to pass only in certain places. It was quite hairy, lots of tree roots coming through and not a lot of room, but fantastic fun. Eddy was always more inclined to enduro and has won several world titles.

I enjoy a high profile in MX and because of some good connections and getting my face about, I'm also known in the general motorcycling world. I get people coming up and saying hello regularly in the Midlands region, because the area is really into its bikes and I have been on local television and in the papers a lot over the years. Many of the celebrities I run into are actually big bike fans, and it makes for a good and easy topic of conversation. Sunny Garcia, one of the top surfers in the world, loves riding motocross, so I've come to know him. I first met Matt Le Blanc from *Friends* back at the San Diego Supercross in 1996, when the off-road manager of Suzuki introduced us. Matt loves his racing and is also a big bike fan. He is a lovely guy and so down to earth. We try to meet up every time I am back in the US and go to watch a race. I have been backstage to see the show being filmed and have met the rest of the 'friends'. That was an exciting experience, because both Naomi and I love the programme.

★ ★ ★

If there is one thing I dislike about being a professional sportsman in this country, it is the typical English attitude to success. It seems like there is so much jealousy here (compared with other countries, such as America, Italy and Spain, where they love their winners) and people are only too quick to slag you off if you do gain some status. Maybe part of the bitterness I have is because I feel that we do not get the respect we deserve in our sport for what we accomplish. Dougie Lampkin has won eleven world trial titles, and he had to notch ten before he was given an MBE. Paul Edmonson has four enduro World Championships, Dave Thorpe has three motocross crowns and they have never been recognised. It makes it all the more frustrating when a team of curlers come back from the Olympics and have all the attention. It may 'only' be motocross, but a World Championship is still a World Championship. I do not mean to cause offence, because to achieve something takes that special ingredient that not a lot of people have. I love watching skateboarders and BMX riders and people like that, because the amount of hours it takes to perfect a skill is incredible.

In 2001, Britain had three real solo World Champions – myself, Dougie Lampkin and Richard Burns. The country is gaining honours in the sporting field and nobody knows it, but on the *BBC Sports' Personality of the Year*, we can see how fishermen and archers are getting on. That year, Dougie and I were not even invited to the show because 'there were not enough seats'. Lampkin has got more motorcycle skill in one of his little fingers than most road racers who have been World Champions.

Maybe I do sound a little sore about it, but it's very frustrating. I want to spread the word about motocross so badly. I want to show people what we do and how exciting it is. It is the most physically tough motorsport in the world bar none.

1 On top of the world, Teutschenthal, 2001.

2 Just losing out going into the first corner at Valkenswaard, 2001.

3 Ecstatic and knackered after winning at Namur, one of my many high points of 2001.

4 Fred gets to work on the KTM.

5 Trying to get out of Luigi's way in Gaildorf, 2001.

6 The Dobb family and team, helping me as always – this time, celebrating a World Championship at Gaildorf.

7 Me with Kurt Nicoll – my hero as a boy and also as a World Champion.

8 From one World Champion to another: posing with Dougie Lampkin in Gaildorf.

9 Gaildorf, 2001. I manage to get the champagne bottle off Kurt!

10 I'm in the helmet! Me on my first motorbike with my brothers, Richard and Julian, and my sister, Sarah.

11 This is me at thirteen, riding a Honda and already knowing how to throw a pose on the bike – note the number.

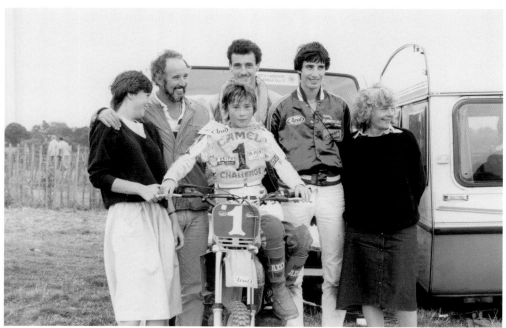

12 With the family, after winning my first British Championship in 1983.

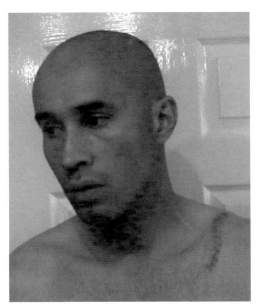

13 Motocross can take its toll on the body. Here I show off my staples after the collarbone operation in 2001.

14 Kirk Gibbons – without his guidance and support, I might never have won a World Championship in 2001.

15 The extravaganza that is indoor Supercross. The Americans sure know how to make one of the toughest motorcycle sports look like a spectacular show.

16 Getting some water down me, with Naomi looking on, in 2000.

17 Riding the Suzuki in 1997. I was a privateer and competing with Rob Hooper's team.

18 Waiting to race at the 1999 Motocross of Nations, with Alessio Chiodi on the left and Ricky Carmichael on the right. I beat both of them.

19 Winning the British GP without goggles in the slime of Foxhill, 2000.

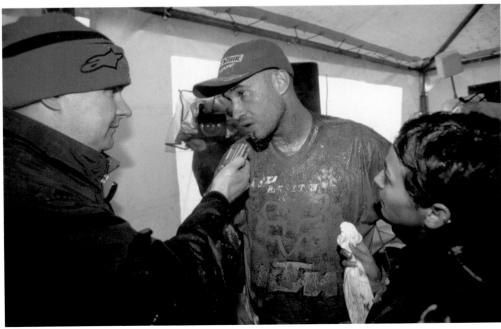

20 Talking to the press after Foxhill in 2000: check out my eyes, I couldn't see for a few days after the GP!

21 The start of a GP – it's the most important stage of the race since the switch to one moto.

22 I'm in second place, trying to block Josh Coppins at Bellpuig in the second round of 2002.

23 Coasting back down the slope towards the pits with a busted motor in Bellpuig.

24 Mickael Pichon gets it all wrong at the start in Teutschental. I am right behind him and able to miss the crash.

25 Leading the race until my unpleasant appointment with fate on the last lap in Germany.

26 The first really wet race of the year at St Jean D'Angely in France.

27 Fighting the track conditions and my insecurity in France.

28 The start of the up-hill climb at Castiglione De Lago. I am next to Coppins, while my team-mate, Gordon Crockard, is far right.

29 Having a good look at Pichon over a jump, as we start our scrap in Italy.

30 The 2001 World Champions, all wearing the number one plates for the first time in Austria.

31 Showing everyone that I still have what it takes with victory in the 125cc GP in Austria, wearing my gold number one.

32 A tough race at Uddevalla in 2002.

33 Another muddy GP, but I'm hurting and feeling unconfident in Genk.

34 Making my best start of the season at Loket, and tucking in right behind Coppins.

35 At last something comes right. Holding a decent third position in the GP of the Czech Republic.

36 Standing on the podium with Pichon and Coppins in Loket – something I had expected to be doing a lot more of in 2002.

37 Handing over my number one plate to new 125cc World Champ Mickael Maschio in Russia.

38 Playing with Gracie in the camper, as Naomi watches.

39 The way I like to ride – on the gas and giving everything I have.

7 July 2002: Round Eight
Swedish Grand Prix, Uddevalla

THE MOTORHOME was back in action for round eight and had already made the journey with the team across the sea and into Scandinavia. Naomi, Gracie and I flew to Gothenburg and then drove the hour and a half north to the town of Uddevalla.

Pick a cliché about Sweden and I find it to be true. The girls do seem to be noticeably good-looking (although there are not as many blondes as you might think), and Sweden in general is very clean and orderly, green and full of lakes. This is the second time that the Swedish GP was to be held on the first weekend in July and, while not really warm, the air seemed as fresh as the surroundings.

The Swedes like their motocross, despite not having any top riders since Peter Johansson enjoyed his heyday at the end of the 1990s. Sweden was part of the second-ever 500cc Championship in 1958, just a year after the inauguration of motocross as an officially sanctioned sport by the FIM. The Uddevalla track is an undulating prospect and quite level in terms of landscape. It bobs up and down very much like Teutschenthal, in some ways. It's full of dips and slight inclines, and the whoops had been replaced with a jump section for this year. The mud is quite fine, grippy and soft, and with no rain during the weekend, it made for good, dry racing conditions.

There aren't really many places for the fans to watch from. However, luckily for the circuit, there is a steep rocky hillside that overlooks the majority of the venue. The grey 'wall' vanishes with colour on Sunday after the spectators climb up, find a vantage point and dig themselves in for a day's racing.

I was pleased to see that the fateful first corner had changed. We would now go out, take a ninety-degree left and then turn immediately into a right hairpin that hugged the far corner of the pit boxes. It would run adjacent to the pit lane for about 100m, and then go into the left corner where Eggens' bike had hit me the previous year.

I had no fear about returning to Sweden, but I thought it was kind of ironic that here I was again, sitting in Uddevalla with an injury problem. I hadn't been able to do any weight training because of the recovering ribs, and had only been out on the bike a couple of times, so I did not feel as perky as when I had arrived in Bulgaria.

There was a lot of heat and negativity about Josh Coppins in the paddock. It was the first time that any of us had got together since the news broke, so there were a lot of opinions being voiced. In the eyes of the riders, his situation had not improved. Several days before we all gathered in Sweden, the international court could not make a decision regarding his case. This meant that he was clear to ride in Uddevalla, and also in the GP of Belgium, due to take place after the four-week summer break but before the CDI hearing. This pissed a lot of people off. Everyone was talking about it, and some even threatened not to ride if Coppins was also going to compete. There was a lot of whispering and, from what I knew at the time, nobody actually made a complaint to Josh. I imagine that in his eyes he was completely innocent, untried by the governing body, and had every right to take part in the GP.

Upon news of the delayed case referral to the CDI in one month, his Vismara Honda team swiftly took him back, and he was all set to go in Sweden. He frustrated many of us, not through being Josh Coppins, but because of the repercussions of his actions and the course taken by the FIM. He had been caught out, but where were the authorities prepared to draw the line? Josh is a really nice kid and after everyone's subsequent support outside of the rider's community, his personality and image may have had some bearing on the proceedings; he does not have any enemies and took the best drug lawyer there is to court with him.

The FIM were stalling and didn't know what to do. There were rumours that Josh would not even get a ban, while he was also threatening to quit the GPs if unfairly treated. It was a mess of gossip, emotion and uncertainty, and God knows what kind of effect it must have had on him when he rolled out for practice.

Watching him ride, it looked as if he was trying to bury some aggression and anger in the Swedish mud, and this posed another concern. If Josh was riding like a lunatic in attempting to prove a point, then that could have consequences for all of us out there with him. I was apprehensive and worried about how he would handle it on the circuit and whether he would be safe.

I did not hide behind a forced smile. I was quite open with my opinion to those who would listen. I might not have been polite or supportive, although I didn't have a problem with Josh personally, but I did not like the situation and the way it was being handled. At least I was forthright, and if Josh thinks I was slagging him off, then he bases his judgement on the fact that I wasn't doing it on the sly. Coppins was the subject of numerous conversations over the weekend, but for me there were other matters to concentrate on.

I toured around the first lap of free practice on Saturday, a cloudy day but not cold, and had a nostalgic look at the section of muddy floor that I had met with a thud, and which had caused such a lot of anguish just one year previously. My ribcage was still sore after the bruising had gone, but did not cause me too much discomfort. Later on in the day, for the second consecutive year, bad luck struck in an Uddevalla qualifying session. This time it was the machine that suffered a breakage.

Unbelievably, the crank failed and the whole thing spluttered to a halt. The only other engine we had available was the old unit we had used in Holland, where the configuration made it difficult to change gear. I had managed to clock a time that left me in sixth before the motor popped. My mood soured after qualifying, when it was very much a case of being back to square one. Once again, I was trying to get the best result possible with the equipment at my disposal, and managed to be quite philosophical about it all; to be honest, I wasn't surprised at anything, even when I came in after warm-up on Sunday and said to Leighton that the second engine wasn't letting me go through the gears. 'Don't worry, it'll be alright', came the reply.

It was damage limitation all over again and I was trying to think about every single point I could gain, rather than the ten I was losing. I was ready for it by now, of course, and the mechanical hiccup and predicament going into the GP acted as a fair summary of the entire year; and there was nothing I could do about it. Uddevalla is a very rough track, with plenty of big ol' bumps, and it naturally threw my suspension set-up to the fore and presented another obstacle.

Fitting the mood, Sunday was grey and temperate. Gundersen looked more pumped than usual in the waiting zone, as this was practically a home GP for the Norwegian. He was fired up in qualifying and almost deprived Pichon of another pole. Almost.

Thanks to the music and psyching myself up for a good race, I had almost forgotten about the state of the bike as we kick-started in the ready area behind the gate and filtered through. Pichon had chosen the first slot on the left, heading to the inside of the first turn. Gundersen lined up next to him and then Coppins. I guided the bike into the fourth place, with Beirer on my right. The gate fell as the heavy rock guitar music (that I have always thought sounds a bit cheesy) blared on the PA. It is a tense and exciting time for everybody in the circuit when the five-second board goes up and sometimes, when you are prepped and ready to go, it can seem like the world has paused. Then the barrier drops and you have to explode into life and hold on.

The two Hondas squeezed me out, as we screamed down to the left bend and began tipping right into the hairpin. Pichon had made a good start and I was in about sixth, holding the inside line on the left from Johnny Aubert. As we tried to fit around the tight right curve, I avoided hitting the bank on the outside, while Pichon railed it. He was behind me momentarily, but wider and higher in the hairpin, which also meant he had more speed. As we straightened up coming out of the right-hander to head past the pit lane, I was on the outside of the track. Pichon flew past using the slimmest gap on my left and was lucky not to crash. He was going faster, but didn't have much room and the bike clipped the side of the small wall that edged the track. Luckily for him, it was quite soft and he gassed his way over and alongside McFarlane, who was just ahead of me with Coppins.

Going into the dip and then into the left, which used to be part of the first old S-section, I was eighth and moved past a young French rider called Matthieu Lalloz. I kept to the inside of the corner this time and gained a position. As we weaved through the next two turns to arrive at the first straight, I had the back of Bolley right in front of me in sixth, as he reached the ramp of the first jump – a big tabletop. The bottom end of the track had a wide right spoon curve. I dragged the bike close to the Yamaha as he left a small gap on the inside. Leaning into the corner, I dived for the line and successfully took sixth place. I was making good progress in the usual first-lap shenanigans.

Gundersen had taken a hell of a hole-shot and was already on the pipe, trying to break away because he knew Mickael would soon be at the front as well. The Norwegian's team-mate, Andrew McFarlane, was next in my sights, and I was waiting for a decent part of the track to try and make a pass. I was on the rear wheel of the Kawasaki, with Bolley right behind, as we accelerated to the left hairpin that took us back up to the central part of the track. McFarlane defended the inside line, but did it quite slowly and forced me to brake. He was holding me up slightly, and I knew I would have to attack to keep on moving forward. While I was virtually blocked on the rougher and more worn racing line, Bolley saw that we had both gone inside and decided it was too crowded. He plumped to go wider and fire off the back of the raised bank. He carried far more momentum than me on the exit of the turn, and glided past to occupy sixth once again, while McFarlane held his standing by virtue of an extra metre or two.

I could sense that Bolley was riding quite well today, and knew I would have to get past the two riders in front of me quickly, if I wanted to remain in with a chance of the top three. We were only halfway around the first lap and next we came into the new rhythm section. Another hairpin loop threw us into the jumps. Bolley made an error this time by taking the inside, with his reduced pace forcing him to take the jumps one at a time. I sailed around the outside and built up enough speed so that I could single and double, reclaiming sixth by flying through the air over Bolley's head.

I gained a bit of time from that move and once more had McFarlane in front of me, who was by now challenging Beirer. I could smell third place, it was that close. In front of Beirer was Coppins, with Pichon in second, desperate not to let Gundersen get too far away. We jumped over a ridge where the earth fell away in a forty-foot drop and then went into the back section before the course returned to the main part that lay in the shadow of the spectator-laiden rock face. Bolley had corrected himself and made up some time, as he again managed to come past on the one of the speedy dips as we finished the first lap.

I had lasted one circulation before the bike started to be stubborn about changing gear. I knew it was coming, but it still does not stop you cursing several times in your helmet when it happens. Bolley was still within reach in the first few technical and sweeping areas of the track where I could run with everybody and was trying to gain ground. The long straight with the tabletop in the middle was where I needed to go up through the gearbox to make progress, and it wasn't happening. I was losing a lot of time because I had to shut off the gas, kick the lever and then it would go.

Bolley pulled further away going down the straight, and I spent most of the lap just trying to keep on level terms, never mind pushing the bike to get me into a position to overtake. I suffered on the fast parts where I really needed the gears to accelerate in the blink of an eye. I was constantly having to clutch my way through the gearbox and was losing, little by little, in every corner. By the end of the third lap, Bolley had something like a two-second margin and was drawing up to the back of Coppins and Beirer, with McFarlane strangely picking up his pace and chasing the leaders.

It took the Frenchman another three laps before he saw off Beirer, and I could see it all unfolding from a forced back seat. I was now becoming accustomed to what the bike would let me do and the lap-times I could aim to make. Lalloz was trailing me by two seconds. Gundersen was fading back through the pack after he had surrendered to the effort of his own lightning speed and became the first victim of another Pichon massacre. Beirer nudged him down to sixth on lap seven, and then we all climbed further up when McFarlane started to hit reverse with a mechanical problem. He wasn't jumping the rhythm section at all and looked like he had brake trouble. Gundersen was about four seconds ahead of me, and we were gaining on McFarlane all the time. He eventually disappeared after three laps and we drifted past.

I had an incentive to hammer the bike as hard as I could. Kenneth had tensed up or maybe his arms had pumped because he really had fallen back quite far from where Pichon was still clocking his race-winning times. The gap between us flexed as the laps counted down. I could not get close enough in time to forcefully continue the downward spiral of his race. He had a sufficient breather to compose himself before I could reach him and started to find his pace again. The distance hovered between three and five seconds until four laps from the end, when my persistent efforts to keep the pressure on him began to show. I gained a second a lap and by the penultimate circulation, I had the margin down to two seconds.

I kept up the momentum for last two laps and caught Gundersen looking over his shoulder a couple of times. He knew I was coming and that I wanted that fifth position. He tried to fight as much as he could, while I was still giving all I had. He reached the chequered flag just over a second before I did; I had simply run out of time.

I can't describe what the frustration is like to see a rider struggling in front of you and not be able to attack and take advantage of the situation. That scenario was just the latter half of the race. To see McFarlane, Bolley and others just rocket away in front at the start was still a tough deal to swallow.

After the race, I had another talk with Kurt and my irritation boiled over culminating in me saying that the situation with the bike was becoming an absolute joke. I think he let me calm down a little before giving me more reassurances that the path we were on would actually lead somewhere. Again the words 'develop', 'improvement' and 'effort' were stressed. The fragility of the new bike highlighted its prototype status and its lack of readiness for a GP moto, while burying its good points somewhere down with the disappointing feelings associated with sixth position.

Trying not to think about the result and the limited performance, I searched for positives to take out of the Swedish race. I had a feeling that we were doing something right with the bike because until the crank failure, it had felt better and easier to ride than at the start of the year. Now all we had to do was survive a weekend with no glitches and continue to try and find a solution to the suspension, so that I felt safer and able to push harder on the track. I started to look at my position in the Championship and what I could possibly gain from 2002. Anything could still happen, of course, but I currently stood in sixth place, not far behind Gundersen and in front of Johnny Aubert on a private Yamaha. Pichon was thirty points in front of Coppins in second, and had become the most successful French GP rider ever with his twenty-first victory.

It was clear that Gundersen and Bolley were now my main targets, and I would have to keep an eye on what they were doing over the future race weekends. Pit was over thirty points away from me, and I'd need him to register a DNF if I was to have any hope of third. Suddenly, a possible fourth, or third at a long shot, did not seem to be such a bad prospect considering the 'mare of a year I had been having.

Pichon's seventh win in eight races unintentionally rubbed everyone's faces in it, regarding the level we would (and should) have to reach. Josh took his sixth podium in a row with the runner-up spot, and Bolley (just to emphasise the point that I could have made it to the top three) took the last step on the podium. During the champagne celebrations, people told me that you could have cut the tension with a knife. Seeing the video later, Josh stood defiantly and deadly serious on the second block, while Mickael just ignored him.

We left soon after the 125 GP, where seventeen-year-old Ben Townley came of age with his first win after only a season and a half in the GPs, after moving across from New Zealand straight out of school. The series was still twisting and turning.

We started doing a lot more testing when we got back to the UK after Sweden. Nick Moores, Gordon's main mechanic, and I started working together, and he was spending some time with us instead of solely with Gordon, which made a change. Nick is a good technician, so his input was welcomed.

★ ★ ★

Sitting out the 2001 GP in Sweden is obviously not the first race I have missed through injury. The physical emphasis of the sport, coupled with the risks associated with speed over unpredictable terrain and high jumps, means that breaking bones, damaging ligaments and spending time in a hospital bed is part of the deal. It's something you rarely think about when you are on the track and an issue you are equally as quick to dismiss while sitting in a medical gown with a cast on one of your limbs. The overriding emotion is to get better and get riding again, as fast as possible (even off the track, in a separate situation, speed is still the primary goal).

Being injured is an inconvenience. It interrupts everything. At an early age, the pain and after-effects can be quite traumatic, but eventually it becomes a drag that you just have to be patient and get over it. In my sixteen years of racing, hospitals have been like a second home, with doctors and nurses seemingly like an extended family. To talk about every crash that has resulted in a bruise, break, strain or sprain would probably fill another book, but there have been a few that were more memorable for the wrong reasons.

I fractured my skull in 1984 at the age of twelv in a race at Elsworth Moto Parc. I knocked myself senseless that day. I was flat out on an 80cc Honda and threw myself into a set of bumps coming off a fast jump. I felt really groggy and was taken by ambulance to hospital, where they gave me an X-ray but then sent me home. For the next few nights, I had difficulty sleeping. My parents were concerned about my racing, but it was already too late to stop me doing something that had featured so prominently in my life. I took a few tentative outings on the bike again the same week, and was soon back up to speed.

Three weeks after the crash, my mum took a call from the doctor and they asked if I had been having any migraines. She explained that I was still having headaches. They asked her to bring me straight back down to the hospital because after re-examining the X-rays, they saw that I had three-inch hairline fracture in my skull.

Kids tend to have an element of 'no fear' about them, and I wasn't any different. I think I was too young to really appreciate how serious the implications a big bang on the head can be. Since then, it has been a painful road. From toe to top, a brief list reads like this:

- a broken metatarsal and two toes on my left foot
- a broken toe and fractured ankle on my right foot
- stretched knee ligaments (both legs)
- a torn right testicle
- a compression fracture of the back
- a broken ulna and radius in my right arm. Twice. The first was a compression
- both collarbones, fractured or broken three times each
- numerous broken fingers
- ripped shoulder ligaments (on both sides)
- a prolapsed disk in my neck

- a three-inch hairline fracture of my skull
- three smashed teeth and a split chin
- uscular problems, such as tears, strains and bruising, that are impossible to count
- skin damage and friction burns in various places

I was smashed up for much of my time in the US. I was speaking with Mitch Payton again recently, and we were talking about how much SX can wipe you out and that you need a few years to get into it. SX can just click, and suddenly you can make the triples and your timing zones in without any of the costly crashes and injuries.

My initiation into American motocross was as tough as they come. At the end of 1992, I competed in a supercross meeting at the NEC centre in Birmingham, three weeks before I was due to fly to the US. I cased a triple and instead of the normal scenario, in which you bounce off the peak of the jump and crash, the bike stopped dead, right on top of the bump, after having been as high as thirty feet in the air. The impact ripped both pegs off the bike and also broke the bolts holding on the tank, after I clattered it with my crotch.

It felt like someone had taken a run-up and kicked me in the bollocks with venom. I was taken straight to the medical room at the NEC, which, predictably enough, had several young girls manning the first-aid facility. Lying on the table, one of them asked me if the pain was in my groin. I had to say, 'No, it's actually here,' pointing to my ball-bag. She got the giggles and had to go out. She obviously told her mate because I could hear them laughing away in the corridor! I was given a cod piece-like brace and sent to the hospital. I explained the situation to the doctor and he thought I may have just taken a bang and might have some bruising. They gave me some painkillers and I went home, with one eye on trying to complete the second night of the NEC SX because it was my last race in England before leaving.

With most injuries, the story is always the same. You are usually writhing in agony for the first day or two and then you just kind of get used to the pain. If it is something really bad, then you end up in a hospital bed full of drugs and that helps. I attempted to race, but the pain was unbelievable and hadn't died down by the next day. I went to the local GP and a female nurse kept a straight face this time as she had a look at it. By now it was swelling up and getting dangerously near the size of a grapefruit, whilst also turning black and dark purple. Her exact words were 'Oh, you poor thing' and she sent me directly down to Derby Royal Infirmary for an ultrasound scan. I remember seeing the image on the monitor of one good testicle and the other almost split in two with all the little 'fish' swimming around it.

I had a haematoma of the scrotum and needed a four-hour emergency operation that afternoon. I was really scared because I have always wanted to have kids and they were telling me I might be infertile, that I might not produce hormones and that I might end up with only one testicle. It was a serious moment because a big part of my future life was really at stake.

Thankfully, the operation was a success, but I never really knew if I was capable of having children, right up until the start of 2001. Naomi and I had been in America for my training and we were thinking about starting a family, and I planned to go and see a specialist when I got back. Funnily enough, when we did return Naomi felt different, had the test and was already pregnant – we said to each other 'So, they do work then.'

A month after the operation, at my first testing session with Kawasaki in America at their track in Corona I got my timing wrong on a triple again. This time I cased and crashed on the landing and broke my right forearm backwards, so that the bone of the rest of the arm was sticking out. It happened after I railed the outside of a berm in third gear and gassed the bike to hit and clear the triple. I went a bit high in the turn and kind of screwed the obstacle before I had to jump it. It's like when you play golf and you start your swing and hear somebody talk. You think 'It won't bother me, it won't bother me', but you whack the ball and it hooks way off into the rough. Half of me thought 'Back off, back off, it ain't gonna happen', while the other half said 'Shit, I can still make it'. The voice of reason was ignored, and I lost the gamble.

I had leaped off the berm instead of lining up on the take-off, and the bike bounced into the ramp, preventing a good run at it. I landed on the very top of the jump, which was a bit like landing on cement. The force snapped the handlebars and my arm went with the broken piece of the bar, while the rest of me stayed with the bike. I remember lying on the ground and thinking, 'God, that one broke the bars'. I then looked at the mess I'd made of my arm and thought 'Oops'.

I tend to have one pain threshold (which means I seem a bit of a wimp when I have a headache!) and, while the limb was in a bad way, I automatically started to think about getting it fixed and being positive. It's a case of 'Right, lets get on with it', instead of freaking out over what you have done.

The permanent twelve-inch scar hid a plate on either side of the arm, which held the bones together with nine screws on one side and eight on the other. I have since had the plates removed, but there is another one in there with four screws on either side because I broke the same arm again later in the season.

The second fracture happened in Troy. I went into the first turn on the outside of Jeremy McGrath and Damon Huffman. Huffman charged in too fast and forced Jeremy to pick up, in so doing, he scooped away my front wheel and I went down in front of many other riders. Crashing in the pack is a scary thing. In the rush of noise and activity, you just have to crouch and pray that nobody hits you. I think it was Brian Deegan who came around the corner and clattered me, cracking the arm again. The impact had whacked the plate and snapped one of the screws that was inside holding the thing together. The pain was intense, and I couldn't believe I had broken the same arm.

It was a real shame because I had worked my way up to fourth in the 125 Championship by the halfway stage and won at Unadilla. I was already forty points down after the first round, which I missed because of the first accident. The break while testing, several weeks before the first race of the season, was perhaps the longest time I have spent off a bike injured. It took about ten weeks to have the operation and heal.

Fear is a strange thing. Part of the professionalism and the discipline is to ignore any jumps, leaps or step-downs that might seem ludicrously high or risky. The 'no fear' approach from a young age and attacking all sorts of obstacles on both good and awful circuits soon drills the apprehension out of you. People correctly assume that, most of the time, motorcycle racers disregard any concern for their safety, but it is a necessary evil. The extent of the denial extends right until the last possible moment. If you make a mistake and you know deep down there is a very good chance you are going to crash-land from a jump, you ignore your fear because you are focused on trying to do everything in your power to prevent an inevitable accident. Another half a metre on the triples at the NEC and at the Kawasaki test track, and the injuries would not have happened.

You might experience a knowing fear that you have got the jump wrong, but in a lot of cases you are not quite sure if you are going to crash until it actually happens; if luck is on your side, you might miraculously save it or come out unscathed. As in most motorsports, confidence, willingness to push to the limit, and chance-taking are what deliver success. At the end of the day, that is what every racer is striving to reach. Success breeds confidence, and experience also helps override the nerves.

Racing is a game of egos. A rider will very rarely admit he is afraid because it is a sign of weakness. You have to be strong and tough mentally to put yourself on the line. There cannot be any doubt, because to run at the speed you want requires conviction and no small amount of bravery. We all know about the risks we take, and have the scars, aches and limps to prove it. In the past, I have looked at a circuit with fifty-foot vertical step-downs and the butterflies have started in my stomach. Nowadays, when I am taking a jump for the first time on a new track, any question marks over the obstacle vanish when I have made it once. Most of the time when I'm on the bike, the level of concentration dissipates any nerves.

It's strange that your perception of fear seems to work the wrong way round. As a kid, you charge into anything like a blind bull when you probably do not have the capability to carry it off. With age, you become proficient enough to take some jumps without a second thought, but as the bones ache and your children watch, then the repercussions of a big crash are more serious and you become aware of it. The realisation of the risks, both to yourself (if you have already been banged up in the past) and to those who would be affected the most by an accident, is usually one of the major steps on the road to retirement.

Fear. I have seen riders crying because they cannot take a jump at speed anymore. The day that the gamble is heavier than the gain must be a sad one, especially for riders for whom motocross is their entire life. With indoor SX, you obviously get a little nervous looking at the steep sections and ramps but after a while you get accustomed to most forms of obstacles, and you simply jump them and forget about it. Pitching yourself forty or fifty feet into the air becomes part of the natural way of racing.

I used to walk the giant SX tracks in America, roll it once in practice, and then just go for it and hit the triples. If you start to hesitate, then that's when you begin to get scared and don't carry any conviction into the ramp with your throttle. If you decide that you don't want to (or cannot) clear the distance when it's too late – because you are on the approach – then you know you are probably going to come down with a thump.

You never think that you'll get hurt. There has only really been one time in my career when I was plagued with fear and the dangers of the sport were blinding. I could not switch into 'denial mode' and it almost wrecked everything. Naturally, it derived from a crash. In 1999, I fell out of the second moto of the first GP of the year in Verneuil sur Avre, France. I had taken fourth in the first race and I think I was holding fifth in the next moto when I slipped off. I exited a corner that had a very small flat jump, almost like a rise, into another turn. The jump had a rut through it, and I just lost the front wheel of the bike and hit the ground in a heap.

I was sitting there on my knees and I noticed that my chest protector had been ripped out of my jersey, so I pushed it back in and clambered to pick the bike up and just rode around. I remember pulling out of the way of the leaders as they came around to lap me and then headed back. The team came running out: 'Where were you? You disappeared!' 'What are you on about? I only pulled over for the leaders,' I replied. They then told me that I had been sitting there for three laps!

I watched the rest of the race from the pits without any kind of problem, insisting that I was fine. When I got back to the truck, all hell broke loose. I said to Naomi as I was getting changed that she had better get the bunny rabbits out of the van or else. Honest to God, I felt like I was trippin' or something, I was surrounded by rabbits hopping around. I started crying and freaking out, and refused to get in a car with my brother, Richard, who drives like a nutter anyway, because I thought we were all going to crash and die. It was terrible and a very scary time. I got taken for a scan and was told I had concussion.

In the aftermath, I not only had to recover from the injury, but from the negative thoughts that were eating me from the inside, and I resorted to seeing a sports psychologist just to get over the problems. Basically, when you pull on that helmet, your mind is already trying to act out the perfect race, and you are constantly thinking positive and talking yourself up. Trying to ride after the smash, I was doing up my strap and hoping that I wasn't going to put myself in a wheelchair or end up critically hurt. I remember travelling to a poorly-kept Italian circuit, and I could hardly get round the place through fear. I knew then that I needed some help. The mistake I made was to jump straight back on the bike as soon as I felt okay, thinking I could immediately get down to it. The reality is that after a concussion you should wait a few weeks because of the swelling on the brain. I used to go running a week or so after the crash and would start to feel all dizzy after ten minutes and nearly fall over, purely because all the soft tissue and the 'mechanics' inside had not recovered.

I went to see Bill Beswick, now the assistant manager of Middlesbrough Football Club and loyal right-hand man to Steve McClaren, when he was at Derby FC, and we sat down and talked about my riding, ambitions, pros and cons, and what I wanted in my career. The talks helped me re-evaluate where I wanted to go and what I wanted to do. The notion that I should be paid more also became a priority. I was serious about my profession and now I wanted to be taken seriously.

Part of the fitness criteria of the sport is as much to cope with the strains on the body as it is to push the bike to winning extremes. A large percentage of riders still compete when they are far from ready, still strapped or a little pale from pain-killing injections. Why do we do it? Who knows? Everyone has their reasons. It is our job to race, and while the body is the most valuable machine and needs looking after, there is still the pressure within to get out there and ride. It is a shameless macho thing when you are young; not showing any weakness feels like an important thing to do. As you get older, racing while injured becomes a delicate balance of priorities. The body starts to ache for a day or two more and takes slightly longer to repair itself. In the end, like I did after the concussion I had in 1999, you learn to put yourself and your future first.

Limping riders and people out on the track mere days after 'snapping something' always looks a little crazy, but our bodies are conditioned to a level much higher than a normal person's, and it enables recovery to be a faster process. Rest is still the best form of recuperation. I have become best friends with an icepack, roll of tape and various braces over the years, and a good massage is almost essential these days, even just to relax the muscles when there isn't a problem. A massage is a fantastic way to unwind, and I cannot recommend it enough for a sportsman at any level.

Everyone had injuries at some stage in 2002 and, throughout the course of a season, the rider who has that little bit of luck in staying away from the doctors, hospitals and X-ray machines is guaranteed a good shot at success. I throw this theory out of the window if I speak about 2001, but that season was a lesson in itself about pre-season preparation and fitness. This year, though, I was a well worn-out example.

4 August 2002: Round Nine
Belgian Grand Prix, Genk

DURING THE four-week break, I took the opportunity to rest and get some hard training done, as well as some more testing with Nick. I also visited the Moto GP race at Donington, parked the camper up for the weekend and had some fun with the riders at the 'Riders for Health' day.

We went to Southport the weekend before the next GP in Belgium, to apply our new data and settings in a race environment – another Future West British International Championship round – and to get further time on the bike in a competitive situation rather than endlessly circling an empty circuit. My results that day turned out to be crap, mainly because of an incident in the first race when I went down in a group crash, and Stuart Flockhart managed to do a burnout on my arse.

The first corner on that track didn't really filter the riders out because it was more of a fast kink; if anybody touched trying to go through it at pace, then it would be a painful impact. I had the quickest time in practice, and as I rushed into the kink with everybody else at the start of the moto – somebody came across and completely wiped out my front wheel. As I hit the ground, Flockhart rammed into me and his rear wheel spun a hole in my back. The adrenaline was pumping. My shirt was all ripped and I could feel pain in my lower back, but I picked up the bike on autopilot and went a bit loopy for the rest of the race, fighting my way up to third; an awesome result, considering.

Between the motos, I was in agony. My back and the top of my arse were sore, bright red and bleeding. I got the area covered in bandages because I didn't want to stop riding. I don't know why. It may have been the easiest and most sensible thing to do, but I was angry, exhilarated and pumped. I wanted to try again, mainly because I was sick to death of having my racing hindered by physical problems. I had made my decision but, by the time the second moto came around, the pain had set in and was making it impossible to sit on the bike.

The track was very sandy, with a lot of lose grit on the surface of the dirt, and all this crap was grating away in the hole. I could barely get going. Finally, I just decided to cruise around, not wanting to risk anything more.

The burn measured about five inches in length and about three inches wide; his tyre had got some decent traction on my skin. It was cleaned up and dressed properly in the hospital, and lying in bed and sitting down often had me wanting to climb the wall. I had yet another X-ray and, thankfully, there was no damage internally. I was laid up on the couch for two weeks because I could not do anything, which was becoming a ritual between races. The list of injuries went on, and aptly demonstrates the wear and tear your body has to endure to be a motocross rider. Having hurt my shoulder, hand and ribs, and sufficiently got over all of them, my back was next. It took a long time for the pain to fade because the pus kept on building up, and then a scab would form and crack every time I moved.

I travelled to Genk in Belgium with what felt like half an arse. I had thought about maybe not racing and letting my battered body recover. My dad was also a bit sceptical when looking at the strip of rotting skin, and reckoned I should not ride. We got some more cream from the doctors that eased the pain as well as helping the wound heal a bit quicker. In the end, I was uncomfortable but not in a state to miss a GP, as the skin hardened up in the days approaching Genk.

I suppose you could say that Belgium is *the* country in Europe for motocross. It rivals cycling and football for the most popular sport, and Stefan Everts is a national celebrity. Some of the biggest names in the history of MX have come from the northern European country – people like Roger De Coster, Joel Robert, the Geboers brothers, Georges Jobe and, of course, the Everts family.

Stefan Everts has the record for most career victories ever, and he also shares Robert's total haul of six World Championships. Eric Geboers was the first man to win the Triple Crown (titles in the 125, 250 and 500 classes), and Everts joined Geboers at the end of 2001 when he became 500cc number one.

The country is synonymous with MX and naturally the crowds do turn out, regardless of the poor weather that seems to curse most of their GPs. Racing in Belgium is always a pleasure, because you know the circuit will be full of fans with the kind of loyalty that would put some football teams to shame. Everts has his own fan club and they often travel to other GPs together, a bit like Valentino Rossi's crowd, but a few hundred less. Smets, Everts, Bervoets and, to some degree, Ramon and Caps receive a lot of attention. Belgium's relatively central base means that many French, Dutch, German and British fans also make the journey, turning the crowd into quite an eclectic mix. There seems to be a lot of beer and French fries swimming in mayonnaise sold, and the volume of the crowd as they lean into the track makes for a lively atmosphere. I usually get through a fair few autographs when we arrive at a Belgian venue.

With the attention and prestige surrounding the GP of Belgium (the VIP hospitality facility is rarely more full), it's odd that a venue like Genk is chosen to play host. The circuit is awful and we should be at Namur. I suppose it's Dorna and their financial concerns again, paying heed to their own gain rather how they could profit from investing properly in quality racing and attention to the product. Geographically, Genk is right on the eastern border with Holland, and not so far from Germany. Half an hour down the road is the city of Maastricht.

The facilities at the circuit are crap. When it rains, as it has done the last two years, the water does not drain from the motorhome parking area and creates a muddy pool. The few buildings look like Second World War hangars with their rusting oval corrugated iron roofs. In 2001, they had to drive trucks of wood chippings into the paddock to stop everybody from sinking.

The track itself is basic and boring. It swings back and forth over a raised bank several times for long corners that disappear briefly into a forest section. We jump from the main flat stadium area that holds ninety per cent of the track, over the rise and into the woods, negotiate a turn and come back. That happens on four or five occasions, and that's it. The rest of the course is like a kart track. How we can use a venue like Genk when Namur is available is beyond me. Quite simply, there is no other track on earth like Namur. It is the Monaco GP of motocross, and I felt very proud to win there in 2001.

It's located on top of a huge mount that overlooks the town and the nearby river. On top of the hill is a park containing a hotel, a museum, leisure facilities like tennis courts, and several restaurants. Inside this recreational area is also a MX GP circuit. Namur oozes history with its military past (it used to house a castle, the ruins of which are still dotted around) and especially with motocross. It was the original host of the Belgian GP back in the first-ever World Championship in 1957 (500cc).

The 'Citadelle', as it is also known, is more like an enduro course. It is a track of character and is unique. It is barely six or seven feet wide in places and you run under footbridges and next to an old pub. You cross the main road in the park several times, which has been covered with mud or a jump that is conveniently placed over the asphalt. The inclines of the step-ups and downs as you descend the mount, run along the bottom for several hundred metres and then climb back up to the top are quite steep, and not for the faint-hearted. There are no hairpins, chicanes and hardly any jumps – just a fairly quick, flowing and technical blast up and down through the woodland that is so dense in places it can be quite dark in broad daylight.

It's so interesting for both rider and fan. Granted, it may be the one circuit where the public will not see a great deal of the action from one spot due to the woods, but if you hike around you will get a lot closer and catch a glimpse of motocross like no other track will allow. Namur figured on the World Championship calendar twice in 2001 with its own GP, and also entertained the Nations at the end of the year. The GPs are the poorer for its absence this season, and instead we have to suffer the rank substitute that is Genk.

True to form (so much so that I would have put money on it), when we arrived at the track, it was raining. Fred had managed to get the camper parked and levelled right next to the KTM semis, which was handy. Looking at the circuit, it had hardly changed. The soft terrain that was a mix of fine dirt and sand, also had its fair share of stones. It would not drain very well after a liberal amount of showers, meaning that with some wear through practice, the track would be heavily rutted and rough.

Free practice and qualifying was not an easy affair. I had three issues to contend with. Yet again, I wasn't fit going into a GP race, and I would also have to ignore the pain from my lower back, as well as the suspension that was the ever-present cherry on top of a mouldy cake. I was sitting down on the bike as little as possible to try and minimise my discomfort, and the whole unnaturalness of the situation visibly affected my riding, resulting in a seventh-position qualification. For once, Pichon did not collect pole, as Beirer pushed him off the top spot in the dying minutes of the session.

That evening, we went to eat in the hospitality area as usual, and I retired to the television set without peace of mind. I knew the next day would possibly be my hardest race of the year, and I would have to pump myself up more than usual, while praying for some good fortune at the same time. More rain overnight saw the track turn into a bog after both 250 and 500 warm-ups. Splashing through the standing puddles on the first laps of the day, I was still telling myself that if I could give everything I had, then there was a chance that something would come good today.

Josh Coppins lined up in the gate once more, and there was a guy who certainly had a lot on his mind. The gossiping had died down after Sweden and the summer break, but Coppins was still virtually an outsider in the paddock. He didn't know if this would be his last race for Vismara Honda and even the season, seeing as his rearranged hearing with the CDI was due to take place a few days after Genk. Coppins still had a point to prove to everybody and, while the rawness of the whole deal had mellowed since Sweden, he was very much a rider on a mission.

I moved into slot three from the inside, with Pichon and Beirer to my left. The flat straight ran the entire length of the pit lane before going into a 180-degree left hairpin that headed back down the other side of the team boxes. Beirer had selected the first gate position and was looking for that inside line – pretty much the same start that Pichon and myself were seeking. I shook my head, carrying the new model of the onboard camera with a much smaller battery and less weight. I took the unit as a favour to the Dorna television crew and, because the lighter model looked more practical, I could not really have any objections. Extra coverage on live television, considering the race was on Eurosport, was never to be sniffed at. The fact that the camera was a prototype version quite aptly tied in with my present mechanical situation. I fidgeted on the bike and dragged my wrists against the top of the bars to pull my gloves tighter. I try to keep loose and focused in the gate at least until the fifteen-second board comes up, then it's time to work.

The gate wobbled and thirty bikes leapt into life. I lost a little traction compared to Pichon and Beirer. Pit headed straight down the inside, with Mickael just behind, while I tucked in behind the Suzuki and took a line so tight, I almost hit a photographer who was leaning out of the bend. I was in about sixth or seventh and had the rest of the pack flanking around the outside of me in a wave of colour and noise. I kept close to Mickael as we picked up exiting the left and ran down by the pits. We then sliced through another bunch of puddles into a right kink that took us into the tree-lined side of the ridge for the first time. Pichon had a bit of extra space. He had held a firm line on the inside of the first turn and came out practically in the lead, as Pit carried a bit too much speed on the entry. Coppins was also up there.

I went into the kink in about eighth place and felt the rear wheel break sideways under acceleration, as I hit the wet and drifted to the banking on the outside of the track. Bolley was in sixth and I was stuck behind Paul Cooper, as we ploughed through the mud. I muscled my way into seventh several turns later, and was then promoted to sixth on the next lap when we passed a fallen Beirer. I could see him remounting, and suspected that I hadn't seen the last of the red Honda.

By the end of the third lap, Pichon was leading and Coppins was slightly adrift in second. Once again, I was losing the back of Bolle because I found that I didn't have enough confidence in the bike to attack the circuit. I was holding back on certain jumps where I did not know what would happen if I pushed to go flat out. The 250 wasn't doing what I wanted it to do. Bolley was simply was faster than me, and closed up to Kevin Strijbos and Crockard who were fighting for third. I rode as quickly as I dared, and it was not at a pace that would break the top five.

Five laps into the race Cooper, who had been following me quite closely, disappeared. His bike had broken again, just like in Italy when I was chasing him. Briefly, I had a reminder that I wasn't the only one to suffer bad luck throughout a GP year. I was then more or less by myself, and started to reel in seventeen-year-old 125cc regular Strijbos, who had one of Pichon's bikes in his 250cc début. Pichon had adopted Strijbos as a sort of protégé, and that is one of Mickael's really good points as a professional and a human being. He is always free with his advice to the younger riders, and has been helping the French guys like Eric Sorby, Matthieu Lalloz and Christophe Martin. He assisted Strijbos in getting a World Championship-winning bike for the Belgian GP, at a time when the Belgian was on a Suzuki 125 and struggling to get into the points. It goes to show what decent machinery and good support can deliver. Strijbos was running in the top five for most of the race, along with Gordon.

Crockard was in third, behind Pichon then Coppins, and had actually slipped off on the back part of the circuit, a flat turn that was very wet, and almost wiped out the pursuing Strijbos and Bolley. Crockard recovered and immediately got the better of Strijbos. In all this commotion, to my pleasant surprise, I was gaining time on those in front. The track had by now formed a drying rough line, with the rest of the surface of the terrain resembling a shallow pool in places. It was slippery out there, and made the handling of the bike an important factor.

It was easily the wettest race of the year so far. The flat landscape held the water, where at least in St Jean we were on the side of a hill for most of the time and only encountered the slush when we ran along the base. The sun popped out from behind clouds now and again and, at one stage, it rained at the same time as well – only in Belgium. The spectators were pretty noisy and Strijbos was enjoying a lot of local support, however, I sensed that maybe he was tiring. Within one lap, I decided to force a move and got more gas coming off a jump to drive past on a short straight.

My theory about Strijbos starting to feel the pace was proved right when I didn't see his front wheel again. Gordon was five seconds in front of me at the halfway stage of the GP. Two laps later, Bolley slowed with some sort of problem and lost third to Crockard. I caught the Yamaha as he seemed to be cruising, and claimed fourth when he threw himself into the Belgian gunk.

I assessed my situation at the end of that lap and saw Strijbos a second or two away, and just behind him was Beirer on a flyer. One circulation later, and Pit was hounding me. He aced a big step down in one go to hit the main straight, whereas I didn't even dare. I couldn't clear the jump, when normally I would have been soaring through the air and hitting the bottom, just like the out-of-shape Honda. In the corner at the end of the straight, he sailed past on the inside of the right-left flick and earned his fourth place. Pit was riding in a zone I could only dream about in Genk.

I pushed on regardless and kept the margin to around a second to two seconds for a few laps. The momentum dragged us away from a fading Strijbos. Pit's speed proved superior in the last ten minutes of the moto, and he increased the gap to four or five seconds, but could not catch Crockard in third. I had a good look around me in the last two laps and crossed the line well ahead of Strijbos.

I think it's fair to say that my confidence deserted me in Genk. I had no faith or feeling in the bike in the conditions. I wasn't entirely sure what would happen if I tried to clear the big step-down in one go. I erred on the cautious side because I did not feel safe, and the race disappeared. Another boring forty minutes on the bike, almost nondescript.

The racing is not as much fun when you have to struggle, hold on and count down the laps. You cannot relax and seize the moto, which was essentially the main drawback of the bike. I was squeezing the throttle intermittently, rather than just giving it full-on gas, and that's not the way I like to race. Not being able to attack the Genk jumps was a crushing indication of the depth to which my confidence had sunk. I barely felt like the same rider who had crossed the line first by some distance here fourteen months previously.

Of course, I was dejected afterwards and immediately put the GP out of my head, so much so that I wanted to leave quite quickly and get back to the house. 'On to the next one', I thought, and now I would take two weeks to try and get myself back to 100 per cent. Deep down, I knew I was still capable of being a winner, even at this low point. It had only been two months since I had thrashed everyone in Austria. You have to believe in your heart that you can win, and you never let go of that fact, otherwise you do not race. Sometimes the truth can be harsh and, in my case, it was too often right in my face.

Bolley's DNF was a small piece of good news, and it meant that I was now level fourth in the Championship. Josh and Pit were also fairly close together in fighting for second, but had something like a thirty-odd point lead over Bolley and me. Gundersen was only four points behind both of us, while Gordon's podium had dragged him up to seventh with a seven-points gap.

In the days straight after the GP, Coppins faced his doping charge and incredibly escaped without a ban. The FIM hardly set an example with this decision. Despite submitting an illegal sample, the CDI found him not guilty, imposed a $5,000 fine, dished out a three-month ban (suspended conditionally for one year) and deducted his points from Austria, which now placed him one behind Pit in third and meant that Mickael could win the Championship at the next round in Germany. Again, the news surprised a lot of people. What kind of message did that send out about our sport? The guy could finish second in the world, having been caught with a banned substance in his body, and still stood on the podium every other week. I thought the FIM were sending out confusing signals regarding the doping issue.

I dismissed the memory of Genk, after watching the race on television a bit later in the week, as a low point in a season consisting mainly of low points. To give a measurement of the reversal in fortunes inside one year, both Gordon and I had won there in 2001, giving Britain a double victory, and now here we were in pain and scrabbling for crumbs at the table of Pichon. 2001, in contrast, was a weekend to savour, especially for all fans of British motocross.

★ ★ ★

I have qualified for every GP I have entered bar one, and that was at Genk in 1988, my debut year with the Cagiva. It was quite nostalgic in 2001 because, as I stood on the podium with the 125cc winner's trophy in my hand, I had time to think back to the utter disappointment at not getting a lap-time fast enough to be a part of the Belgian GP thirteen years previously and now here I was, on my very next visit, on the top step.

The conditions were wet and technical in 2001, much more so than they were this year. I was on song that weekend. 2001 was the first year for a while that British fans were missing a GP, so a fair few of them came across the Channel. They picked the right meeting because only three hours later 'God save the Queen' blared out again for Gordon, as he soundly beat Pichon. In a way, it was such a shame that we had no top rider in the 500cc class, because a hat-trick would have been awesome. Genk was my third win in four races, and already I had amassed a lead of fifty points in the table.

We visited two other circuits in Belgium that year. Round six was at Spa, and I earned my fourth consecutive victory on a fantastic circuit that I have always liked. Spa was also the meeting when I first learned of KTM's plans to run a new factory 250 in 2002, and I knew I would be in the frame for the ride if I sealed the Championship.

Namur played host to round nine, one race after my efforts to come back from the broken collarbone in Sweden with a second place in Ernée. Due to the violent nature of the training crash and the other broken shoulder, I seriously doubted whether I would be able to race at the Citadelle. The accident happened when I was hurrying into a fast right-hand turn with a big berm, lost control and clattered a fence post on the side of the track. The bike smacked sideways and stopped abruptly, throwing me off. I landed on the face of the jump, which cracked the shoulder.

To my despair, there was nothing they could do at the hospital, because the bone and ligament had ripped away from each other and the end of the collarbone was fractured. It hurt twice as much as the other break. The separation was a common rugby injury, apparently. I had painkillers and strapping and just had to grit my teeth.

Namur seemed like one hell of a test, even for a fully-fit rider. It would be the first time that the 125s had visited the circuit, and would be a new experience for all of us. I looked at the track in bemusement, because without a painful arm, I would have been relishing the challenge of its tight-cutting path through the woods. My plan was to see how I felt in qualifying and hopefully I might be able to compete and gain some points in the race – the same plan as in Ernée. My Swedish break actually felt pretty good, and I was rowing and doing push-ups in the days before the training incident.

In practice, I posted a time that was only half a second behind Luigi Seguy, and completed as few circulations as possible. I was very happy with second fastest, but not so content with my start in the second qualifying heat race that left me outside the top fifteen in the first few corners. I went to work with heavy strapping holding my shoulder, and passed enough people to rise to fourth in three laps. One more push, and I could then only glimpse the back of Eggens – some twelve seconds ahead in some sections – in first place, as I settled into second and concentrated on riding the track and being smooth. I had already qualified and wasn't interested in wasting my energy to catch the Dutchman.

My arm didn't feel too bad at all after Saturday. The only time when I felt pain on the circuit was when I really had to work and extend my arms. The whoops were tough. The limb felt tired and heavy because of the weakness, and without the usual preparation of my training.

On the morning of race day, the ground was very wet, thanks to overnight rain. I was quite happy with this situation because it made the track slower and technically more difficult. It had been dry and fast on Saturday, and I was happy to think more about my riding instead of having to try and dodge big tree roots before I could even see them. I had a sneaking suspicion in the waiting area that I could even pull off a win at the Citadelle. I certainly knew that such a result could place one hand on the World Championship. If anyone thought they could steal the title from me, then it would take more than two arm injuries to make that possibility a reality. That rider would need to have a determination and thirst deeper than my own and, looking around at my rivals, I could see a lot of fast people, but none that I would put on the same level in terms of desire. A victory here, in these circumstances, would finish them off.

The rain fell briefly and the terrain shone with a greasy slipperiness. My shoulder was weak and I had to ditch my mud-coated goggles early on in the race. All the factors surrounding the GP said that it was unlikely I would win. I rode for my life and career that day, and easily count it as one of the defining moments of my days as a motocross racer. I was very emotional on the podium and with Naomi afterwards. I believed in my heart of hearts that I had cracked it. The 125cc Championship was coming back home with me to England, and now I just had to complete a couple more races to engrave my name on the trophy.

To get to the point where I was on the verge of being World Champion had been a lengthy path of watching, listening and learning, with a large chunk of mistakes thrown in as part of the process. My Dad helped me out immensely when I was a kid. He didn't give me that many tips and advice about my riding, but was always supportive and took my brothers and me to GPs and race meetings. He would always point at the professionals and say things like 'Look how they handle the bike on the ramp' or 'See the different lines they are taking through that corner'. With his direction, watching and simulating what I saw on the race track became my main method of learning. I was like a sponge as a kid, and absorbed any styles or tricks that I saw on the track, on a video of riders in America or even in photos from a magazine.

As my racing career took off with my success as a youngster, I got closer and closer to the stars and wouldn't hesitate to ask for any pointers or instruction. I believe, even now, that watching the best in the world performing their stuff is an excellent coaching method. You never stop learning because there is always someone with something new or better. Take a promising kid at a young age to a football match every week, and I am very confident that he or she will garner a lot from watching the movement and patterns of play before them.

My influences were varied. A rider dominating at national level was my hero for a day and enjoyed the same status as David Bailey in my young eyes. Living on the farms and having my own little circuits really helped me to practice and rehearse what I had witnessed, and that is how I improved as a rider and racer.

I never really had a coach or a mentor. Numerous people have chipped in with their opinions on my riding throughout my career, some useful and others not. The two most beneficial contributors to my riding were Gerard Rond and Kurt Nicoll. Rond helped me a lot when I started out in GPs at the age of sixteen. He worked for Premier, a helmet and racewear firm, and I met him after the company approached the Cagiva team and struck a deal. He was probably one of the best sand riders of all time, and a winner of six 125cc GPs. He really helped with my riding in the soft stuff, and I scored my best results on the sand in those days, thanks to his advice. Again, he helped me more with a 'watch and learn' method. We would go to a track and I'd ride around for a while getting used to it, then I'd clock a fast time and pull in. He'd say, 'Now follow me' and then I would try to keep up with him. He would take different lines and hit other spots on the course, sometimes I used to think 'Where the hell is he going?', but most times I'd end up cutting at least a few seconds off my previous best.

Kurt Nicoll has been through most things that could happen to a rider (in terms of success, disappointment, injury etc.), and that level of advice is invaluable. We have a good relationship. I find him easy to approach and talk to if I have a problem with things, such as the bike or my lines, anything really. Being a team manager is a super-hard job, and there are not many out there who are good at it. Nothing is ever a problem for Kurt, and I think a lot of people around him appreciate his manner.

Trips to America accelerated my progression, and training camps run by people like Wayne Boyer opened my eyes to what I could do on a dirt bike. I was travelling to San Diego from as young as eight years old on a partial busman's holiday to continue my motocross education.

Practice is a monumental part of the sport. Naomi and I have been looking for a new house or farm for some time now, with enough space for me to build my own track. At the moment, I have to travel nearly forty-five minutes to Mansfield and the place I use for training. It would be perfect just to roll the bikes out of the garage and start riding. That said, I love my practice track. People have been using it for twenty years, and it used to be an amateur circuit before it was closed down, due to a lack of insurance cover. It's a great little course on disused land owned by my brother-in-law, with a couple of jumps and a lot of variety. Make forty minutes around that track, and you can make forty minutes anywhere. It has a sandy soil that cuts up and gets rough in the summer. Rolling corners and square edged – it's a good place to test that I have been using since I returned from America in 1997. The track up at Donington Park is also a venue that I like to use.

Supercross is a discipline of the sport that is difficult to master. Many have tried, failed and got hurt in the process. Racing SX feels like your heart and lungs are going to explode, because it's unrelenting and there is never a time to take a breather. It's twenty minutes of pure, wide-open gas. Outdoor MX is getting closer to SX in that it's a one-moto main event now, but even so, there are nowhere near as many jumps, doubles and triples that really take it out of you.

One of the best SX riders, Ricky Johnson, gave me a few pointers when I was learning my trade, telling me to experiment with various positions and lines. At times, I was struggling with enough cash to eat while in America, so employing a trainer/coach was not an option. My supercross schooling mainly revolved around trying something and then lying on the ground, thinking 'Shit, that hurt. Better not do it again'!

My first SX race was an amateur meeting in Manchester when I was fourteen years old, and I won. The jumps on the farm stood me in good stead, and I enjoyed a lot of success at that age. I was even provisionally invited to race at the Paris SX, but sadly was too young to take part. My introduction to the AMA scene was at the Rose Bowl in Pasadena in 1993. I was spooked about the whole affair from start to finish. The broken arm was still as fresh in my memory as the new long scar on my skin. Oddly, I then managed to hole-shot and then proceeded to shit myself for the duration of the main event. I ended up with fifth and then wasn't bad in the remainder of the season, with several more top-five finishes.

I had an SX-style track from I was a kid, so it was not a new skill for me. You have to be so precise at high speed and make sure your timing is spot on. Casing triples hurts. Normally there is also a jump that leads straight into another. If you tumble over the bike outdoors, you just roll away, but in SX, landings arrive hard onto the face of another jump and, if you are lucky, you're not hit by streams of other bikes right behind you on a track that can be no more than four metres wide.

I have been very afraid of SX in the past and it can be a dangerous way to race. By 1996, I felt pretty comfortable. Even once you gain a decent level, it's not hard to forget. I do the odd supercross meeting now and it takes me around twenty practice laps to get my timing back in. For SX, you need a much harder suspension and lower-end power, while the outdoor machine is set up to cope with a variety of conditions and terrain. The changes are more important with the 125s than the 250s, but mainly it's just in the shocks and the pipes to handle the jumps.

Having good jumps on a track always makes riding more fun. Jumping is one of the most natural and instinctive parts of motocross. It is such a good feeling when you get to a place with some really big obstacles and you land them perfectly. It can almost be like floating around a circuit at speed. To get your timing spot on and clear a huge leap is a great buzz. Initial attempts at a vast distance and a lot of air is a bit like going on a theme park ride for the first time, such is the small shot of exhilaration in making the jump.

It's as natural to me as for a person driving their car to know when to brake, or for someone like David Beckham to know how to strike a dead ball. I know where and how to be in order to jump the distance that I can see. I act on instinct and do not think twice. The skill is in the judgement of the pace, position and distance, and then it is all down to your motorcycle-handling ability. Eventually, you get to a stage where you are not even thinking about what you are doing. It is like an everyday activity, like putting the kettle on, for example. I reached that point at quite a young age because I was riding so much. The jumps get bigger and the speed gets faster, but the 100 per cent instinctiveness of the skill is one of those things that you soon reach as a professional (and need to, in order to stand any chance of success).

People have different styles when it comes to jumps, and it is a fantastic area of expression. As with most difficult skills, it looks very easy in the hands of the pros, but I suppose it is quite a technical process, either to do it at high speed or with flair, using techniques like pre-loading and seat bouncing for example. Negotiating a jump, I am trying to go as fast and as low as possible. More time in the air means less power on the ground. A technique that is often used consists of pushing the front end of the bike into the face of a jump and turning into it as you run upwards. The subsequent shape of the bike means that you keep a lot lower than from a normal take-off.

Lining up a jump involves a lot of things – your position, speed, bravery, judgement and gearing. I am a rider who never knows what gear he is in. Some can be very precise and tell you exactly what they are using, whereas I never have a clue and just know if the bike has the correct power that I need. On the bigger jumps, you can really hang high in the air for a long time. Often it presents an opportunity to have a look around and see what is going on.

SX tracks tend to be quite formulaic in their layout. The doubles and triples will all be the same size and spacing, and there is a similar kind of run-up to everything. It forces you to adopt rhythm and precision. It can take years to hone the timing to be fast at supercross. It's an internal knowledge and feeling about where you need to be on the circuit. I can close my eyes and see what I need to do in order to jump a triple. I know exactly how the bike is going to feel. Usually, I am aiming to get over all the jumps and rises as fast as I can, but sometimes it's nice to play.

Deciding if you want to pull a trick on a jump means setting yourself up slightly beforehand. On the take-off, it's usually a bit late to shift your body shape and throw the bike at an angle. In most tricks, you need to be turning already as you hit the ramp, depending on the move you want to pull. Getting the distance is the key to completing the jump and giving you enough time to do your show-boating. Obviously, more airtime helps out, but also loses you seconds. A good lap involves nailing most of the jumps as quick as you can, and that can be a thrill as much as the actual act of sailing through the air. It is always nice to perfect a skill that not many people in the world can or want to.

18 August 2002: Round Ten
German Grand Prix, Gaildorf

IN SOMEWHAT different circumstances, I looked to Germany 2002 and the GP race in Gaildorf. The champagne and glory of 2001 seemed a long way off, while at the same time having that familiar feeling of occurring all but five minutes ago. I was excited for Mickael because, exactly as it had been for me in 2001, he had the chance of winning the title, and I knew how he was feeling in the days leading up to the race.

The circuit is based centrally and to the south of Germany, not too far from the city of Stuttgart. It is within walking distance of the small town of Gaildorf, and the thriving party tent that is set up adjacent to the track draws the locals every year and usually sounds like a packed, raucous affair. The pavilion is always in the same spot and, in 2001, the organisers had the bright idea of placing the riders' motorhome enclosure quite close to the din. Luckily for me, I was in a hotel that weekend.

The track itself is quite like Teutschenthal, but not as flowing. It cuts the grassy terrain on a sloping field and is quite fast. The speed is broken up by some jumps and some awful karting-style chicanes. Gaildorf could be a very good track, but the alterations to slow us down, (we were doing 1m 52s as it was, which is really quick for a single lap) in my opinion, were detrimental to the racing, because nobody could really pass going into the choppy little sections.

The parking situation was a little weird and, in an effort to get us further away from the crowds, we were spread over two enormous fields adjacent to the circuit. The problem lay in the fact that they were both steeply angled, so everybody was spaced out and trying to find a flat spot. Half of the paddock was at the bottom, while the other half was at the top, with a huge 200-

metre stretch of green in between; the motorhomes were in a different field altogether. Never was my little scooter more badly needed. It's quite a cool jet-black 80cc Beta, and I've had it personalised with a big orange sixty-four.

There was an air of inevitability around Gaildorf. Mickael was on the eve of a possible seventh consecutive victory and another World Championship. I knew that Pichon would not be nervous this time. Gaildorf last season would have carried more pressure, but he had practically been polishing the trophy from the first few GPs of this year, and nobody had been able to touch him since. I imagine he would be aiming to run his usual race and the number one plate would bolt itself back into his bike by default. Mickael is also too professional to wobble at the vital moment. He had won enough races – a couple of titles in America – and was the defending Champion. I figured the butterflies were weak ones at best.

Josh Coppins had been cleared controversially, in my opinion, but he still looked like a troubled man. His Italian Honda team promptly sacked him after the hearing. He started practice with a blank red bike and was stationed in the tent of Corrado Maddii's satellite Honda set-up. After the drama of the last two months, it was probably the very last thing he needed when trying to put the whole mess behind him. I heard a whisper that the team was allegedly in financial trouble, and that getting rid of the rider was one way to avoid paying his salary. Luckily for Coppins, Honda Europe stepped in and apparently demanded that the Italians hand over a factory bike to their number one rider.

Fred Bolley held a special press conference in Germany to announce and explain his retirement. I had been told after Genk, and he made the amazing news official a week before Gaildorf. Bolley was only twenty-eight years old and was expressing a desire to try his hand at road racing. His reasons for leaving motocross and the 250 class that he had dominated in

1999 and again in 2000, I could completely understand. He stated that the effort and work required to be at the top in motocross and compete with the likes of Pichon was something that he felt he could not do anymore, and he identified supersport racing as a way of still enjoying racing motorcycles, but with half the amount of stress and dedication. His point highlights perfectly the intense level of physical and mental strength that motocross demands in comparison to other motorsports.

It's something I have struggled with in my career at various stages, and the fact that I had to wait until I was twenty-nine years old to earn the rewards I believe my talent merited, was proof that to be the best, you can't be half-hearted. Fred believed that he didn't have the will to make that depth of commitment any more, and I reckon a lot of riders knew that, deep down, a small part of us felt the same way, because most have been racing a motocross bike since early childhood. A 'Bolley moment' will come to us all eventually; some will welcome the fact more than others.

I was still ready to give all that I had to race and win, and I was confident that my urge to hang up the goggles would not come any time soon, even though I was two years older than Fred. He appeared relaxed and content with his decision after the news had come out, and that automatically made him a threat again to my designs on fourth place. He would be fast and loose this weekend. I get on well with Frederic, because he is a cheerful and happy guy. I was pleased for him that he had the strength to try a different direction with his career, and I made a mental note to try and get hold of one of his jerseys at the last race for my collection.

In the week leading up to Gaildorf, I had finally fully accepted that my Championship-winning year had been followed by a season of unwanted learning and unexpected hard work. Two factors meant that the journey to Gaildorf wasn't a barrel of laughs. I was still having the same backwards and forwards, 'something gained, something lost' process of developing the KTM to my liking enough to win races, and this put us both at the sharp edge. Thanks to the fact that we had endured nine GPs and had yet to experience more than two weekends in a row without some sort of problem, I now rolled into the paddock on Fridays, thinking there was little chance of victory. As I mentioned before, the battle begins in your head, days before you even get near a bike.

The suspension trouble was a constant lead weight around my neck and, over the last four months, we hadn't had the resources, opportunities or expertise to get it sorted. The time constraints were such that we were forced to experiment and test in qualifying, and even in some races. I was competing with different swinging arms and rear-end suspension units, while also swapping front forks with regularity – in short, the apple cart was never stable and when I quite liked one adjustment, the bike felt upset in another area. All this activity and sustained confusion throws your preparation ideas to the wind.

Instead of having a test team back at the factory, we were forced to do the development ourselves, and subsequently we landed in this mess.

The second reason for my acceptance was the appearance of the production model of my factory machine. I was getting scared because I always stand by my word in saying that KTM's production motorcycles are of the highest quality, but if the 250 going into the shops was anything like my race bike, then they might be in a bit of trouble.

So, when I jumped on it, I don't think I've ever been so shocked in all my life to find that the bike was excellent. Mind you, the deluge of information the factory had gained from our exploits and mishaps for five months must have helped the firm find an excellent middle ground. I was not going to be World Champion and may even struggle to register a win, but it seemed like the frustration and effort had not been entirely in vain. My professional duty to KTM felt partially vindicated. I had hardly helped the marketing campaign with my endeavours on the track, but I like to think that my complaints and comments had aided the birth of the factory's quality two-stroke 250 for the public.

After a brief test, we decided to raid the production model for parts we thought might help us at the GP. Up to now, the prototype race bike (the model that had been made purely for the track) and I were not gelling or working as one. I couldn't play with it. After nine GPs, I was tired of being a bit-part player in the World Championships, and I approached riding the bike with trepidation and reluctance, rather than enthusiasm.

Instead of requesting specially-made parts that took time to machine, fit, test and evaluate, we took what the firm had prepared for Joe Bloggs and found it sufficient for our needs. The production suspension was virtually the first component we nicked. Sadly, it proved to be far too soft in qualifying, and was bottoming out all over the circuit. Under sunny, warm and very dry conditions, I took seventh position and faced more negative remarks from the WP guys about how it would not have worked in the first place. 'At least we tried', was my reply, and we then set about trying to cure it and get some traction at the back end, where we were losing a lot of performance.

The production KTM 250 was a very good motorcycle, one that I thought was instantly more rideable and workable, and at last it seemed as if we had a firm basis from which to plough forwards with our job as the forefront of the two-stroke development plan.

On Saturday night, we relaxed in the camper. I fixed my goggles with tear-offs and the roll-off canisters. It's a time-consuming process, but one that I like to do myself. Naomi is fantastic for me at the races. She looks after Gracie all day and makes sure that I can have half an hour, either to unwind or just think about my riding instead of running around after the little one. It is so reassuring to have her there. I often confide my thoughts and feelings to her through the weekend, and during the course of this season, she had helped get a lot off my plate. We have experienced some real highs and lows together, and I cannot overstate how important she is to me. Her involvement in the paddock itself has changed a bit in the last three or four years. Back in the day, she used to do all the little jobs, like cleaning my boots or the crash helmet and making food for the guys when we were a privateer unit at Suzuki. With the success at KTM, her participation began to shrink, as other people took over certain responsibilities. She didn't have to wait long before her hands were full once again, however, with tiny Gracie. If I try to take stock of the 2002 season, then a big chunk of it was unsatisfactory, but travelling to the races with my family and combining my two big passions meant the year was, in another way, fantastic.

Like 2001, the weather for Sunday was great. I completed warm-up without any problems, and definitely felt more relaxed in the waiting area than twelve months previously. Pichon had pole and took the first position in the gate on the left side, ready to run inside the hairpin turn. The first corner was almost exactly the same as in Genk, except that the bend was a bit wider and also ran slightly downhill, as opposed to the flat surface of the Belgian circuit. I counted seven slots along and took my place, with Chicco on my left and Johnny Aubert on my right. The first ten metres or so beyond the gate was grass turf, which would be interesting. The wheel would not grip so well over this patch before hitting the mud, so a good lift away from the line was even more important.

An innovation in the last few years to help riders make the best start possible and to cope with the blast of acceleration is the anti-lift system. Apparently invented by Maddii, when his rider, Claudio Federici, complained that he could not keep the bike from wheeling on an uphill start, it involves the front fork hooking onto the mudguard and keeping the suspension depressed until you're out and away from the gate. As soon as the front wheel touches a bump, the mudguard pops off the grooved lip on the fork and the bike rights itself. It's a clever little idea and very useful.

As soon as the start was signalled, I was running. After a bit of wheel-spin, the front end did not bounce and return to its normal shape. I gassed the bike and it squirmed in its squashed shape. I almost hit Chicco after a couple of metres, and had to back off slightly because the front end still hadn't released itself from the catch – I didn't want to hit a big bump and get slung off. Finally, it did pop up, but I had lost ground and entered the first turn in the lower half of the pack. Desperate to turn in tight and retake some positions, I knew it was easily my worst start of the season, and I would have to 'panic attack' the field ahead to give myself a chance of making a decent position.

Heading down and into the left, I felt like I had the whole field in front of me. I kept close to the apex but still carried some speed and saw a gap in the middle of the corner, so I slid across and was able to go a bit faster than I had anticipated. Going back up the hill and to the right, I was baulked by Beggi as I tried to head around the outside, and wasn't going to gain any more places that way.

The snake of riders entered various s-sections, and I saw Chicco way out in front, having grabbed the hole-shot. We plunged into a cambered hairpin left that was in a dip, with numerous riders taking the high outside line. I headed for the rutted line in the inside and hit Lalloz, who had almost stopped in the turn. That slowed me up even more, as I had to wait for him to get out of the rut before I could accelerate anywhere. I drove past as we both exited the turn, and then had to fight my way through the remainder of the lap, going past the pits down in a shocking seventeenth position.

Reviewing the race later on television, Mickael had taken the lead on lap three, due to a classic case of luck that is usually ninety-nine per cent essential in any World Championship. Chicco was out front by a good second or two and got slightly out of shape in a narrow, deeply rutted corner. He flipped out of the line and ran onto the inside of the track. Just as he corrected himself and went to rejoin the circuit, his back wheel caught in the green plastic fencing. It chewed the material up, locking the wheel and putting him on the ground. Pichon flew past, thank you very much, and went on to win the race and the title once again.

On the very next lap, I had moved up into thirteenth and was surprised at the time to see the number seventy-three machine of the Italian right in front of me. I followed Chicco for almost five laps, and we had a good race jostling for twelfth and then eleventh, as we passed McFarlane. Nearing the middle of the GP, I went to make a pass over the first jump after the swirly s-turns at the beginning of the lap. I was right next to Chicco, as we drove up the short hill to approach the take-off. I gassed the bike and launched over the edge of the leap to make sure I had the speed advantage and the position over the Yamaha when we landed. The move worked, but also meant the timing of the jump was slightly off and I hit the ground a little later than usual to make the next turn. As the ground absorbed the bike and suspension, I realised I had made a slight error. The track surface was a lot rougher off the racing line, where it had been ripped up by the diggers, and 'grabbed' the bike as I ran wide. To my sudden surprise, the KTM stopped dead. I hadn't stalled, but for a split second I was going nowhere and lost all my momentum – like leaping into a puddle of glue. The abrupt landing and halt forced all my weight forward, as my body did not register the inertia, and I smashed the handlebars with my chest, almost knocking the wind out of me. I initially struggled to breathe, and the shooting pain coming from my upper abdomen would later turn out to be another cracked rib, with a tasty patch of bruising emerging in the following few days.

I turned the bike, engaged a lower gear and cursed my error for losing ground on Chicco. The incident lasted no more than several seconds, but I summoned all my resolve in the next three laps, as I fought to get my breath back and keep my race position safe from McFarlane, who was just behind. Chicco was off and away, but I managed to catch him while we passed a few other riders that dragged us up to eighth and ninth. He then went on to pass Carl Nunn for seventh. I ran out of time to pass Carl, but was elevated to eighth after riding past a prostate Johnny Aubert on the last lap, three corners from the finish. The Frenchman had been in second and was in the frame for his first-ever podium, until a suspension failure launched him over the bars and straight into hospital. He was quite banged up and had to stay there for several days.

For me, it was another race and another occurrence of lousy luck. Overshooting the jump had its risk like any overtaking move, but I did not expect to be halted in such drastic fashion by the track. With two races left, I had almost ran out of opportunities to register a podium result and, as the season's end approached, I turned my head to what I could accomplish in terms of results. My resignation that 2002 was all about trying to shape a new bike meant that I viewed any victory at all now as a very remote possibility, particularly as Pichon had won again.

The chase was over, and now everybody was looking at their possible final ranking. I was pleased that I had finished just ahead of Gundersen. Bolley, however, had taken third behind Beirer, and an off-form Coppins could only settle for fourth. Fred had two GPs left of his career, and I was sure that fourth position in the Championship meant a lot more to me than it did to him. He had gained seven points over me in Gaildorf, and that meant I could not afford to finish behind him in the Czech

Republic in two weeks' time because it would leave too much to do at the last race in Russia. Gundersen was also still in the picture and trailed me by five points.

After his third in Genk, Gordon had a miserable GP and couldn't adjust his bike to suit the track – he finally took sixteenth to complete another underwhelming weekend. A GP like Gaildorf, with its eighth position and second-lowest result of the year, does force you to look at how shite your season has been, particularly when you have to watch the winning team and rider celebrating, and look at all the well-wishers gathering round.

I went and offered my congratulations and, while I could feel some affection for Mickael and what he had done, in the moment of that handshake, I also knew that I had failed in my goal because someone else had the trophy and the glory. All there is left is a list of excuses and reasons to justify the absence of a world title, and you have to try your best to learn to deal with the situation and come out the other side the better for it.

★ ★ ★

Mickael's path to success is simple to identify. It's the same reason that Valentino Rossi and Michael Schumacher win every other week – it's called the unbeatable package. The elements consist of talent, fitness, a fast and well-developed machine, a strong and supportive team, luck and, the cherry on the cake, insurmountable confidence.

Riders who are not World Champions may have some of these attributes, but not all of them at the same time. The levels of the criteria bounce up and down in your career like the equaliser graphics on a stereo. The closest I came to having all firing at once was firstly in 2000, where maybe I lacked a bit of luck and having the edge that confidence gives you but, in

2001, all the elements peaked. The whole combination rose to the occasion and, despite two broken collarbones, the seven GP wins and ultimate prize testify to the strength and potency of the 'winning package'. For 2002 in Valkenswaard, I knew that I was missing several parts and it set the tone for the season.

The only way I can describe the weekend when you become a World Champion is to resort to cliché and say that it truly is a whirlwind of emotions, from the nervousness and steely-faced tension of the preliminaries to the realisation, buoyancy and immensely satisfying knowledge of the treasure you have gained. World Championships and race wins are the only reason most of us dedicate ourselves to the intense life the way we do. Set the bar high or don't set it at all.

Gaildorf 2001 went to plan. I had won in Switzerland at the previous GP, in the meeting directly after Namur, which put the title within reach. I passed Luigi Seguy and Kenneth Gundersen in the first third of the race, with my own version of the Pichon attack strategy, and only eased off when I had an eight-second lead under the sweltering Swiss sun. Ramon, by now my only challenger (Eggens pulled out of the GP once again), had made his way to third, but with my seventh win of the year from ten GPs, I had amassed an eighty-seven-point advantage over the Belgian. With only a hundred possible points and four races remaining, if Ramon won in Gaildorf, I could finish as low as fourth and still be World Champion.

In the build-up to the most important GP of my life, I had to run around getting passes for all my family and friends who wanted to come out to the race. I struck a deal with the attractive Italian girl who looked after the VIP hospitality for Dorna, and managed to get some good food and seats in the Cross Club, and even had Kirk flown out to see how all his efforts were going to be rewarded. Naomi said there was no way she could miss the GP, despite being seven months pregnant, and ended up driving across with the family.

Again, it was excellent weather for motocross in southern Germany, and I already had my mind set on the fact that I could win the Championship in Gaildorf, but I didn't *need* to. I wasn't about to take any risks at this stage, and with my comfortable point cushion, I could afford to err on the side of caution. Of course, with everybody travelling out, I wanted to win and take the title in style, but because of the hard work put in during races like Ernée and Namur, I was not in a position where I had to churn out a victory. This knowledge removed some of the pressure. Gaildorf was not last-chance saloon.

I thought that I was keeping quite a cool head through Saturday and that evening, but my family were making it hard to settle down! They were much more nervous than me and were bad at trying to hide it. People were apparently under instructions not to disturb me or talk about what might happen, which made things worse and hardly diffused the tension.

The times were very close in practice, with the top six of us separated by two seconds. I was at the back of the bunch, and could see that Chicco and Seguy were enjoying the track. I was concentrating on the bike set-up, and had one or two problems finding some traction in the morning. We tweaked the suspension and I felt the improvement in the afternoon heats. I had a fun ride with Chicco in the qualifying race and just beat him. So far so good.

With the heat win under my belt that night, I had an incredible urge to win the Championship by recording my eighth GP victory of the year. It would be a fitting way to finish the season, after all, my lowest result all year had been second place on two occasions (excluding the DNS in Sweden). Dougie Lampkin was in the paddock making a visit, and we chatted for a while – he is a guy who certainly knows a thing or two about winning world titles. A journalist asked me how long had I been thinking about the GP in Germany and what it might mean. I had to give an honest answer and said, 'Since I was about six years old.'

I slept well that night, but with the coming morning on my mind. When I woke, I sensed that this wasn't just a normal race day (despite trying to tell myself it was), and I could feel the weight of expectation in the air somehow. I spent the morning keeping out of people's way and submerging myself in my music for a bit longer than usual. I tried not to make too much out of this GP. I would have another chance if things did not work out.

I took a great start, and flew by Thomas Traversini on the first lap to lead the world once again. Before I could break away, Ramon was also turning in some fast laps, and we had a scrap at the front of the field for a few circulations. We collided coming out of the second turn and brushed each other. At that point, I decided that Ramon was riding too close to the edge for my liking. We were turning in similar lap-times, but I let him pull away so there was no danger of us both ending up in the mud – I had done too much of that in recent months. I was concentrating on the race, and found it easy to block the Championship out of my head for the first half.

Before I could think about settling for second, Luigi Seguy caught me up and virtually put my heart in my mouth. Luigi is a fast but wild rider, and can sometimes be a little careless on the track. Approaching one of Gaildorf's chicane kinks, he ran far too fast into the curve and slammed into the back of me. The knock startled me and almost threw me off-balance. Fortunately, Seguy took the brunt of the impact and half-fell off his machine. I breathed again and then kept a careful watch on his progress. It took him another couple of laps to come back at me, and this time I practically moved over to let him through. With the speed Luigi was carrying, I knew it would only be a matter of time before he caught Ramon, and I had no complaints about him dumping my rival to second.

With about ten minutes to go in the GP, the intensity of the moment and the proximity of my goal struck me. I suddenly felt very tired. I'm sure my fitness wasn't at its peak, and with the mental drain of concentration over the weekend, I felt like my body was going limp. I was going to be World Champion in four laps and I found it difficult not to go all dreamy. My pace suffered with my distraction, and Chicco caught and overtook me at the start of the last lap. Dropping to fourth made me panic a little and annoyed me immensely, but I was powerless to retaliate. I was still World Champion and was a spent force in this particular GP.

The last lap seemed like the slowest circulation of a race track I have ever done. I was anxious to get it finished, but was shattered and a little dizzy. I looked at my lines and watched the jumps and sections of the circuit pass by. Halfway around the last lap, the elation and emotion washed over me and I found it hard to ride. I felt a rush of well-being and the tension flowed out of me. I could barely cross the finish line and just coasted over the final jump.

Finally, it had happened. It was all over. I didn't know what to do with myself. This one thing that I had been searching and working for all my life had finally arrived, and I hadn't really known what to expect or how to deal with it.

People have asked me what it felt like that afternoon, and my first response is always 'tiring'. It wasn't so much the strains and sprains of the season, but the fact that it had been over fifteen years in the making. It is a long time to be waiting and trying for one goal, and I sensed that all the highs and lows poured out of me in those hours after the chequered flag was waved in my face. Whenever I have achieved something, I'm always the first to sing my praises, but this just seemed too big. I still can't believe it to this day. I am a World Champion, the only British rider ever to win the 125cc title, and I will be in the history books. It has always been this shining beacon that was so far away.

If riders are only as good as their last race, then I have made my career a tough and eventful one through my own indiscipline or some very unlucky breaks. But, finally, I had made the top grade. 2001, combined with the team and my family, became a defining period of my life.

The race after I won the title in 2001 took place at Leirop in Holland. Before all the hassle with my neck, I did a big television interview for Dorna as part of a feature about my Championship. They asked how important Naomi and the baby were to my success, and I couldn't answer for a minute or two because I was fighting back the tears. My eyes welled up. I was World Champion and I was having a family

For that very brief moment, it all hit me. I was the fastest and the strongest 125cc rider on the planet in 2001, and that comforting thought will always leave me content with my career until the day I die.

★ ★ ★

I left Gaildorf in a tired daze in 2001, and pretty much repeated the feat in 2002, except without the hugs, scent of champagne and feeling of simmering elation. On Sunday night, we arrived at a hotel in Munich and travelled to the factory the next day for a press afternoon and another test of the production bike. A positive point from Gaildorf was how well the standard components on the bike had worked, and I felt within reach of a frame of reference to improve my race machine in my own style. Using production parts could be seen as a backward step for a factory team, but to me it was a beneficial move.

The highlight of the week arrived in the hotel on Monday evening when little Gracie took her first steps. It was awesome to watch her push away her walker and then slowly wobble to catch it up. Little did I know that the next week in the build-up to the Grand Prix of the Czech Republic, I would also be taking some vital steps myself with the KTM.

We took the suspension units, the bikes and all the equipment back to the factory on Monday, and I stayed in Austria, this time to test with Peter Johansson, in some sessions that would prove to be nothing short of a revelation.

1 September 2002: Round Eleven
Czech Grand Prix, Loket

THE KTM factory has always been an impressive sight: an entire complex dedicated to off-road excellence. I have become very familiar with the place as it's got bigger and bigger over the years, and was even more impressed to see the rate of progress on the new £25 million motocross workshops that were being built across the road.

KTM is moving places. It seems that they cannot build enough bikes to meet demand, and the sales charts looks a little like the side of Everest. In 2001, they sold 55,000; in 2002, they surpassed 65,000; and I believe the goal for 2003 is 75,000. It's insane how much it has grown.

KTM have always put decent motorcycles into the World Championships, but since the mid–1990s, they have got so much better, and the company has expanded rapidly with their success. Back in the day, their production bikes were nothing like the race models and not as reliable, now they have progressed immensely and the difference is marginal.

If KTM's vast new visual commitment to their MX racing wasn't enough of a perk–up, then the results we gained in testing in Austria in the week before the eleventh round of twelve in the Czech Republic finally saw some light shining on our season. For the first time in 2002, I had the advice and help of Peter Johansson.

I have known Peter for over twelve years, and have been racing against him for a large chunk of that time. He joined up with KTM in 1999, and enjoyed some of the best years of his career, finishing second to Andrea Bartolini in the 500s and third behind Bervoets and Smets in 2000. Johansson's manner and personality mean that he was a popular member of the set–up, and his technical know-how was crucial in KTM's emergence as a leader in the off–road production industry.

Peter had decided to call it a day at the end of 2001, after a pre-season arm injury had largely ended his quest for a world title. He only made eight appearances in the GPs that year, and showed nothing like the form that had made him one of KTM's most valued riders and a leading 500cc campaigner. The firm signed Yves Demaria for 2002, to ride alongside Joel Smets, but kept Peter in the frame by positioning him as KTM's arm in Sweden, and making sure that he got the equipment to compete in as many GPs as he wanted. It all went pear-shaped for him again at the first race in Valkenswaard, when he crashed and broke his wrist. Removed from the pressure of fulfilling a factory contract, unsurprisingly, Johansson took his time to heal, but this did not help us because he missed a vital part of his 2002 deal, namely that of test rider.

Peter has a lot of experience and is also a really great guy. He is laid-back and likes to take his young family with him to the races. He's someone who I think is quite similar to me in many ways, and we have had a good friendship since our introduction as team-mates in 1990, when riding for Yamaha. He has a big heart and is always willing to help you out – there are not many like him in the MX industry.

Fully recovered, he could now travel to Austria and take part in tests for the 2003 250 production model, and we escaped to another track with some mechanics and the WP guys for one day with my race bike and the production model. I explained to him that I did not feel safe enough on the bike to be able to really push in the GPs. He put me at ease right away, by saying that he had watched my riding on television and could see that I was struggling with the handling.

On the track, Peter is one of those guys who has a very sensitive touch and feel with a motorcycle. He can come along and say, 'Go one click harder on the rebound', do one lap, come back in and say to the mechanic, 'I said put it one click harder, you've gone softer.'

Peter started out as a test rider with Yamaha working on their YZN, and then went on to get a racing deal, so his help was of huge benefit. It rapidly became apparent in those few hours of testing how much we had missed his input and opinion. We were riding together and trying numerous combinations of the factory and production machines. His fresh ideas, and the suggestions of one or two other people who also tried it out that day, made the puzzle less complicated. At this stage, I was suffering from a lack of direction with regards to improving the bike. I was stuck and generally in a rut. I couldn't get it working and my tolerance with WP had been eroded. Without Peter's help, there would have been a decent chance of finishing the season none the wiser.

He knew exactly what he was talking about and did a pretty good job of convincing the WP guys with his knowledge and feedback that his settings were the way to go, something I had been unable to manage. He modelled the bike to how he would like to ride it, and trying his preferences, I felt immediately more secure. He explained to the suspension techs that their units did not have to absorb every bump, because that would make the bike unstable when pushed to its limit. From that philosophy, we tried to work from a base where I would feel safe.

We made the shock much harder, worked on low-speed compression, increased the rebound and made the front forks stiffer. Suspension is such a delicate issue to get right. Riders can affect the handling immensely with their weight, body and riding position on the bike. We got the 250 to turn better because Peter thought I was too far forward on the motorcycle. We moved the air filter and the fuel tank, and that also helped. I had some attention paid to my chest, which was sore but ignorable, and got on with the riding, trying all the settings that Peter was recommending.

Within about three hours, incredibly, he had more or less cured the handling problem by at least fifty per cent. The rear suspension was where I had been suffering the most. The bike would hop around everywhere. His suggestions transformed the bike and made it a hell of a lot better, and I could therefore go faster into turns without holding back. The back end felt far more predictable. WP saw the lap-times and they were persuaded. We packed up after the tests, and I felt very happy with the progress we had made. I had been able to really chuck the bike into corners compared to before, and thought that I would easily carry more race speed come the next GP.

The circuit of Loket was just over four hours' drive from KTM's base, so Fred, Vincent and I left the following Thursday night in the motorhome and arrived there late that evening. The weather in central Europe had been pretty bad in the weeks surrounding Gaildorf and leading up to Loket. The Czech Republic in particular had suffered, with some areas of the city of Prague lying submerged under water, as the country tried to deal with severe flooding, and made the news all over the continent for the wrong reasons. Luckily for the GP, Loket is situated almost 150km east of Prague, near the German border. The area was unaffected and a cancellation was not on the cards.

Friday was a very interesting day, as Neil set up the location shoot for Alloy's first catalogue, and I spent the day modelling for photographer Steve 'Bingo' Jackson. It was all good fun, and cool to dress in the new gear that would soon be available to buy. I had been wearing an assortment of prototype racing designs and colours throughout the year, as well as the leisure side of the brand, which was very much to my liking and carried my 'sixty-four' identity. We took a lot of photos in and around the track, and it was a pleasant way to kill a day of waiting before the GP cranked into life.

The circuit lay on the side of a long hill that must have been angled at more than forty-five degrees. The entrance, pits and gate were stationed at the top, and the track worked its way right down to the furthest part at the bottom – where only the most energetic fans would venture to watch from – before heading back up. Loket was not the roughest of tracks, but the soil was good and it was still very technical with its many inclines and slopes dug into the hill, making the most of a natural ravine that ate into the east side. The very wide and lengthy start straight, located in the ravine, was the only flat part of the circuit. The rest of the course plummeted off sheer drops, weaving up and down twisty and fast sections and providingsome hefty jumps. I had never raced at Loket before, and the track looked like quite a challenge for the re-worked suspension settings on the KTM.

My mood and that of the team had improved greatly. The bike was running well and felt like a tool capable of some good results. Practice and qualifying passed without incident, and I notched a time with my final lap of nine that placed me right behind, and only just over half a second away from, Pichon, who had pole again. For the first GP of the season, I was posting times and then being able to beat them. I can't describe what a shot in the arm the bike's new lease of life meant to my confidence. Now it seemed like we were capable of consistently lapping amongst the leaders, and I hadn't looked forward to a race as much in the whole year.

I really pushed the machine in practice and almost lost it a couple of times, but managed to save the front end before it vanished, when in the past I would have certainly have been face down in the mud again. My physical condition was poor by a GP winner's standard. My chest still bothered me sometimes from all the bashing my ribs had taken. I had not managed two consecutive weeks of training all season, due to my injury problems. Kirk had been calling me to go work out instead of the other way round, and I could sense his frustration sometimes. He said it was visibly clear that I was about sixty per cent fit and had been struggling a little more than usual after about twenty to twenty-five minutes of the race. Deep down, I knew he was right, and any tiredness on my part would reflect badly on him, but recently I hadn't had the inspiration or motivation to get working in the gym when various parts of me ached, and riding the bike had turned out to be a flat experience.

As if to re-affirm that 2002 had been a season of misdirection, the 250cc two-stroke had finally become a motorcycle worthy of on-track success, but my condition to take advantage of my 'new' bike was not up to scratch. We had passed each other on our respective slopes. I was on a downward incline of confidence, motivation and fitnes,s while the bike moved upwards, slowly becoming better, peaking in the last month with the appearance of the proddie bike a week before Gaildorf, and speeding onwards with the help of Johansson. Sadly, our paths had not crossed at any stage, and the nearest we came to touching was in Loket.

I also had my family in attendance. Na and Gracie travelled out with my sister, Sarah, her husband, Mark, my nephew, Jordon, and my niece, Abigayle. We certainly tested the sleeping capacity of the camper. It was crowded, but by this stage of the season I was more laid-back, only worrying about Bolley and Gundersen and wrapping up fourth place. It was nice to have them around and they were clearly enjoying a weekend away. Mark and Jordon were really buzzing about the racing, and the atmosphere inside the camper was always fun and relaxed.

The next day the weather was cloudy and cool. I changed into the new black and charcoal-grey race gear from Alloy and completed warm-up in second place. By the time of the race, I was feeling more and more pumped about getting a good result.

I picked the inside position in the gate on the far left, with only Bolley to my right. The start straight was perhaps the longest we had seen this season, and curved upwards sharply into a left hairpin and then on to another flat stretch that ran back adjacent to the way we had just come off the line. I had plenty of time and space to attack the straight, and knew my placement on the inside of the corner would put me right into contention, if I could carry enough speed on the rise into the bend.

I gated well and flew up to the turn. I barged Bolley slightly wide and almost made the hole-shot, but Coppins had the slightest of advantages as we turned left and into the uphill 180-degree corner. Second place was good enough as we shot along the next straight that was flanked by a packed grandstand seating area. Heading right and uphill again to rise and run behind the seating section, Beirer crashed and took a few riders with him. Good news for Coppins, who was now fighting for his number two plate and leading the GP.

Half a lap later, and Pichon passed me after a tabletop going into the fast downhill. He muscled his way through on the inside on the tight left turn that rounded off the slope, and I had to move over slightly so that neither of us would crash. We were side by side in the corner, but he had more grunt exiting the section to take second and set off after Coppins, who was just ahead. I held onto his back wheel more successfully than in the past, but he had a little bit of extra speed out of every corner that I could not match. Mickael had the lead by lap three, and was clearly not suffering a lack of motivation. He was chasing records now, and if he could triumph here and in Russia, then he'd have the distinction of the highest number of consecutive wins ever with nine (the previous record being eight, set by Smets in the 2000 500cc season).

I found my speed to be comfortable and, as I sat behind Josh, we slowly pulled away from Jussi Vehvilainen in fourth, while Pichon started to stretch a distance in front. Encouragingly, from the pit-board times Fred kept giving me, Pichon and Coppins were not pulling out any more time on me, and the distance remained the same, with us all running at intervals of a couple of seconds. I knew Josh would be at his slowest in the early stages of the race, and concentrated on being able to chip away at the two- to three-second margin and maybe start a fight for second.

I was finding it relatively easy to go at the same pace as them. The fact that I wasn't losing ground every lap gave me the hard physical evidence that we had made a huge leap forward with the bike. It wasn't perfect and wasn't on the same level yet as the Suzuki, or maybe even the Honda, but it was enough, and felt like a eating a gourmet dinner after feeding on crumbs all season.

Inside my mind, I was anxious to see how far I could push it. If I drilled the thing through the bottom section of the track, would the suspension start to play up again? I had several new questions about the bike, but sadly my body was in no condition to find the answers. I continued to ride as hard as I could, but I found the race more tiring than usual and knew that normally as I approached the latter stages, I would have given something extra to propel me to the line and maybe make up an extra position. It was hard to see that resource coming into play.

Try as I might, I could not get close enough to Josh to attempt to overtake. The downhill approach into the tight left turn, where Pichon had passed me, was a good spot to make a move, but as I jumped the tabletop and kept the bike as low as possible to drive down the slope every lap, I was not in a good enough position to attack. I was also getting signs that Vehvilainen was increasing his pace, so I now had to watch my back as well. In the three laps between eight and eleven, I pushed hard enough to break away from my pursuer but Josh had also found his rhythm and extended the gap to four seconds.

In the last ten minutes, I tired, and Coppin,s who is arguably the strongest of all of us at the end of a race, pulled away slightly, leaving me with a distant view of the Honda more or less seven seconds ahead. I was pleased to see that Bolley had retired late into the GP.

For the last four or five laps, I maintained the hard-earned four-second advantage I held over Vehvilainen. At one stage, he was really trying hard and had made up some time, drawing slowly closer. Although I felt the pace, there was absolutely no chance that I was going to surrender my first 250 podium of the year. I had enough will and determination to ensure that he would not get close enough to pass, and my job became easier when he must have made a slight mistake and dropped back by a second or two.

On the last lap, I had a good look at Jussi going over the jumps, just to gauge if a final charge was on the cards. We had started to get caught up in some backmarkers, and I had to hurry through them a bit quicker than I would normally have done on the last circulation. Halfway round the circuit, I saw the distance and relaxed; at last.

In the immediate furore that follows a race, you are thinking about many things and nothing at the same time because of the fatigue, which can hit you quite hard if you are struggling physically or the conditions have been tough. Various thoughts revolve around your head: 'Where did so-and-so finish? How many points do I have now? Where are the guys? Why wasn't the bike shifting that well? I need water. Thank God I didn't crash on that turn on the third lap. Where do I go to reach the podium? From where did Naomi and Gracie watch the race?'

The team rush to greet you, offer words, hopefully of congratulations, and then you head back to the podium or the paddock. One location is busy with fans, photographers, well-wishers, family and television cameras, while the other is usually empty, and is a stark and solemn reminder that as a factory rider, you haven't cut the mustard this time.

Thankfully, in the penultimate GP of 2002, I was surrounded by people and bustle. A comfortable third completed the most productive and enjoyable week of the season. Finally, I believed that I stood where I belonged, and had that glow of relief and satisfaction at earning a good result.

The Czech GP was another step forward in a slow year, but it was a significant one, and everybody in the team seemed to let out a collective sigh of relief as we finally got on the podium. Gordon's fifth place completed a decent enough weekend. In response to a press conference question (a post-race ritual that had seemed so commonplace in 2001, now felt like a positive treat) I said that, in some ways, a podium did make it seem like a weight had fallen off my shoulders. Then I remembered that this is my job and third should represent a reasonable day in the office. It was hard to be too over the moon. I should have had at least two podiums earlier in the year, and while I savoured the champagne ceremony on the elevated steps, there was still the feeling that this sensation was overdue.

However, in the context, gaining that first top three in a way was like an absolution. While my critics were satisfied to see that my naïve claims of being able to fight for the title with Pichon were dashed, and I had to face doubts about my ability from various corners, even some from within my own team, I always believed in myself. Although I knew that, deep down, I could only blame my lack of outright success on bad luck for so long, I still was, and am, a World Champion and I earned that distinction for a reason. That thought remained in my head throughout the year, sometimes dimly lit in the background, as I endured the numerous sticky situations and moments of frustration when your confidence has taken such a battering that you look at the bike before practice and think 'There is no way I'm going to get anywhere on that thing'.

As our high expectations were crushed by the harsh reality of our technical predicament, 2002 became the vision that nobody expected. However, part of the dream scenario we had originally envisaged had at last arrived in Loket. I did think after the GP that everything in racing is relative. Everyone wants to win, but your levels of happiness are often graded by what it is possible to achieve. If anyone worth a title shot had the bike I had in 2000 and 2001, then by rights they wouldn't be satisfied if they weren't hitting the top three every weekend. On the other hand, there are guys out there who, by limitations of ability or machinery, can only dream of even stepping on the podium, never mind a winning a World Championship. I like to think that I have been 'every' rider at some stage, and have experienced the full spectrum of racing emotions. When I haven't been fit, or have been thrashing a dog of a bike for two motos, I've walked away from a circuit, buzzing about a result that wasn't necessarily a win but that I would have snatched out of someone's hand prior to the event.

With all that had happened in the year, fourth position was not looking too bad. The 250s is a difficult and competitive class. When a three-times World Champion like Chicco can mange only tenth on a works Yamaha, then you know that fourth isn't so disastrous in the context of things. Bolley's third DNF of the year was good news for me in the standings. Gundersen's eighth place in Loket was also a small blessing. I was now fourth, twelve points ahead of Kenneth and thirty behind Pit. All I had to do in Russia was to finish in front of, or close to, the Kawasaki to walk away with that number four plate.

Now I saw that Bolley was more of less out of the running, I had to keep an eye on Gundersen. I had already gifted him a rookie win in Teutschenthal and there was no way he was going to get more charity. The campaign wasn't quite over yet – as a professional, I owed KTM fourth place at least, and finally I had a bike that might just draw me up alongside my old French rival.

The 125cc GP had seen the close chase for the Championship take another step towards being decided. Maschio had comprehensively beaten everyone in Gaildorf, and proceeded to do the same in Loket. He pulled a major result out of the bag when it was desperately needed. His back-to-back wins, after a dodgy mid-season spell without any podiums, was perfectly timed and made him a deserving favourite for the final outcome in Russia. The Kawasaki rider would now lead a host of KTMs into the last GP of the season with a ten-point advantage.

Stefan Everts won his sixth world title in the 500s by finishing second to Smets. It had been Joel's third win on the trot in a mini-revival, but Everts' 100 per cent podium record had merely postponed the inevitable until Loket, when a runner-up position was sufficient to elevate Stefan to the top of the record books.

The events of Loket certainly gave me optimism for 2003, where I had another year on my deal to race the 250. The time I needed and had missed in pre-season with the bike has been clocked up now, so maybe 2003 will be the year I was innocently expecting this time round.

The end of the season was fast approaching, and everybody was deep in the process of wrapping up talks on new contracts with teams and products. I was linked to Alloy and had most of my other sponsors tied up and sorted. I signed up to be in a video game, due for release in the middle of the year, so I should be appearing on a few Playstations soon. There are various others behind the scenes, and I owe a debt to people like Smith, DC Shoes, DEP, Airoh helmets and Alpinestars.

I am now working to attract some outside sponsors, so that maybe I can own a team at some stage. It's hard to bring people into the sport in this day and age when I get so little press coverage in the nationals. This is something I am trying to fix. Spreading the word about motocross, and my endeavours, can benefit us both.

★ ★ ★

I've always been keen to invest my money into my racing. It is my 'business', and I'll never understand these people who never pay cash into their own projects. In 1998, I spent all the money I had on racing, and then a load that I didn't have. My credit cards were full and the bank account was empty. At the end of 1999, I finally paid off around £30,000 of debt that I had accumulated through racing. I had a clean slate, and started to try and save. America in 1996 had been a tough season financially, but I had my best ever SX year with the budgeted Suzuki effort. It was around that time that I was thinking along the lines of setting up Excel, my sports management agency.

The germ of the idea came out of my negotiations and dealings with the Quiksilver sponsor I had that season I played a part in getting the backing (thanks to being friends with the owners), and then made sure that they got the right exposure and saw out most of the little details of the arrangement. I enjoyed the organisational aspects and making all the contacts back then, and it became something that I would like to explore more fully when my riding days are over, when I will have more time.

A few years later, I got to meet some of the footballers of Derby County FC and struck up some friendships. One of them asked me if I would consider being his agent, and I hadn't really thought about the sports management idea since America. There was no way I had the time or energy to set up an operation like that, so I sold the idea to Naomi's father, Gino, who was a keen football fan. I told him that I could bring the footballers and the sportsmen into the equation, if he could get his FIFA licence and run the numbers side. In 1999, Gino passed his exams and we were in business. I started to approach the players, putting out the feelers, and we finally went full-time with it in 2000.

To date, the company has been rolling for about eighteen months. We are doing okay. I thought I had seen some corrupt dealings in my time, but the world of football must take some beating. Managers have their own agents and seal up any players to benefit themselves. There are many double-deals that take place and a lot of secrecy, deception and tapping-up involved. Agents are by no means the bastions of innocence, and there are as many devious and bad ones as there are good, but I like to the think that with Excel we offer something a little different. There are not many agents out there that can say they are a World Champion or have been at the very top level of a sport, and I can offer that side to the younger players. From having competed since I was a little kid to making the sacrifices required to become a professional sportsman, I think I have many things in common with our clients and what they want to achieve. I know about the highs and lows they will go through, and can lend an ear or give some advice whenever they need it. Gino and I don't really like to be called agents, because we want to do much more than merely make some calls and push a contract through.

I take a deep interest in our players, what's going on in their careers and how I can help them to improve the mental side of their game. I want them to concentrate totally on their football, while knowing that Gino and I are looking after their interests, and I can be there any time they need any assistance, or even just a chat. At this time, Gino is pulling all the strings. I can do more meetings and negotiations in the off-season, but when I'm racing, I am basically on hand to make sure the guys are doing okay. I enjoy some of their company a lot and would definitely count them all as friends. Derby goalkeeper Lee Grant has virtually become a part of the family!

We have a good stable of young players now – Granty, Adam Murray, Izale McLeod, Pablo Mills, Lewis Hunt, Gerard Doherty and so on. Most of them play for the first teams of their respective clubs, and a few are in the England Under-21 squad. We also have a lot of contacts over in Spain, and have some deals with Spanish and Brazilian internationals. Excel has really grown in the last year-and-a-half. People are starting to know who we are, and while we are still a comparatively small fish at this stage, those who do business with us know that we are straight.

My vision for the future is to have representation from a variety of sports, not just football or motocross, and at the moment things are looking good for when I unclip my boots for the last time.

15 September 2002: Round Twelve
Russian Grand Prix, Park Extreme, Moscow
... and the ghosts of the Nations

THE DAY before flying out to Russia, I finished my responsibility with the Alloy catalogue by again linking up with Steve Jackson at his studios in London. People like *Vogue* and various agencies use the venue, and it all felt very professional and was again good fun, harking back to the days of my brief modelling career. I always enjoy looking the part, and have spent so much money over the years buying designer clothes. I am just as much a sucker for some Prada gear now when I am not permanently wearing Alloy or MX-related stuff.

I did not have much creative input into Alloy's riding gear lines, but I did state my preference for white riding gear, and think that it stands out quite well at races where not many others use the colour. The first time I wore the 'James Bond' outfit, as someone in the press dubbed it, was in Spain, and it was more or less my first choice (along with a smart-looking black number with pinstripe orange) for most of the GPs, until a new orange-and-black set arrived in Sweden.

After the photos had been completed, I then turned my attention to the final race of the season and boarded a plane at Heathrow for the flight to Moscow. The first GP in the eastern European country for almost twenty years (the last event was a 125 race in 1983), the final event of 2002 was a good example of the perks of the job that can arise, when the FIM announce the calendar at the start of the year and you learn of any new countries and places you will get to visit.

With the trip to Yakhroma, this would be the second circuit that nobody had ridden on before this season. I do not have a particular preference for any sort of circuit design, but I do tend to lean more to the ones like Bellpuig, Sevlievo and, as I would come to discover, Park Extreme, because of the blend of motocross skills they require

227

and the spectacle they create for fans and television; nobody wants to see a pack of riders disappear into the trees for a minute-and-a-half (we'll make an exception for Namur).

Boarding the plane, I was excited by the fact that we were travelling to a country with a lot of history and mystery about it. At the same time, I had heard enough rumours and stories about Moscow to be apprehensiv, so the trip was an uneasy one – I have never been the best of flyers!

My visa had been already sorted out by the team as we arrived in the airport – a dark and unwelcoming place, that did nothing to ease my imagination of finding a country that would be wearing a stark, visual representation of its troubles. The customs process was slow, and it was like being transported back in time by twenty years with all the hassle to get through. My impressions of Moscow were not favourable, and the only time I was happy for the duration of my four-day stay was when I was in another line to go through the customs barrier back to the other side.

The blatant presence of corruption hit us from the moment we walked through the airport door. The taxi drivers are experts, and can spot a tourist (mug) from a mile away. To get to our hotel, which we were told was a twenty-minute drive into the city, Nick and I had to pay 100 euros, an amount to which we reluctantly had to agree. Hiring cars was a no-no for this GP, due to the amount that get damaged, ripped off or stolen, so we were at the mercy of the cabbies and however much we could barter with their virtually non-existent English. Driving through the city, the contrast between the poor conditions and the occasional shockingly rich ones was surprising. For every Mercedes with blacked-out windows and a thumping stereo flying past on the road, there were thirty clapped-out vehicles that looked like they were ready to fall apart.

The hotel was a huge development with its own casino that screamed modernisation and money, and was unsurprisingly full of high-class hookers everywhere you went. The travel company that had organised most of the bookings and visas for the riders, teams and journalists had booked us into a safe enough place, but sadly, with the crazy Moscow traffic, it took between two and three hours to return to our accommodation from the track on Friday night (which was about forty kilometres north east of the city), after another extortionate amount paid to a cabbie. All the teams were staying in the same place, which looked as though it might have enough rooms for half of Moscow. There were plenty of bars near the hotel, but I never got the urge to wander off exploring.

Everyone was having the same nightmare with their travelling plans to the circuit. Further problems arose when it transpired that several teams' rigs were stuck on the Polish border because there had been a paperwork error. The main sufferers were the Brits, as they had loaded all their gear together after a British Championship race the previous weekend and had used the same travel rep, who had then apparently messed up the visas. As their equipment and bikes lay parked by a border control on Friday afternoon, the paddock was a frantic hive of activity as Dorna and the track officials made calls to try to get the trucks through, while the team members, having realised that their gear would not arrive in time anyway, started hunting around for spare bikes and clothing they could borrow.

Saturday arrived, but the trucks still hadn't. It was a free-for-all as bikes were borrowed from Russian teams and privateers, and it was sad to see a World Championship event reduced to almost farcical scenes. It was a mess for the riders who were hoping for vital Championship points to finish a little further up the rankings, and for sponsors who were going to miss out on any possible coverage.

Some got lucky with the sharing out – Stephen Sword secured a factory 125 KTM instead of his usual kitted bike, while others were less fortunate, such as Carl Nunn, who couldn't make his last ride with Husqvarna due to a missing 250, and although he had the chance to ride a 450 in the 500 race to save a wasted trip, he was denied permission by the FIM to change class at the last minute.

Understandably, with the truck mess, the hotel distance and the cabbie corruption, there were a lot of pissed-off people. Team managers camped out in front of the Dorna office truck and, to be fair to the Spaniards, they did try to help as much as possible with organising lifts or giving some of the British lads access to their hospitality so they could eat.

Amongst the chaos, KTM were secure. The semis had come via a different route, and we had all our equipment and sleeping quarters in the trucks for the mechanics. Gordon and I cleared it with the guys in the team that we could kip in with them on Saturday night (a practice that doesn't usually happen), so that we wouldn't have to run the gauntlet of traffic and spend hundreds of euros making it back to and from the hotel for race morning.

The location, like the furore surrounding the build-up to the event, was disappointing. The track was quite a way out of the city. You drove further and further away from urbanisation and entered countryside that was fairly remote, beyond the irregular pockets of housing estates, where the only rule seemed to be 'anything goes', as apartments were erected in all shapes and sizes, part-wood, part-steel and others that were a complete mish-mash. In a press conference in Sweden, I was told that the organisers were anticipating an attendance of 100,000 people! Seeing as that would more or less equal the total amount for all the GPs put together, most of the paddock didn't know what to expect.

What was alarming was the lack of facilities. They had been working to get the circuit ready for most of the season, and it was still unfinished in areas, most importantly in that of first aid and ambulance support, which hardly enthused the riders. With the look of the surroundings, you had to be concerned about your welfare and what would happen if you had an accident and had to be taken to hospital. The lack of readiness created a sense of unease.

Although some riders were frustrated and bemused by the circumstances of the weekend (many had plainly lost all motivation and wanted to race, finish the season and get home as quickly as possible), there was one small positive. The track was fantastic. It was the redeeming feature of the whole shambles that masqueraded as a GP. Like Bulgaria, you could see ninety-five per cent of the race from wherever you sat, thanks to the fact that it rose, dipped and curved inside a deep quarry setting, with a mix of muddy clay and sand for a technical, but sticky surface. Also, again like Bulgaria, the track was fast and wide. This time, though, the blend of sections was excellent, combining some steep hills and jumps with technical corners and fast parts.

It had an old-fashioned motocross feel to it in the way that it climbed, fell, turned and weaved around the dug-out inclines of the quarry; all credit to the designers, because it was mostly man-made and didn't follow any natural curves of the landscape. The soft terrain would cut up easily, especially with the cool late-summer humidity and dew. It would become rough as the race went on, and would be a good challenge. The sky was permanently grey, and it was quite cold throughout the weekend.

A tight collection of two or three corners at the lowest point in the quarry entered a high-banked pit of deep sand, which had a steep wall on one side that went up fifteen metres and then formed a seventy-metre slope of terracing, where most of the spectators stood, meaning that they were looking right down on top of you, like a section of a coliseum.

The jumps were hefty and well positioned. The tabletops threw you up quite high into the air and straight into another section, increasing the technical demands. The first part of the track really required you to think about your lines, whereas the latter part, which ran down a low-angled slope about 200 yards and then back up again, was a test of speed and nerve.

At the top of the slope, the course plummeted downwards in a huge S-shape, and during qualifying I experienced a G-out for the first time in my career. Hitting the berms on the outer rim of the turns, the sheer incline of the hill going downwards and the speed it was possible to reach, really pushed my whole body down into the bike. I had to stand on the pegs because I needed to have full control leaning into the curves, and for well over a second I felt like I could not see and began to get dizzy. It wasn't that dangerous because, like a bobsleigh, I was running down on a line and just had to keep my balance, but it was a very weird sensation that I had never had before – even the big triples on the SX circuits hadn't fazed me like that. It was exciting and a rush, but it did make me aware of the speed at which I must have been travelling to get that kind of feeling.

Qualifying proved to be another productive outing. I was able to ride more naturally with the KTM, and I perhaps had a more relaxed frame of mind because six months of pressure and anxiety were almost at an end. I did feel buoyed by the condition of the motorcycle though, and again, like at Loket, I felt that it could be taken further than I was able to push. I gained third and, interestingly, Pichon did not take pole again, that distinction fell instead to Josh, who was certainly on the pace, and perhaps detected that Mickael's less-than-peak level of motivation might yield a moment of weakness or slight opening to grab a debut GP victory. Pichon was certainly making enough noises to the press about his reluctance to race. Josh had to finish in front of Pit to make sure he secured that number two plate. Coppins was still racing the blank red factory Honda and, from what I heard, was Honda Europe's favourite son now.

Third was satisfactory, and I was looking forward to Sunday morning and wrapping up the year. Gordon and I kipped in slightly cramped mechanics quarters in the truck, after we all enjoyed a cheap steak and chip supper, prepared and generously sold by Dorna's Belgian caterers. Similar to the start of the season, the last race of the year has a particular vibe about it and is perhaps the most relaxed state the paddock will be in during the whole calendar.

Not everybody was sleeping so easily that night. I had my 125cc number one plate in my bag, and three riders could still win my title, so for Steve Ramon, Patrick Caps and leader Mickael Maschio, there was an important job to be done in the GP of Russia before they could even think about a holiday like ninety-five per cent of the rest of us. My concern for the next twenty-four hours was to finish the last forty minutes' racing of the season in front of Kenneth Gundersen. As I curled up on the sofa bed in the truck that night, I thought about Naomi and Gracie and could not wait to get out there the next day, do my job and return home.

I did not sleep fantastically, and race-day morning dawned quickly. I was pumped and ready to go. As I completed warm-up and posted the fourth-fastest time, I knew that another podium was on the cards, and I suddenly warmed to the idea of really ending the year on a high. I wasn't sure I had the physical state or level of confidence to beat Mickael, or even Josh, but after Loket it was a relief to enter the gate, thinking I could at least give them a tough time. In front of what looked more like 10,000 fans instead of 100,000, I knew that, like so many times before, the fate of my GP would lie in the start. After a sixty-yard straight run, the first corner was a kink into a thirty-yard incline that people could not even manage to walk up.

Coppins took the first slot, again on the left side, and Pichon kept his distance, instead choosing the third position. I moved in between them. This should be interesting – wedged in between the two fastest starters in the Championship. I looked down at the gate as the five-second board popped up.

My lift from the grooves I had dug into the mud was not bad, but the wheel spun in the first two or three metres and I instantly lost a yard on Coppins and Pichon, who both drifted near each other and cut off my path. I jostled my way into mid-pack as we went through the kink and climbed the hill. Gundersen was just ahead, and I counted back about nine positions. On the first lap, everybody was all over the place, trying to work their chosen lines – the busiest section was the sandpit. I had Bolley and Vehvilainen for company, while Gundersen had moved up a few positions.

About five or six of us were more or less racing side by side on the first lap, some going outside, some picking the inside, and some trying a variation. It must have looked good, because it was chaotic being in the middle! We swapped positions a lot, while Coppins was out front being chased by Pichon. At the start of lap two, I was at the back of a close group, placing me eighth. Four laps later, I got the better of Christophe Martin (like Strijbos, given a chance on the spare Suzuki machinery, but not faring as well) and Vehvilainen to jump up to sixth. Gundersen was in third, while Josh and Pichon were ten to fifteen seconds in front, racing for the lead. Kenneth was beginning to get away, and had maybe a three-second advantage over Bolley, Pit Beirer and then me.

I closed on Pit and passed him without a problem on lap six. If only I could have felt the same way five months earlier in Valkenswaard. Bolley was next, but only a lap later, he faded from fourth position and dropped right down the order. I was not sure what had happened, but Fred wasn't going to win the GP, so why take it seriously in his last MX moto? I privately thanked him for moving over and giving me fourth, but was now looking at a slightly empty track. I had lost too much ground on Gundersen in third. We were clocking the same lap-times and, for once, he was fast without making any mistakes that would let me claw back some distance. I didn't repeat my G-out experience, but I was having fun on the circuit, which tired me out towards the end.

My podium chances wore away as the race went on, and although I kept up my speed, just in case the Kawasaki rider faded, I did not have anything in reserve to close and, frustratingly, just looked at the same piece of track every lap. Gundersen was enjoying better form than when I had worn him down towards the end of the race in Sweden. The seven-second gap barely budged. I wanted that third place, but realistically knew it was out of my grasp. I began to think about the Championship. The two points I would lose to Gundersen for fourth position would make four my adopted number for the following year, and I would have achieved my goal.

At the front, all sorts of drama was going on. Firstly, Pichon had passed Coppins, but wasn't able to drop him as per usual. The Honda rider stayed with the World Champion, and had the audacity to retake the lead and kick off a scrap for the GP at the halfway point. The challenge to Pichon's authority had been around ten races too late, but it was interesting watching Mickael's reaction to the move on the video. He had a large chip on his shoulder about Coppins anyway.

The pair seemed to have got on quite well as team-mates for two seasons at Suzuki, but Mickael was bitter over the doping incident. Pichon immediately retaliated and pressurised Coppins. The race was decided when they both leapt over a tabletop together into the uphill straight and Mickael changed his line. The rear wheel of the Suzuki clipped the front wheel of the Honda as they landed, and Josh went down. Race over. Coppins got going again and, such was his lead over Gundersen, he was able to ride a quiet race for the last third of the moto to confirm his overall status as second best.

Whether Mickael's move was unsporting or not is one for the judges. I didn't see his line going up the hill every lap, so if it was his normal route, then it was an unfortunate clash that stopped an exciting contest. However, there is a small tell-tale sign on the tape where Mickael has a little look across going over the jump, before accelerating away. It was an act of hard racing, and I wouldn't be surprised if he actually did mean to pull it off. Finally, it was put down to a 'racing incident', and although Coppins was dry and professional about the moment, claiming he lost balance, I would love to have known his real thoughts on the matter.

For me, in some ways, it was a boring moto to finish the year. I did have the adrenaline rush of having to catch Pit and pass him, and the ease with which I could pull away from a guy who still had second place in the series to fight for was the clearest indication to everyone of the improvement we had made with the bike. Finally, we were gaining, overtaking and beating the riders who had been in the leading pack all year. Then, when I realised the chances of drawing up to Kenneth were slim, I had to concentrate on making solid consistent laps to ensure that I crossed the line right behind him. With Gundersen taking twenty points for third and my gain of eighteen for another fourth, then I would confirm that frequently-appearing number for 2003.

The procession of circulations became a little bit more frantic in the last third of the race, when I had to negotiate a way past some of the crazy local Russian riders, whose inexperience showed though their dangerous positioning on the track. Luckily, they proved to be nothing more than a minor distraction, and soon I was able to watch the race clock, just before the big rise of a first turn, tick down on 2002. I had shaved the time difference down to four seconds by the last two laps. Fred's board told me that Pit had fallen back to five seconds, and I knew the season was almost over.

Completing the race, I again sensed the familiar pang of minor disappointment that I would not be heading to the podium, but I rode back, relieved that the season had come to an end. The bike hadn't played up for two races now, and was at last turning into the machine that I had been promised back in September 2001. I handed the 250 back to the team, confident that we would be a stronger combination next season. I then wandered off to the paddock office to see the official declaration that my efforts over the last six months had finally resulted in fourth place, as I had expected. I had come to Russia promising to seal that position for KTM and, while I could not give them another podium, I sufficiently completed the job. I then relaxed by thumbing through the luxury holiday brochure of the Bahamas where my family would be heading in two weeks.

Although my racing activities in the World Championships were over for another year, I still had a small part to play in the season. The 125 race was a thrilling affair, with Ramon, Caps and Maschio fighting it out on the track for the grand prize. The class had been extremely open, especially after my dominant spree in 2001. Race leader Ben Townley, on a KTM, was getting signals to let Ramon, on the factory version of the Austrian bike, go past. Townley submitted and Ramon won, but Maschio's sensible and solid fourth place meant that the points gap wasn't enough, and KTM lost the 125 crown they had held for the last two years to Kawasaki.

Maschio totally deserved the title, despite a few hiccups in the middle of the year, because he proved his capability when he needed to by producing a perfect ride in Loket. Of course, it was a travesty that KTM had not won the 125 Championship. Half of the 125 field were using orange bikes. The podium in Russia was a clean sweep by the factory and, in my opinion, Ramon had chucked it away when he was in a position to win twice as many races as he had finally managed.

I jumped out on the Frenchman as he coasted to a halt some metres past the finish line and gave him my number one plate, on the back of which I had also quickly scribbled a congratulatory note. I posed for some photos with him and then got out of the way, as he went crazy with his team. Achieving your lifetime goal is really a moment to be savoured and, as I watched Maschio walk onto the podium after the top three had left, I knew exactly what it felt like to be alone up there, shattered by emotion as much as by fatigue.

KTM had a pretty disastrous final GP, and left 2002 empty-handed, meaning that going into 2003, I am still their most recent World Champ. The curtain closed on the season, and it was evident in the farewells and mellow mood in the paddock as everybody was packing up to leave (sadly with more urgency than normal, due to the desire to get out of Russia).

Gordon had already announced that he would be returning to CAS Honda, with the added bonus that Harry Ainsworth and his British crew would be fielding factory Honda machinery in 2003, after the collapse of the Berni team in somewhat suspicious circumstances, with rumours of financial misdoings. Gordon had emerged as a talented rider from the homely confines of CAS, a company that had grown immensely from its humble beginnings and was now the top British team, with the weight of Honda UK and Europe behind them. I think he will find the CAS ship a different vessel from the one he left, but from what I last heard, he was planning to ride the Honda 450 four-stroke, which would suit him down to the ground and good luck to him.

I think Gordon suffered with the depth of the job that faced him at KTM. He was constantly working on different and prototype engines, and then having to experiment with different chassis, suspensions and various settings on top of that; even an experienced development rider would have had their work cut out. The main problem was the way in which he liked to race a bike. He changes gear a lot and needs a lot of power in the bottom of the engine. I believe I had more difficulties with suspension than Gordon, because I race very much on top of the bike and I'm more aggressive with the power.

Gordon never really gelled with the bike, and his race in Russia summed up his frustration and disillusionment in 2002. Initially, there was some doubt as to whether he would ride. In a British Championship meeting the week beforehand, a rock shattered his goggles and broke his nose. It's never nice getting someone's roost in your face, but the wound where the rock that had caught Gordon required stitches and gave him two cracking shiners, making him seem like a comic-book villain. With the pain he was in, I'm not surprised he only rode around to eighteenth, and when he parked the KTM after the last GP, I'm sure that he felt relieved to end the struggle. Despite the tension that was apparent at times between us during the year, I still regard him as a decent guy and wish him well.

Rumours were rife that Pit Beirer was going to be my team-mate for 2003, and although Kurt told me that nothing had been sorted out officially, I was more or less informed that this would be the line-up for the two-stroke effort in the first-ever season of the Motocross GP, a new class generated from the 250s, but allowing four-strokes up to 450cc an entry.

I was happy for Pit to come into the team. He is a polite and cheerful guy in the paddock, with a demeanour a world away from his on-track wild-man persona. We are the same age and we have similar styles in setting up the bike. He has been in the 250 GPs for eight years, and has mounted four different makes of motorcycle in his time, so he has a lot of experience. Pit likes to ride at high revs and on the limit of the machine's power, very much like myself. So, testing work for 2003 is instantly slightly easier, because we will want similar machinery and won't be needing engine redesigns like Gordon required. For KTM, signing the number one German rider would also keep a large part of their home central European market happy, and it seemed like a good deal for everyone.

I shook hands with those I would not see for six months, and said goodbye to some that I expected to meet in America for the Motocross of Nations. I was keen to leave the circuit and get back to the hotel to grab my things, before making my way to the airport. The Kawasaki guys were holding a bit of a celebration party back at the hotel that night, but I wasn't interested in getting the beers in and drinking away the end of the year; Fred easily does my share, so I left him to it. On Thursday, Naomi, Gracie and I were going to the States for the Nations, and then jetting off for our first real holiday for two years that was also serving as our honeymoon.

As with any holiday, packing and getting ready was all part of the excitement. I also had to focus on the role I had to take as leader of the British team, picked by Rob Herring. I had a new helmet and Alloy gear designed in Union Jack colours that certainly looked the part, and I was happy to be heading out to America and some blistering weather. The Nations was set to be the biggest meeting in world motocross since the FIM and Dorna announced that this year's event was to be held in the USA for the first time since 1987. The Motocross of Nations basically works like a World Cup, with each country selecting a three-man team of their best riders (125, 250 and 500cc) to race against over three motos.

Britain has taken the title of World Champions a record sixteen times since the Nations inauguration in 1947. The Americans were very close, thanks to a thirteen-year winning run from 1981 to 1993, and Belgium was third in the 'most victories' table. The

Nations was an important event for British motocross, and one in which all of the home riders took a great deal of pride. We last captured the huge trophy back in 1994, somewhat against the odds in the face of a much-favoured US team, and Kurt Nicoll was a winner that day in Roggenburg.

There had been some changes to the proceedings, which is always guaranteed to upset the traditionalists. As well as adjusting the name, there was also a re-working of the regulations and format. Instead of the three races spread over an afternoon, there now would instead be a more television-friendly super-final, with a qualification process that would push the twelve best countries into a main event and everybody else into a less interesting 'B' final, where the grand prize was a pointless highest placing of thirteenth. What was immediately clear was that like a US SX race and, in recent years, the GPs, the start would be vital, and a forty-minute sprint would involve all sorts of manic action, rather than tactics like one rider knowing he doesn't have to push because his team-mate was winning and they had enough points.

In a way, it sounded more fun and would really be a true one-off extravaganza of the best riders in the world going crazy; the ultimate decider of who was the fastest. I was relishing the prospect and, although the new programme did dispense with the formula of old, the Nations had become more marketable and, for once, the label of 'a gathering of the top motocrossers in the world' would ring true, as people could see for themselves in the space of one race if Pichon could beat Carmichael, and if Dobb could beat Everts.

The Americans know how to make a show out of their events, with all sorts of activities happening aside from the race itself. For that reason, combined with a little sentimentality, I was excited about the prospect of racing out there.

I knew a lot of people were treating the 2002 Nations very seriously in Europe, including myself. Some were even going as far as to say that it could re-galvanise the sport in a global sense. It could certainly lead to things like the chance of an American GP and a bevy of new sponsorship deals and exposure. If Pichon, or any of us, could beat or gave Carmichael a race, then it would have many positive implications for the regard the Americans have for the World Championships, which has hardly been complimentary in the past, in line with the insular belief they have regarding their sports over there. I had already agreed to race KTM's new 450 four-stroke in California, because it would have been a hassle for the factory to ship the two-stroke bikes over to the US from Russia in time.

My first appearance for Team GB took place in 1989. It was a very proud moment, and I lined up with Jem Whatley and Dave Thorpe. I scored a sixth and a fifth, and the team claimed third overall, and I climbed onto the podium at my first-ever Des Nations. I then took part every season until my American years (1993-95). I also missed out in 1998. 1994 was when the team surprisingly ended the American domination of the tournament, and I was too elated about the fantastic result to worry about the chance I had lost. From my eight Nations appearances, the best finish the team has gained is third – in 1989, 1992 and 1997. I won the 125 class in 1997 at Nîmes, France. I took to the podium again in 1992, this time in Australia (I rode with Kurt and Rob Herring).

In 1999, in Brazil, I had a great time racing with Chicco. We had already beaten Ricky Carmichael, who had crashed in both races. We were banging into each other and really going for it, but because we both had respect for one another, it was fun without being malicious. We could have a laugh about it afterwards and, no matter who had won, the other person would have a smile on his face. My last Nations appearance in 2000 had gone well in terms of performance, if not in terms of luck.

Building up to 2002, most of the hype was centred on Pichon and Carmichael. Pichon was the main man in Europe, whereas Carmichael, on the other hand, had been on another planet in US competition over the last few years. In 2002, he won the 250 title by claiming every single moto of the season — twenty-four consecutive race wins, amazing. Both riders were firing at their peak and, to be honest, even I was bubbling inside to see how they would get on against each other, and wondering if I could maybe surprise everyone and get in amongst them.

The venue for the race also played into the pair's favour. Competition Park, in California, raised a few eyebrows when it got the nod to host the event, particularly as several other US tracks, with a lot more experience in motocross and a better infrastructure to cope with a meeting the size of the Nations, were ignored. The isolated and flat nature of the terrain in the Californian desert meant that a lot of work would need to be done, and would probably fashion the circuit more in the style of supercross, which would act as a disadvantage to people like the Belgian team of Everts, Bervoets and Smets, and play directly into the hands of the likes of Pichon, Carmichael and myself.

It seemed another strange move by Dorna and the FIM to accept the bid of one man, Malcom McCassey, to run the world's biggest motocross race at a barren practice facility in the middle of nowhere. Sadly, their naïve roll of the dice with the most important date on the MX calendar backfired, and with an unhealthy dose of bad luck thrown into the mess, their name, which was already in the mud — if you forgive the pun — was now floundering around in new lower depths. In short, the 2002 Motocross of Nations never happened. Well, it did, but not in America, and not with half the teams and riders that should have been contesting the historic fifty-five-year-old tournament — it was a washout, a sham and a crying shame.

There have been a lot of rumours and counter-rumours about what happened to the 2002 US Nations, but here's my brief alleged version of events, as it was explained to me. The FIM and Dorna had something of a murky involvement with the American racing body, the AMA, and Clear Channel over their role in the US SX, which was at one stage a major row in itself between the fractious partners over the pond. Thanks to a deal signed when the AMA and Clear Channel were in dispute, the FIM now had a tiny grip on the money-spinning US SX scene, and had a hand in transforming the SX Championship into a World Supercross series.

The FIM and Dorna were now partners with Clear Channel, and sensing that their series was in danger, the AMA resolved their differences with the American promoters and strongly pushed the case for the US Championship. It is possible that the FIM were put out by the re-entry of AMA into the mix and, as a consequence, the US SX competition survived in Clear Channel's capable money-generating hands, but also had to run concurrently with the new WSX GP series. Out of the political mess, it seems that the AMA was ignored when it came to choosing a venue for the Nations due to occur on their patch. The FIM and Dorna eventually opted for a circuit that eventually turned out to be on illegal ground.

I was hearing rumours as the event drew near that the track was in trouble and Competition Park was facing closure. The gossip was spreading like wildfire, and I seemed to spend most of the time being fed different versions of news from various sources. Competition Park didn't sound like a wonderful prospect anyway. It really was off the beaten track, over an hour east of LA, and most of the US press had been condemnatory of its selection as the Nations venue.

The problems started when a tribe of native Indians claimed that the track was on their land, and they objected to the noise and inconvenience a major race meeting with over 30,000 expected fans would generate. They made legal motions to get the meeting off their turf. McCassey had drafted a press release only days beforehand, saying that despite echoes of trouble the event was secure, negotiations had been held and permission granted. Then the real slice of bad luck occurred. One of the Soboda Indians was killed on the grounds, allegedly in an accident on the track. The tribe again pushed hard in the courts to get the venue shut down. A sign was hung on the gates to the circuit, three days before practice was due to get underway, to say that Competition Park was closed, pending further legalities, and the Nations was left floating in the air, near collapse.

Hearing all this from my hotel, I couldn't quite believe it. I then became angry in the immediate aftermath when Dorna insisted that the event could not be moved at the eleventh hour to a more sensible venue like Glen Helen. Apparently, the Glen Helen raceway had offered their circuit and facilities to the organisers in an effort to save the event and all the plans, effort and money that had been spent to get all the riders and equipment to the other side of the world. Finally, Dorna announced after two days that the Nations had been postponed two weeks and would be held, conveniently for them, back at Bellpuig in Spain.

By the time that the FIM and Dorna had raised their heads above the pulpit to comment on the postponement and say that everybody had to return to Europe; there was dismay, anger and a lot of disappointment in virtually every conversation I heard involving motocross. I felt sorry for all the British fans I saw, and knew they had saved money to fly out especially for the race. I was also annoyed because I had personally shelled out nearly £3,000 for flights and hotels to get ready for the event and was now being told that I would have to go back to Europe.

There was another issue. The Thursday after the Nations, we were due to fly off to our luxury Bahamas holiday that Naomi, Gracie and I had so much been looking forward to, and now the Spanish Nations would fall right in the middle of the vacation. There was no way around it, and I knew a pretty big decision was coming up.

When the news about Bellpuig emerged and became official, many riders and teams were laughing at the idea. There were practical reasons for missing the rearranged date; it would mean another two weeks' training at the end of a hard year, and most people I spoke to were not motivated to race a competition as important as the Nations towards the end of October. Many were also too disgusted, and vowed to ignore the event in protest and through a matter of principle.

I was torn about what to do. I was in a mind to say fuck off to Dorna, along with most other riders, but I didn't want to miss out on the chance of representing my country for the second year in a row. I couldn't fully come to terms with the fact that a British team somewhere else might be trying to win the Nations without me.

People like Pichon, Carmichael and some of the big names in the sport ruled themselves out straight away, while the federations were busy trying to find any riders willing to race near the end of October. France didn't even send a squad of 'B' team quality to defend their title, and most of the top Belgian riders turned down the Bellpuig date. The Americans withdrew their interest for the second year running (in 2001, it was in the wake of 9/11 hysteria) and eventually, over the next week, so did Great Britain, effectively making my decision for me.

To be honest, I was relieved. It was tragic that the 'real' Nations was not going ahead, but the racing season was over for me. I could relax and switch off for a couple of weeks, and enjoy some more time with my wife and baby. However, as I would come to learn, in the whirl of activity that happened in the few days after the Nations was officially called off, my riding duties were not quite finished for 2002. I was contacted by Rob because some guys at Glen Helen were trying to rescue the ashes of the tournament and were holding an unofficial 'World Cup of Motocross' international meeting, with a hefty prize fund and reduced entry fees for all those fans that had flown over with Competition Park tickets. A website was quickly set up, and word of the race was soon all over the place, as the organisers tried to convince all the teams and riders who were already in California to stick around and still put on a show. Not many did.

I agreed to compete in the World Cup at the last minute, as much for the fans that had made the effort to come and support us as for myself. Fred got to work setting up the Union Jack sticker set over the 450, and the makeshift England team was completed by semi-retired Neil Prince, team manager at CAS Honda, who was loaned the Dyno bike from Pro Circuit, and Rob himself, who had already made a few low-key appearances in the 500cc GPs towards the end of the year. He took the bike that James Noble was going to ride, amid a scramble for both guys to get some kit and parts. It was slapdash and put together in a rush like the event itself, and my motivation to race wasn't sky high. In one respect, I thought it might be fun, but in the other, I didn't want to have a fall or accident in a meeting that meant nothing to me right before the holiday, and one that might affect the off-season.

All in all, I was wary as we took off around Glen Helen for practice on Sunday morning. The 450 was very light, almost like my 250, and felt very powerful. The warm-up certainly brought back a few memories of racing there in the mid-1990s in some unbelievably scorching temperatures, very much like the day of the World Cup itself. There were still a few big names around, like Tim Ferry, Sebastien Tortelli, Chad Reed and Greg Albertyn (who was making a one-off comeback for the cause of South Africa), my old mate Grant Langston and Ernesto Fonseca.

I surprised everybody there by grabbing the hole-shot on a grunty 450, and although Reed and Yamaha team-mate Ferry flew by me by the end of the first lap, I enjoyed a quiet race to take third. Australia, USA and England – that would do for a first-moto result. Our makeshift team's chances of any decent finish were scrubbed before the end of the opening race, when Rob crashed into Tortelli and had to be taken to hospital to have a painful arm looked at. Neil was down in twentieth.

The second moto arrived and, on the parade lap, the bike's gearbox started to malfunction. It would keep slipping into neutral. I virtually hole-shotted again, but then with the bike continually clicking into neutral, I dropped back to about tenth in the few first corners, and was down in something like twenty-second inside the first three laps. I settled into a rhythm, knowing when and how to kick the bike through the gears, and pushed back up to seventh.

Neil had taken another twenty-first and I was persuaded to finish the meeting with the third and final moto, so that we could at least get a placing. On the parade lap, the bike had had enough and locked solid in fourth gear. I entered the gate with the plan of at least getting a few laps done to wave at the fans and see what would happen, and I eased the bike away but it wasn't happening.

Reed had won two motos and finished second in the other, giving people an early warning of what he was capable of for the SX and MX year ahead in America, meaning that Australia took the overall victory, while England were placed a creditable sixth; that wasn't bad, considering Rob had barely lasted five minutes. The event was decent enough, considering it had been organised in a week. There were about 12,000 people watching, and around 400 British fans in attendance. I met these twins who told me that they had worked seven days a week for the last two or three months so they could afford to travel out.

I would say that only the Americans, Australians and Japanese took it seriously. It was hard to get 100 per cent ready for a meeting like that, when you have no proper team or stuff like spares. I had one tyre to use all day, and it's not the kind of preparation I like to have for any type of race. We celebrated Gracie's first birthday that week by going to Chucky Cheese, and left for two weeks of bliss on the Thursday after the race.

Italy, for only the second time ever, won the 2002 Motocross of Nations in Bellpuig, and from looking at the entry list on the internet, they were the only country with a full-strength team. Somebody texted me the results of the Nations, and I was still interested to see who had won. The event had become too important to me since my first appearance in 1989 just to switch off and ignore completely. Alessio Chiodi, Andrea Bartolini and Alex Puzar, all former World Champions, easily and predictably took the honours, ahead of Belgium and Finland. There was no Britain,

America, New Zealand (who had finished third in 2001) or Australia. From what people told me, the paddock was more than half empty, and the event was devoid of atmosphere, aside from the 10,000 Spanish fans that you can always rely on to turn up. I was busy reading a biography about Manchester United player Roy Keane on a beach.

POSTSCRIPT

THE NEW year has ushered in and as I set off for the USA again, flying out on my thirty-first birthday, this time alone, I have come full circle and am ready to begin the process once more. Before flying to America over the winter, I had been acting as a part-time estate agent. Marco Melandri wanted to leave London, and I recommended that he moved to Derby, where he was close to Donington for tests and where we could also train together. He came up and had a look around and liked the place. Marco is from quite a small village in Italy, and I think he felt a bit isolated in the capital. I sorted him out with a nice three-bedroom semi about 500 yards down the road from me.

Motocross is also evolving and changing again. Dorna have cut down their resources at the races, and it finally looks as though they are going to walk out of the door at the end of 2003. They have helped the sport in some minor ways, like the paddock organisation and the VIP facilities, but I can only hope their successors are open-minded, have a bit more common sense and actually care about motocross, both as a sport and as a business. I find it very sad that just when the sport is evolving and is in need of a lot of publicity and a big promotion push for the new Motocross GP class, the controlling company are counting their pennies and preparing to chuck the whole thing into the river.

I worry now where the sport will head, because Dorna definitely bought some slick television production to the show. If we lose their range of coverage, then how many years will we regress? Whatever the short-term outcome, the 2003 World Championships will become a landmark and represent a new era in the sport. The rule changes have created a 'super class' and, as motocross slips back in one way, it will make a leap forward in another. Motocross GP will see the old 250cc category expanded to welcome 450cc four-strokes.

Everts and Bervoets are moving down from the 500s (which has now been pushed up to a 650 limit), with new factory Yamahas, and Smets is also lining up with KTM's 450 effort. The differences will not be vast, but I can see the bottom-end traction of the thumpers (and the 200cc extra power) having more of an advantage at quite a few of the usual circuits. Racing against people like Everts and the best riders in the whole World Championships makes the MX GP classification a fascinating competition. I don't think I speak solely for myself when I say that I am eager to get my teeth into the new campaign. The 125 category now sees the two-strokes facing a threat from 250cc four-strokes, and an age limit is to be introduced in the not-too-distant future, with a view to making it a breeding ground for young talent.

I suspect a lot of people don't have faith in me to rise to the challenge against Smets, Pichon and co., but if I can go into the fight 100 per cent fit and ready, then I know I can beat anybody in the world.

There are still areas to work on, but I believe the bike was good enough to win in the final two races, only I was not in a condition to get the best out of it. It's like we have climbed two-thirds of the way up the mountain, and now have another pre-season and another trip to America to get right to the top, where Pichon, Coppins, Smets and Everts are bound to be at the first race. Mitch Payton said to me that winning one is simple, it's getting two that proves you are actually doing something. He was actually speaking about a US National race after Unadilla, but his thinking can be applied to a World Championship, and that is now where I have to set my sights.

I don't know if I could continue in motocross after I have finished riding. I love my family too much to keep on travelling and being away from home. Naomi and I would like to have another child – just when I thought my life couldn't get any busier! Coordinating a team looks like just as much work as being a rider, what with organising and going to tests, spending most of your time at the factory and all the other stuff that goes on behind the scenes, it's not just about appearing at the races.

When I had my operation in 2001, Kurt flew across, sat with me while I woke up, asked how I was, spoke with the doctor, checked everything was okay, had a chat for fifteen minutes and got back on the plane to Austria – that is what a good manager is all about. When the results are arriving and everything is cool, then it's easier, but when dealing with problems like injury and slouching confidence, not to mention the whole logistical side of the team, the job becomes very hard. I am not sure if I could offer that level of commitment after retiring. I'd need a long break of several years first!

One way in which I am trying to water the grass roots in British motocross is by forming a little 85cc team. I want to try to bring somebody else forward in the sport, so that maybe I won't be the only Englishman to have taken a 125 world title for long. I am not happy with how the system works for our riders. I have also been fortunate to enjoy a good life, thanks to the MX, and have achieved some big prizes – now it's my duty to put something back.

The Alessi brothers have emerged fast from the US amateur system, and James Stewart has also made the jump to national stardom, because somebody has recognised his talent and given him a chance. The young talent here in Britain are poor losers in comparison to their US cousins, who get more help from the manufacturers in America than many of the established GP riders. Most of the amateur guys and teenage stars of the 80cc class are earning more money than the GP winners in the 125s (except for maybe Maschio). I am talking here about thirteen- and fourteen-year-old kids! The void does not apply solely to cash, it's also about the level of equipment and publicity.

It's not a double standard that will shift overnight, and it may never even happen because the World Championships have some work to do if they want to nudge into the same arena as America, but at least with this 85cc effort, I am trying to rectify the balance and maybe lay the beginnings of a path for a young star. His name is Luke Remmer, and I've bought him a couple of bikes and managed to get my technical sponsors to come on board and help out. The three main ones are Michelin, Renthal and Motorex, with Alloy, Airoh, Smith and Alpinestars also lending their support.

Luke was British Schoolboy Champion and SW 65cc Future West Champion in 2002 at the age of eleven; for 2003, one bike at cost was all that he was originally offered. It wasn't good enough, and I wanted to make a gesture that would at least try to get him near a similar platform. I hope to provide a stepping stone, and will act like a mentor and manager when he needs me. I can only ask him to go there and do his best, and I will not accept anything less, so the pressure is on! It's already too late for me to help any of the guys in their mid-teens. It's the really young kids that can benefit the most from my advice and tutelage, as well as having the boost of good machinery to help get themselves noticed.

I have a connection with Luke and the Remmer family because his dad Andy used to race against my brother years ago. I had seen Remmer Jnr in a couple of races and he looked pretty good. Many people I spoke to (and who have witnessed him riding a lot more than me) also added recommendations. He beat everyone in the UK during 2002, and the word is that the boy has something special. He was a big kid on a 65cc, and now he has the chance to prove his potential on a larger machine. The guys who eventually win at GP level have moved up a class virtually every year, so the journey is lengthy and arduous.

It's an exciting project, because he will have good bikes and a supportive family behind him. For me personally, it's part of the emotion I have towards the sport to leave a lasting trace, and maybe is one hint to the small depth of involvement I would like to keep within motocross in the many years to come. I hope that when I leave the GPs, the sport might be going in a better direction in terms of publicity, money and popularity. That's why I like to speak my mind about all the areas where MX falls short compared to other sports, and even the US MX and SX scene. It needs to be a lot more professional in key parts if it is ever to really shine globally, and that's why I will never stop short of doing some publicity or anything to try to promote it.

I am very happy with the lifestyle I have now – I have a beautiful wife and daughter, along with a prospering agency business and sense of achievement in the sport after so many years of trying. I freely admit that, from the gut-wrenching effort I made back in the winter of 2000, right up to gaining the elusive world title, I now find it hard to re-enter the gym and put in the same time and effort, experiencing physical agony. Maybe it's the drag of age, post-Championship relaxation, or perhaps just because the development season I experienced in 2002 took away some of the fun. 2003 could be like a new chapter, and I hope to revive my taste for glory.

I'm thirty-one now, and think I probably have another four or five years in the sport. I love motocross and the fire still burns within me, to use a popular cliché. I want to show people that the 125cc title victory was no one-off. There are GPs to be won, critics to silence and British fans to be made proud. My life has been about motocross and racing. When I am leading the best riders in the world, and I look to my left and see four hundred people averting the sun from their eyes as I jump practically over their heads, forty foot in the air, I know that there isn't anything else better.

2001 RESULTS

125cc WORLD CHAMPIONSHIP

ROUND ONE:	Bellpuig, Spain	1ST
ROUND TWO:	Valkenswaard, Holland	2ND
ROUND THREE:	Broadford, Australia	1ST
ROUND FOUR:	Genk, Belgium	1ST
ROUND FIVE:	Teutschenthal, Mitteldeutschland	1ST
ROUND SIX:	Spa, Europe	1ST
ROUND SEVEN:	Uddevalla, Sweden	DNS
ROUND EIGHT:	Ernée, France	2ND
ROUND NINE:	Namur, Namur	1ST
ROUND TEN:	Roggenburg, Switzerland	1ST
ROUND ELEVEN:	Gaildorf, Germany	4TH
ROUND TWELVE:	Dutch Brabant, Lierop	DNS
ROUND THIRTEEN:	Castiglione Del Lago, Italy	DNS
ROUND FOURTEEN:	Kärntenring, Austria	DNS

TOTAL POINTS – 228
CHAMPIONSHIP PLACING – 1ST

2002 RESULTS

250cc WORLD CHAMPIONSHIP

ROUND ONE:	Valkenswaard, Holland	4TH
ROUND TWO:	Bellpuig, Spain	DNF
ROUND THREE:	Teutschenthal, Europe	4TH
ROUND FOUR:	St Jean d'Angely, France	5TH
ROUND FIVE:	Castiglione Del Lago, Italy	7TH
ROUND SIX:	Kärntenring, Austria	5TH*
	125cc Grand Prix	*1ST*
ROUND SEVEN:	Sevlievo, Bulgaria	10TH
ROUND EIGHT:	Uddevalla, Sweden	6TH
ROUND NINE:	Genk, Belgium	5TH
ROUND TEN:	Gaildorf, Germany	8TH
ROUND ELEVEN:	Loket, Czech Republic	3RD
ROUND TWELVE:	Park Extreme, Russia	4TH

* 4TH upon amendment

TOTAL POINTS – 177
CHAMPIONSHIP PLACING – 4TH

INDEX